THE ECONOMY OF LITERATURE

Marc Shell

THE ECONOMY
OF LITERATURE

THE JOHNS HOPKINS UNIVERSITY PRESS • BALTIMORE AND LONDON

Manufactured in the United States of America

The Johns Hopkins University Press, Baltimore, Maryland 21218
The Johns Hopkins Press Ltd., London

Library of Congress Catalog Number 77-21640
ISBN 0-8018-2030-8

Library of Congress Cataloging in Publication data
will be found on the last printed page of this book.

CONTENTS

LIST OF PLATES

ACKNOWLEDGMENTS

Many people helped me during the writing of this book. I should like to thank especially Geoffrey Hartman, Paul de Man, J. Hillis Miller, and W. K. C. Guthrie, whose careful readings of parts of the manuscript were invaluable. To George Steiner, Charles Drekmeier, and the late Jacques Ehrmann I am deeply grateful for the advice and encouragement they gave. I should also like to thank Robert Fishman and Susan Meld, who reminded me of work that remained—and still remains—to be completed.

Preliminary research for this book was supported by a generous grant from the Danforth Foundation. The book has been published with the help of a grant from the Humanities Research Council of Canada, using funds provided by the Canada Council. Photographs are reproduced by permission of Hirmer Fotoarchiv and the British and Ashmolean museums.

THE ECONOMY OF LITERATURE

INTRODUCTION

The lord whose oracle is at Delphi neither speaks nor conceals, but gives signs (or symptoms) [sēmainei]. –Heraclitus

Those discourses are ideological that argue or assume that matter is ontologically prior to thought. Astrology, for example, looks to the stars, phrenology to the skull, physiognomy to the face, and palmistry to the hand. In the modern world, ideological discourses look to the biochemistry of the brain, sexual need, genes, and social class; they seek to express how matter "gives rise to" thought by employing metaphors such as "influence," "structure," "imitation," "sublimation," "expression" and "symptom."

Every ideology would demonstrate that all other ideologies are idealist expressions of the basic matter to which it alone has real access. The intellectual battlefield of the modern world is strewn with the half-dead remains of ideological criticisms. The sight of that field drives many students to despair of ever witnessing a solution or victory. Finding no salve for the wound of the desire to know, they retreat to comfortably relativistic or uncomfortably nihilistic lookouts, from which, grandly surveying the combatants, they argue that all ideologies are equally valid and therefore equally invalid. Who has not heard the liberal injunction to "do your own thing," the rule that "you have your opinion and I have mine"?

Students often retreat before they have worked to understand any one of the discourses that they disdain. There is something disquieting, however, about their outlook. As we shall see, they are deceived who seek a material explanation of thought by thought. The logical impossibility of ideological studies, however, does not make inevi-

1

[handwritten top margin: not just literature about economics, but economics of literature (how literature & economy are homological)]

table or wise the retreat from the forefront of the thoughtful study of thought and matter.

Not all thought, after all, seeks to explain thought by matter alone. For example, the Platonic dialectic originates in matter but finally incorporates, diagnoses, and surpasses it. The Hegelian dialectic, diagnosing the Platonic dialectic, presents a phenomenology of mind that looks to (or is itself) the spirit of human history. This book seeks to understand dialectically the relationship between thought and matter by focusing—for reasons I shall now consider—on economic thought and literary and linguistic matters.

[handwritten left margin: subject of the book]

Thinkers often study words that seem to refer to economic conditions. Many philologists, for example, study the historical development of witting and unwitting commercial metaphors in everyday language.[1] Some cite etymological connections between economic terms as evidence of allegedly truthful relationships between the concepts these terms are supposed to signify, and a few believe that disagreements and misunderstandings about production and distribution are, fundamentally, problems of semantics or definition.[2] Others argue that verbal etymologies and definitions are untrustworthy reflections of social fictions.[3] Many literary critics study economic themes and metaphors in works of literature. Some consider the works of an author (or the opinions expressed by one of his characters) to constitute serious economic theory, and a few suggest that only literature about economics is worth reading.[4] Other critics con-

[handwritten left margin: language & economics]

---

1. For example, Jacob Hemelrijk, *Penia en ploutos* (Amsterdam, 1925); J. Hangard, *Monetaire en daarmee verwante metaforen* (Groningen, 1963); L. Spitzer, "Frz. *payer comptant* und Verwandtes," *Zeitschrift für Romanische Philologie* 38, no. 3 (1914); and J. Korver, *De terminologie van het credietwezen in het Grieksch* (Ph.D. diss., University of Utrecht, 1934).

2. Johann Kaspar Schmidt [pseud. Max Stirner], *Der Einzige und sein Eigentum* (1845), and L. M. Fraser, *Economic Thought and Language* (London, 1937), exemplify these respective positions.

3. See, for example, Karl Marx and Friedrich Engels, *The German Ideology*, trans. S. Ryazanskaya (Moscow, 1968), esp. pt. 3.

4. For the former position, see Henry W. Farnam, *Shakespeare's Economics* (New Haven, 1931); and C. S. Devas, "Shakespeare as an Economist," *Dublin Review*, 3d ser. 17 (1887). Ezra Pound takes the latter point of view. "It would sometimes appear," writes Noel Stock (*The Life of Ezra Pound* [New York, 1970], p. 344), "that [Pound] maintained an interest in such figures as Homer, Dante and Shakespeare, and in some lesser men, by convincing himself that they were really poet-economists;" and, more significantly, that "[Pound's] opinion of a writer sometimes depended on whether that writer mentioned money or economics."

[handwritten left margin: Approaches:]

[handwritten bottom:]
① language & economics (economic themes, tropes, metaphors)
           commercial

② economic themes & metaphors (discursive formation?) in literature

③ literature *as* economic theory

words & coins — economics & language, exchange & value
words as coins / capital of intellectual exchange — Bourd. ✱✱✱

sider the witting and unwitting metaphors in works of literature to be mere reflections of the author's world view.[5]

These and similar studies focus only on the economic content of some words in some works of literature. They ignore other contents (e.g., the sexual), which they could, but do not, scrutinize in exactly the same way, and they ignore works of literature that do not contain economic themes or metaphors. Dazzled by the economic content of a few metaphors, such studies fail to consider the formal similarities between metaphorization (which characterizes all language and literature) and economic representation and exchange.[6]

Many thinkers have been led or misled by comparisons between economic and verbal tokens of exchange. Both language (sometimes assumed to constitute a superstructure) and economics (sometimes assumed to constitute a substructure) seem to many theorists and poets to refer to groups of tropes. Seductive similarities between words and coins bolster structural (and often static) analyses of exchange and value and inform uncritical writings about economics and language. It has been argued, for example, that both words and coins are stores and transmitters of meaning or perception, that an etymon is like a monetary inscription that has been effaced by time, and that words are the coins of intellectual exchange.[7] A general theory of

Poor interprets of relation b/w words & coins

5. For example, Victor Ehrenberg, "Money and Property," in *The People of Aristophanes: A Sociology of Old Attic Comedy* (New York, 1962); Robert Goheen, *The Imagery of Sophocles' "Antigone": A Study of Poetic Language and Structure* (Princeton, 1951); Mark Schorer, "The Humiliation of Emma Woodhouse," *Literary Review* 2, no. 4 (Summer 1959); Daniel Defoe, *Moll Flanders*, ed. Mark Schorer (New York, 1950), intro.; and Wilfred H. Stone, *The Cave and the Mountain: A Study of E. M. Forster* (Stanford, 1966). L. C. Knights ("Shakespeare and Profit Inflation," in *Drama and Society* [London, 1937]) argues typically that the literature of any period is influenced by both economic and linguistic conditions, so that the poet does not wholly create but rather partially inherits the class structure and verbal idiom.

6. On this distinction between content and form, see my analysis of Heraclitus's metaphorization in Chapter 1.

7. For the first argument, see Marshall McLuhan (*Understanding Media* [New York, 1964], pp. 139 ff.) and Sir Richard Blackmore, who proposes (*Satyr against Wit* [London, 1699]) that a "Bank of Wit" be established to test all wit for counterfeitness and to insure that the supply of "currency money" in Parnassus not be exhausted. On the second argument, see Friedrich Nietzsche, "Über Wahrheit und Lüge im aussermoralischen Sinn," in *Werke in drei Bänden* (Munich, 1966), 3:314; cf. Jacques Derrida ("La Mythologie blanche," in *Marges de la philosophie* [Paris, 1972]) and Marc Shell ("'What is Truth?': Lessing's Numismatics and Heidegger's Alchemy," *MLN* 92 [1977]: 549–70). For the third argument, see the Reverend Frederick William Robertson, *Sermons*, 1st ser., no. 1 (1886–87).

④ *economic metaphors reflections of the author's world view*

✱⑤✱ *Formal similarities b/w metaphorization (which applies to all language & literature) & economic representation & exchange*
cosmology, God-man, salvation
(I will add to this — religious? metaphysics & practices & conceptualization)

we implicitly construct an analogical /homological
relation between how reality is structured,
how it functions, & human economy, exchange, commerce, symbolization

4

INTRODUCTION

linguistic and economic forms, however, requires a critical approach
to the problem of symbolization.

The economist and professional etymologist A. R. J. Turgot adopts
such an approach in his systematic comparison of verbal and monetary semiology. He argues that both human speech (*langue*) and
money are languages (*langages*). Languages differ from nation to nation, but are all identifiable with some common term. In the case of
speech, this common term comprises natural things or our ideas of
these things, which are common to all nations. In the case of money,
the common term is value. Turgot argues similarly that speech and
money are both measures. Speech is the measure of the ideas of men,
since the lexical and syntactical divisions of reality require the speaker
to organize natural things on the basis of analogies that size them up.
Money is the measure of the value of wares, but, being merely a
quantitative measure, it can measure extension (*l'étendue*) only by
extension itself. We cannot evaluate money except by other money,
just as we cannot interpret the sounds of one human speech except,
in translation, by the sounds of another human speech.[8] The theory
of monetary value that underlies Turgot's comparison of evaluation
and interpretation rests on a notion of measurement that Turgot himself sometimes derides. He refers admiringly, for example, to Galiani's argument that "the common measure of all values is man,"[9] but
he is unable to incorporate this argument into his own theory.

Turgot's emphasis on pricing and evaluation is diagnosed by other
economists, such as Karl Marx, who argues that "language does not
transform ideas so that the peculiarity of ideas is dissolved and their
social character runs alongside them as separate entities, like prices
alongside commodities: ideas do not exist separately from language."[10] Turgot's consideration of economic and verbal symbolization focuses on "translation" (which in all Indo-European languages
refers to interlinguistic, economic, and intralinguistic or metaphorical
transfer). The only analogy that Marx allows between economic and
verbal symbolization is one that relates interlinguistic translation
(from the mother tongue into a foreign [*fremde*] language) to alienation (*Entfremdung*).[11] Marx shifts attention away from measurement

hermeneutic
circle of
literature,
religion, &
economy

8. A. R. J. Turgot, *Réflexions sur la formation et la distribution des richesses* (1766), in
Oeuvres, ed. E. Daire, 2 vols. (Paris, 1844), 1: 45 ff. Turgot also treats this matter in
"Tableau philosophique des progrès successifs de l'esprit humain" (1750) and "Valeurs
et monnaies," both in *Ecrits économiques*, intro. B. Cazes (Paris, 1970).

9. Fernando Galiani, *Della Moneta* (Naples, 1750).

10. Karl Marx, *Grundrisse: Foundations of the Critique of Political Economy*, trans. M.
Nicolaus (New York, 1973), pp. 162–63. Translation adapted by the author.

11. Ibid.

the problem of symbolization (for me, not so much)
what kinds of power relations are validated by certain economic forms?
How does this influence man's relation to himself, to God, How else?
to the other? How does it shape, limit, determine thought? otherwise?
species.

toward alienation and labor, and only ironically draws analogies between verbal and economic symbolization. For example, he attacks Pierre Proudhon and Adolph Wagner for misunderstanding the relationship between words (*Worten*) and concepts (*Begriffen*) in the same way that they misunderstand the relationship between money and wares. Marx hypothesizes bitterly, in a discussion of the relative form of value and the fetishization of commodities, that "the only comprehensible language which we can speak to each other or which can mediate us [in the capitalist era] is not that of ourselves, but only that of our commodities in their mutual relations." He suggests further that it is not neo-classical political economists who speak to each other and to us about commodities, but rather ventriloquistic commodities who speak through these economists a unique and alien "language of commodities."[12]

Many political economists of language ignore production and alienation and argue that words are a kind of credit-money,[13] that merchandise and discourse are symbolic forms with similar genealogies,[14] that verbal meaning is like the gold that money symbolizes,[15] or that a metaphor about language and a metaphor about

12. For the attack on Proudhon, see Karl Marx, *Capital*, trans. Samuel Moore and Edward Aveling, 3 vols. (New York, 1967), 1:68; and for the attack on Adolph Wagner, see *Marx-Engels Werke*, 41 vols. (East Berlin, 1956-68), 19:355-83. (Marx refers to Goethe's *Faust*, 11. 1995-96 in both.) On why those who live in a capitalist world cannot understand *eine menschliche Sprache*, see Karl Marx, "James Mill, Eléments d'économie politique," in *Marx/Engels Gesamtausgabe*, 11 vols. (Berlin, 1927-35), vol. 3, pt. 1, pp. 545-46; and on the *Warensprache*, see Marx, *Capital*, 1:52, 83.

13. For example: Saint-John Perse, who writes, "De la langue française ... on sait l'extrême économie de moyens, et qu'au terme d'une longue évolution vers l'abstrait, elle accepte aujourd'hui comme une faveur le bénéfice de son appauvrissement matériel, poussé parfois jusqu'à l'ambiguïté où la polyvalence, pour une fonction d'échanges et de mutations lointaines où les mots, simples signes, s'entremettent fictivement comme la monnaie dite 'fiduciare' " (*Livres de France* [January 1959], p. 8). See Donald Davie (*Articulate Energy: An Inquiry into the Syntax of English Poetry* [London, 1955]); Geoffrey Hartman (*The Unmediated Vision* [New York, 1966], esp. pp. 110 ff.) on Valéry; and Jacques Derrida ("La Double Séance," *La Dissémination* [Paris, 1972]) on Mallarmé. Cf. Harold Don Allen ("Monetary Concepts in Ten Early Verse Problems," *Canadian Numismatic Journal* 15, no. 12 [1970]); and algebraic poems in *The Greek Anthology*, ed. and trans. W. R. Paton, Loeb Classical Library, 5 vols. (London, 1918-27), esp. bk. 14, pt. 1, nos. 1, 2, and 10.

14. For example: Henri Lefebvre, "La Forme marchandise et le discours," in *Le Langage et la société* (Paris, 1966), esp. pp. 336ff. Jean-Pierre Faye and Antoine Casanova (*Littérature et idéologies: Colloque de Cluny 2, 2-4 April 1970, La Nouvelle Critique,* special 39 bienn.) discuss what Marx means by "the language of commodities."

15. See, for example, Jean-Louis Baudry, "Le Sens de l'argent," in *Théorie d'ensemble* (Paris, 1968). Cf. Julia Kristeva, "La Sémiologie: science critique et/ou critique de la science," in *Théorie d'ensemble*, esp. p. 89; and Sigurd Burckhardt (*Shakespearean Mean-

money are both metaphors about metaphorization.[16] Such arguments, some of which will be diagnosed in the following chapters, seem to imply that the study of language and economic exchange constitutes a kind of "numismatics" that explains society on the basis of its social, nomic, or monetary symbols.[17] Such a numismatics informs even respected discourses about society. Some students of linguistics and many students of structuralist anthropology and sociology, for example, adopt Ferdinand de Saussure's adoption of Walras's economics in order to define concepts such as verbal value and to distinguish between diachrony and synchrony.[18] Other students follow the economics of language proposed by Louis Hjelmslev.[19] These different appropriations of economic theory have stirred much political debate about which, if any, is *the* architectonic science, a debate finally about how human society—its language and economy—can or should be reformed or revolutionized.[20] Literary theory, which sometimes appears to be apolitical, necessarily deals with concepts such as verbal value and cannot avoid the economic and political problems that they imply.

---

ings [Princeton, 1968], esp. pp. 23, 25, 212, 256, 268, 284), who even goes so far as to apply Gresham's Law (about good and bad currency) to language.

16. For example: Michel Foucault, *Les Mots et les choses* (Paris, 1966).

17. Jean-Joseph Goux ("Numismatiques," in *Economie et symbolique* [Paris, 1973]) and Jean Baudrillard (*Pour une critique de l'économie politique du signe* [Paris, 1972]) are representative views. Kenneth Burke (*A Rhetoric of Motives* [Berkeley and Los Angeles, 1969], p. 129) writes that "the reductive, abstractive, metaphorical, analytic, and synthesizing powers of all language find their correspondences in the monetary idiom."

18. For example: Claude Lévi-Strauss, *Les Structures élémentaires de la parenté* (Paris, 1967). See Ferdinand de Saussure, *Cours de linguistique générale* (Paris, 1968), esp. "La Valeur linguistique considérée dans son aspect conceptuel" (pp. 158–62) and "La Valeur linguistique considérée dans son aspect matériel" (pp. 163–66); and P. Veyne and J. Molino, who suggest ("*Panem et circenses:* l'évergétisme devant les sciences humaines," *Annales: économies, sociétés, civilisations* 24 [January–June 1969]) that Saussure adopted the marginalist economics of Léon Walras, whose student, Vilfredo Pareto, was in Lausanne when Saussure was in Geneva. Lévi-Strauss may be compared with Talcott Parsons and Neil J. Smelser (*Economy and Society: A Study in the Integration of Economic and Social Theory* [New York, 1957]) and Parsons (*Politics and Social Structure,* [New York, 1969]), who merely apply the Marxist analysis of money (the only generalized symbolic medium in Marx's thought) to other symbolic media.

19. See, for example, Gilles Deleuze and Felix Guattari (*Capitalisme et schizophrénie: l'Anti-Œdipe* [Paris, 1972], pp. 287 ff.).

20. Cf. Philippe Sollers, "L'Ecriture fonction de transformation sociale," in *Théorie d'ensemble,* esp. pp. 402–3; Jacques Derrida, *De la grammatologie* (Paris, 1967), pp. 15–142; Goux, *Economie et symbolique,* pp. 130 ff.; Baudry, "Linguistique et production textuelle," in *Théorie d'ensemble,* pp. 359 ff.; Fredric Jameson, *The Prison-House of Language* (Princeton, 1972), p. 15; and F. Rossi-Landi, *Linguistics and Economics* (The Hague, 1975).

[handwritten at top: if economic theory is the architectonic science of society, then revolutionizing society requires revolutionizing economy]

INTRODUCTION

[handwritten right margin, near page number: 7]

Literary works are composed of small tropic exchanges or metaphors, some of which can be analyzed in terms of signified economic content and all of which can be analyzed in terms of economic form. In these two kinds of analysis, words and verbal tropes constitute the principal focus. Opposing thinkers have argued that Hobbes was not wholly mistaken to suggest that "words are wise men's counters, they do but reckon by them; but they are the money of fools."[21] Some critics, seeking to consider more than words, include in their analyses those larger literary structures of exchange that can be comprehended in terms of economic form.

[handwritten right margin: Sourd]

A few writers incorporate economic doctrine in the plots of works of literature. Harriet Martineau's *Illustrations of Political Economy,* for example, not only illustrates material conditions but is also informed by an extreme and ideologically symptomatic conflation of plot and economic doctrine: plot is to tale as economic theory is to everyday economic exchange.[22] Large structures of exchange can also be analyzed by applying economic or linguistic doctrine to some aspect of a narrative. Roland Barthes, for example, relies on Saussurian linguistics and formalist criticism to demonstrate how a tale may establish its own (counterfeit or creditable) exchange value and also the value of literature in general.[23] Literary works, then, are all composed of both small and large tropic exchanges.

[handwritten right margin: & economy of literature / how narrative can establish its own exchange-value & value of literature in general]

One goal of literary criticism is to understand the connection between the smallest verbal metaphor and the largest trope. The economy of literature seeks also to understand the relation between such literary exchanges and the exchanges that constitute the political economy. It looks from the formal similarity between linguistic and economic symbolization and production to the political economy as a whole.

From a more distant lookout than the economy of literature, the hypermetropic sociology of literature looks to some of the same

21. Thomas Hobbes, *Leviathan,* ed. M. Oakeshott (Oxford, 1946), p. 22.

22. Harriet Martineau, *Illustrations of Political Economy* (London, 1832). On structures of exchange in dramatic plots, see Jacques Ehrmann ("Structures of Exchange in *Cinna,*" *Yale French Studies* [1966]), who, however, projects his essay against a more general context, suggesting that "literary language, like the language of the other arts, has a metaphorical function in relation to everyday language, the language of reality, just as money has a metaphorical function in relation to the merchandise it is intended to represent." Cf. Algirdas J. Greimas, *Du sens* (Paris, 1970), and *Sémantique structurale* (Paris, 1966).

23. Roland Barthes, *S/Z* (Paris, 1970), esp. pp. 95 ff.

[handwritten at bottom: For Shell - all literary works can be analyzed in terms of economic form, and some in terms of econ. content also (Sourd) larger literary structures can be considered in terms of economic form]

things. Sociologists, for example, may often seem to rely (however uncritically) on broad theories of social influence, like that implicit in Alexis de Tocqueville's argument, in "The Industry of Letters," that "democracy not only gives the industrial classes a taste for letters, but also brings an industrial spirit into literature. . . . Democratic literature is always crawling with writers who look upon letters simply as a trade, and for each of the few great writers you can count thousands of idea-mongers."[24] De Tocqueville's modern version of Lucian's "Sale of Philosophers" seems to be the theoretical touchstone of many modern sociologies of literature which, bolstered by statistical studies of sales and taste,[25] help us to understand a little more about how a political system may be said to influence what is produced or published but which do not pertain in particular to literary production. The sociologist Georg Simmel explains the appeal of all works of art by arguing that "the strange coalescing, abstraction, and anticipation of ownership of property, which constitutes the meaning of money, is like aesthetic pleasure in permitting consciousness a free play, a portentous extension into an unresisting medium, and the incorporation of all possibilities without violation or deterioration by reality."[26] This simile, and Simmel's related figure that beauty is a *promesse de bonheur* as money is a credit, pertain not only to the plea- sure associated with the contemplation of linguistic products in par- ticular but also to that associated with the contemplation of art in general. As we shall see, many theories of beauty associate sublimity with a feeling of liberation from work. Why, then, should the social study of art focus so much attention on language and literature?

The ways in which specifically linguistic products are similar to and interiorize aspects of the political economy distinguish them from other kinds of art. Language has a unique relation to social fictions. Al- though ideas may be expressed materially or sensibly in other

24. Alexis de Tocqueville, *Democracy in America*, trans. George Lawrence (New York, 1969), p. 475. Cf. R. P. Blackmur, "Economy of the American Writer," in *The Lion and the Honeycomb* (New York, 1955); and Leo Lowenthal, "German Popular Biographies: Culture's Bargain Counter," in *The Critical Spirit*, ed. Kurt H. Wolff and Barrington Moore, Jr. (Boston, 1967).

25. See, for example, Gerald Reitlinger, *The Economics of Taste: The Rise and Fall of Picture Prices, 1760–1960* (London, 1961); and Levin L. Schücking, *Die Soziologie der literarischen Geschmacksbildung* (Leipzig and Berlin, 1931).

26. Georg Simmel, *Philosophie des Geldes*, 2d enlarged ed. (Leipzig, 1907); trans. Roberta Ash, in *On Individuality and Social Forms*, ed. Donald N. Levine (Chicago, 1971), p. 180.

ways—sculpture and film, for example—it is often believed, as Kant writes, that "books are the greatest means of carrying on the exchange [Verkehr] of thought," just as "money is the greatest means of human intercommunication [Verkehr]."[27] Literary theory, which is in part the study of the relationship between these two kinds of exchange, is privileged to study, as in a looking-glass, the medium in which it is itself conceived. Language is the final and original home of the conscious spirit of mankind, and it enables men to incorporate and rise above contemporary and socially "functional" ideologies. Hegel argues that this power of the human spirit is in part attributable to the ultimate separability of language and its sensible or material basis (sound).[28] This introductory chapter has, of course, relied uncritically on metaphors of sight, which imply something sensed (seen). The following chapters, however, will seek to diagnose the hypothetical position of sensible things and to comprehend the insensible or silent language of philosophy.

Poetics is about production (*poiēsis*). There can be no analysis of the form or content of production without a theory of labor. Labor, like language, is symbolically mediated interaction, reconciling man and "nature." For Hegel, whose dialectic of the spirit challenges the idea of nature itself, language is "the medium in which the first integration between subject and object takes place" or "the first lever of appropriation"[29] that enables an individual "to take a conscious position against his fellows and to assert his individual needs and desires against them."[30] Hegel suggests the direction of any adequate economics of literature when he argues that the worker's instrument is the medium of labor, the object of which is nature-in-transformation; and that speech is the medium of memory, the object of which is nature-in-conception. Although labor and memory are aspects of an ideal (as opposed to a real) conscience, work is a higher subject than memory; it corresponds to a practical (not, as does memory, to a theoretical)

27. Immanuel Kant, *Die Metaphysik der Sitten: Metaphysische Anfangsgründe der Rechtslehre* (1798); trans. W. Hastie, *The Philosophy of Law* (Edinburgh, 1887), pp. 124–25.

28. See, for example, G. W. F. Hegel, *The Philosophy of Fine Art*, trans. F. P. B. Osmaston (London, 1920), 4: 13–18. Joseph Stalin, erring on the side of dogma, argues that "only idealists can speak of thinking not being connected with 'the natural matter' of language" (*Marxism and Problems of Linguistics* [New York, 1951]).

29. G.W.F. Hegel, *Jenaer Realphilosophie*, ed. Johannes Hoffmeister (Leipzig, 1931), esp. 1: 211 and 2: 183.

30. Herbert Marcuse, *Reason and Revolution* (London, 1968), p. 75.

"poetics is about production"

labor, like language, is a symbolically mediated interaction

conscience.[31] Among modern Hegelians, there is a controversy about the difference between work (which concerns economics) and memory (which concerns literature and language). Georg Lukács and Herbert Marcuse stress the priority of work and argue that it can solve many of the problems raised by speech. Jürgen Habermas argues that language, like labor, is a mode of self-production, but he admits that the dialectic of one differs from that of the other. Theodor W. Adorno and Max Horkheimer do not so much emphasize the medium of speech as underemphasize the medium of labor.[32] The study of literature and poetic production cannot ignore this controversy. It, too, has to do with the relation between our labor and our memory, including our memory or our hypothesis of origins.

The following chapters begin with material hypotheses. "The Ring of Gyges," for example, considers the historical origin in the same time and place of both philosophy and coined money; "The Lie of the Fox," the position that words signify original things or that money signifies commodities; and "John Ruskin and the Economy of Literature," the supposition that literature is valuable. These studies of literary and linguistic production attempt to show how it is possible, in the course of thought, to begin with material hypotheses that, in the end, hardly matter.

For theoretical totality it is unnecessary, and within the space of a single volume it is impossible, to refer to all works of literature and philosophy. In general, I shall consider only those works whose interpretation (and, less often, whose historical existence) is necessary to the development of the argument. These necessary interpretations, however, are representative enough to suggest the whole way of the thoughtful economy of literature, whose subject matter is the comprehension of thought and matter and whose goal is to show how literary and philosophical fictions (perhaps even our own) can help us to understand and to change the tyranny of our world.

31. Hegel, *Jenaer Realphilosophie*, 1: 197; and G. Planty-Bonjour, in G. W. F. Hegel, *La Première Philosophie de l'esprit*, trans. G. Planty-Bonjour (Paris, 1969), p. 20.

32. G. Lukács, *Der junge Hegel: Über die Beziehungen von Dialektik und Ökonomie* (Zurich and Vienna, 1948); Marcuse, *Reason and Revolution*; Jürgen Habermas, *Technik und Wissenschaft als Ideologie* (Frankfurt, 1968), esp. pp. 26–27; and on Adorno and Horkheimer see Martin Jay, *The Dialectical Imagination: A History of the Frankfurt School and the Institute of Social Research, 1923–1950* (Boston, 1973).

*the common historical origin
of both philosophy & coined money*
*the ethical - political imperative that
is the goal of the economy of literature*

1

THE RING OF GYGES

In *The Genealogy of Morals,* Nietzsche argues that "the mind of early man was preoccupied to such an extent with price-making . . . that in a certain sense this may be said to have constituted his thinking."[1] A fundamental change in price-making constitutes a fundamental change in thinking. The development of money was such a change. Although minting was not a great technological innovation, money informed a powerful revolution in economic and verbal media.[2] The genealogy of the money form is the study of a new logic that is the money of the mind. In this chapter, we shall study the "constitutional" relationship between the origin of money and the origin of philosophy itself.

To the Greeks the exact place and time of the introduction of coinage was uncertain. Their genetic explanations of coinage do not depend, however, on exactitude of chronological and geographic data. They focus instead on hypothetical or mythical periods during which they suppose money to have originated. Wishing to discuss the effects of coinage and the relationship between money and the mind, the ancient Greeks chose many different birth places, times, and events.[3] Their quarrel about the origin of coinage, however, is a de-

1. Friedrich Nietzsche, "Zur Genealogie der Moral," in *Werke in drei Bänden* (Munich, 1955), 2: 811; trans. F. Golffing, *The Birth of Tragedy and the Genealogy of Morals* (New York, 1956), p. 202.

2. Coined money was not a technological breakthrough, but rather the culmination of several developments (Babylonian credit, metal-stamping, etc.). Cf. other important inventions during this period, such as the alphabet and the calendar.

3. In his *Onomasticon,* Julius Pollux refers to the following statement of Colophon: "Perhaps some would think it ambitious to investigate this question, whether coins were first issued by Pheidon of Argos or by the Cymaen Demodice, wife of the Phrygian Midas, who was the daughter of Agamemnon, king of Cyme, or by the Athenians, Erichtonius and Lycus, or by the Lydians, as Xenophon asserts, or by the Naxians, according to the view of Agloasthenes" (*Onom.* 9.83). Ephorus and the Parian Chronicle both agree that the first man to mint coins was Pheidon of Argos.

bate not about antiquarian data but rather about the ideological significance of money.

Herodotus argued that coinage was born in Lydia during the reign of Gyges or his son.[4] (Modern research has shown that Herodotus was probably correct.)[5] The assumption of Lydia as the birthplace of coinage shaped much ancient thought. Whether or not Gyges or his descendant was in fact the first man to mint coins, he was associated in the minds of the Greeks with minting. Like Midas, his neighbor who turned all things into gold with a touch, Gyges turned all things into gold by his ability to purchase them with gold minted into coins.

As coinage was associated with the Lydians, so too was political tyranny, "a phenomenon no less important in the history of culture than in the development of the Greek state."[6] The very word *tyrannos* is Lydian in origin.[7] Many Greeks believed that Gyges was the first tyrant, and often associated him with tyranny; he was the archetypal

---

4. Herodotus 1.94. Quotations from Herodotus are adapted from the Loeb edition (*Herodotus*, trans. A. D. Godley, 4 vols. (London, 1931–38) or, less often, from *The Histories of Herodotus*, trans. H. Cary (New York, 1904).

5. Very little is known about Lydia. The evidence is almost all archeological. (See G. M.A. Hanfmann in *Bulletins of the American Schools of Oriental Research* [1961–66].) "For literature we have no evidence at all, since the stone inscriptions which we have written in the Lydian language do not date earlier than the fifth century, and the poet Alcman, writing at the end of the seventh century B.C., left Sardis. Literature was not highly regarded at the Lydian court" (John Griffiths Pedley, *Sardis in the Age of Croesus* [Norman, Okla., 1968], p. 113; cf. John Griffiths Pedley, *Ancient Literary Sources on Sardis* [Cambridge, Mass., 1972]). The standard but outdated history of Lydia is that of F. A. Radet, *La Lydie et le monde grec au temps des Mermnades* (Paris, 1893). Most modern scholars agree that coinage began in Lydia (see William J. Young, "The Fabulous Gold of the Pactolus Valley," *Boston Museum Bulletin* 70, no. 359 [1972], p. 7).

Authorities on ancient China claim that coins circulated there as early as the twentieth century B.C., but there is no archeological evidence of coinage in China before the seventh century B.C. Coinage in India developed during the first half of the sixth century B.C. (Cf. R. A. G. Carson, *Coins of the World* [New York, 1962], pp. 499, 537; and Lien-sheng Yang, *Money and Credit in China* [Cambridge, Mass., 1952].)

6. Werner Jaeger, *Paidea*, trans. Gilbert Highet, 3 vols. (Oxford, 1945), 1: 223. Scholars of Greek history agree that there occurred in the sixth century a revolution in the ways of thinking about nature. Jean-Pierre Vernant (*Mythe et pensée chez les Grecs* [Paris, 1966], pp. 296–97, 307–8, 311) argues that this revolution was related to the development of money. Jaeger allies the revolution to tyranny, "an intermediate stage between the rule of the nobility and the rule of the people" (Jaeger, *Paidea*, vol. 1, p. 223).

7. On the word *tyrant*, see Roberto Gusmani, *Lydisches Wörterbuch* (Heidelberg, 1964); and Radet, who tries to show the relationships between *tyrannos*, *Tyra* (the name of a Lydian village where Gyges tried to rule), *Tyrrhēnos* (a great hero), and *Tiera* (the Lydian word for "strong fort"). Radet suggests that Greek grammarians believed that the word did not enter Greek vocabulary until Gyges' seizure of power in Lydia.

tyrant as he was the archetypal minter.[8] Indeed, the frequent association of tyranny and minting with one man suggests that they may be mutually reinforcing and interdependent.[9]

It is not easy for us, who have used coinage for some twenty-five hundred years, to imagine the impression it made on the minds of those who first used it in their city-states. The introduction of money to Greece has few useful analogies.[10] Tales of Gyges associate him with founding a tyranny in Lydia and with a power of being able to transform visibles into invisibles and invisibles into visibles. This power, as we shall see, is associated with new economic and political forms that shattered the previous world and its culture.[11] The story of Gyges, however hypothetical or mythical, is a great explanation of the genesis of a political, economic, and verbal semiology.

Many men pretend to dislike money and tyranny. Golden tyranny, though, may be the correspondent or foundation of much that we pretend to love. The myth of Gyges helps to reveal the origin of modern thought and to call that thought into question. As with the study of other apparently historical origins (those of sin, language,

8. See C. Müller, *Fragmenta Historicorum Graecorum*, 5 vols. (Paris, 1841–70), 3:72, Euphorion of Chalcis, frag. 1; quoted by Radet, *Lydie*, p. 146.

9. The relationship between coinage and tyranny has been studied by Peter N. Ure (*The Origin of Tyranny* [New York, 1962]), who argues that the rise of tyrants is directly related to the rise of coinage (cf. Radet, *Lydie*, p. 163). He offers many examples, including Peisistratus (Athens), Polycrates (Samos), Gyges (Lydia), Midas (Phrygia), Pheidon (Argos), and Cypselus (Corinth). "Coinage," he insists, "is the most epoch-making revolution in the whole history of commerce" (p. 1). Those states in which money was not introduced (Sparta and Thessaly, for example) did not develop tyrannies (pp. 22 ff.). Victor Ehrenberg (*From Solon to Socrates* [London, 1968], p. 24) disagrees with Ure, arguing that it is a "mistake to attribute the social upheavals of the later seventh century to the introduction of coinage." Ehrenberg is probably correct that the largest commercial effects of the introduction of coinage were not felt until the fifth century. In this chapter, however, we are interested in the relation between the rise of coinage and the rise of certain forms of thought, and the ways in which the Greeks thought about this relation. (Ehrenberg merely says that "the parallelism of minds and the exchange of ideas were equalled on the material side" [*From Solon to Socrates*, p. 108].)

10. A visitor to a state in which coins circulated might have experienced surprise similar to that of Marco Polo when he visited the city of Cambaluc (China), where paper money circulated. Polo was fascinated by (and his European contemporaries incredulous about) the printing and circulation of such monies. The mystified Polo even argued that the Emperor had a power like that of a "perfect alchemist" (Marco Polo, *The Description of the World*, trans. A. C. Moule and Paul Pelliot [London, 1938], pp. 237–40).

11. On the shattering of the archaic Greek culture, see Chapter 2, "Esthetics and Economics."

inequality, and morality, for example), the study of the origin of money becomes also the study of forms of human activity.

TALES OF GYGES

Herodotus

The tale of the rise to power of the archetypal minter and tyrant plays an important role in the thought of Herodotus and of Plato. By interpreting their versions of the tale we can begin to understand an economic and cultural revolution that corresponds to the origin of money and of philosophy.[12]

In Book 1 of his *Histories*, Herodotus relates the tale of Gyges' taking the royal power from Candaules in gold-rich Lydia. Gyges does not actively seek the kingdom, but is rather a pawn, first of the king and then of the queen. During the first part of the story, Gyges obeys the orders of King Candaules, whose need to have a witness to the beauty of his queen is the occasion of the plot. Candaules tries to persuade Gyges (his courtly confidant) of the queen's beauty: "Candaules fell in love with his own wife, so much that he supposed her to be by far the fairest woman in the world; and being thus persuaded of this, he raved of her beauty (*eidos*) to Gyges" (Hdt. 1.8). In this tale of erotic intrigue the master seems able to define the value of himself and his possessions only by the esteem of his slaves. Moreover, Candaules does not believe that the verbal testimony he gives to Gyges is sufficient for Gyges to appraise his "property," and he seeks to provide ocular proof. Candaules insists that Gyges become a voyeur and spy on his wife naked in the bedroom: "I think, Gyges, that you do not believe what I tell you of the beauty (*eidos*) of my wife; men trust their ears less than their eyes" (Hdt. 1.8). Candaules contrasts spoken words with things seen. He seems to agree with Heraclitus that "eyes

---

12. Ancient writers about Gyges include Xanthos, Anacreon, Plutarch, Cicero, Archilochus, and Horace (cf. Pedley, *Sources on Sardis*). Modern writers include Hans Sachs, Montaigne, La Fontaine, Rousseau, Saint Jerome, Friedrich Hebbel, Quevedo y Villegas, Théophile Gautier, Addison, Beaumont and Fletcher, Hugo von Hofmannstahl, and Gide. Modern critics include Ernst Bickel (*Ilbergs Jahrbücher* [Berlin, 1921], 47: 5.336 ff.), who presents a short history of works of literature about Gyges; Karl Reinhardt ("Gyges und Sein Ring," in *Vermächtnis der Antike* [Göttingen, 1966]), who presents an interpretation of the Platonic and Herodotean versions; and Kirby Flower Smith ("The Tale of Gyges and the King of Lydia," *American Journal of Philology* 23, no. 3 [1902]).

are more accurate witnesses than ears."[13] A man's word is not sufficient testimony—one must see.

The act of seeing articulates Herodotus's plot, in which making
something perfectly believable means making it visible or removing
its clothing. The Lydians, significantly, had very strict taboos against
nakedness.[14] Gyges is therefore frightened at Candaules' suggestion
that he break the law: "Master! What a pestilent command is this that
you lay upon me . . . that I should see her who is my mistress naked!
With the stripping off of her tunic a woman is stripped of all the
honour/shame (*aidōs*) due to her" (Hdt. 1.8). The sight of the queen's
beauty (*eidos*) by anyone other than the king would be a violation of
the queen's honor (*aidōs*, almost a homonym of *eidos*).[15] Gyges tries to
remind the king that "men long ago made wise rules for our learning,
and one of these is, that we, and none other, should see what is our
own" (Hdt. 1.8). The queen is the property not of just any man, but of
the king. Gyges is being asked by the spokesman of political power to
violate not just any law, but law itself. He senses danger for himself
(and, perhaps, for the insecure, enamoured king) and begs that the
king not force him to break the ancient commandment: "I fully believe that your queen is the fairest of all women; ask not lawless
(*anomōn*) acts of me, I entreat you" (Hdt. 1.8). Gyges' appeal to *nomos*
fails. The master Candaules himself plans to introduce his servant to
the queen's chamber:

> I will so contrive the whole business that she shall never know that you
> have seen her. I will bring you into the chamber (*oikēma*) where she and
> I lie and set you behind the open door; and after I have entered, my
> wife too will come to the bed. There is a chair set near the entrance of
> the room; on this will she lay each part of her raiment as she takes it off,
> and you will be able to gaze upon her at your leisure. Then, when she

13. Heraclitus, frag. 12, in H. Diels, *Fragmente der Vorsokratiker*, 5th ed. (Berlin, 1934).
The opposition between sound and sight is related to that between oral and witnessed
contracts (which, as we shall see, was an important one in the sixth and fifth centuries
B.C.). In the *Essai sur les origines des langues* ([Paris, 1970], p. 503), Jean-Jacques Rousseau
approves the Horatian judgment, saying "on parle aux yeux bien mieux qu'aux oreilles." Rousseau fears, however, that invisibles (e.g., words heard) have a more powerful effect on the human heart than visibles (e.g., things seen). Rousseau, who considers
the power of Gyges in another work (see n. 44), suggests that one's interest is very
much excited by words (e.g., those which Candaules speaks to Gyges or those which
Herodotus writes to us) but that exact testimony requires a witness or seer.

14. Among the Lydians it is held a great shame to be seen naked. Cf. Thucydides
(1.6.5–6); Plato (*Rep.* 457a–b); and Seth Benardete (*Herodotean Inquiries* [The Hague,
1969], pp. 11–14) on the tale of Gyges.

15. Benardete (ibid., p. 12) remarks that "*aidōs* occurs nowhere else in Herodotus."

goes from the chair to the bed, turning her back upon you, do you look to it that she does not see you going out through the doorway. (Hdt. 1.9)

That night Candaules' plan is put into effect. Gyges sees the naked queen and so violates her *aidōs*.

If the plan of Candaules to make Gyges invisible to the queen had been successful, then Gyges would have had for one night a power (in relation to Candaules' queen) like that of the Platonic Gyges (who, by virtue of his ring, could see without being seen). Unfortunately for the outlaw king, the plan fails: the queen sees Gyges as he slips out of the room. (The thoughts of the queen on seeing Gyges may have been the subject of ancient plays.[16] Herodotus, however, does not concern himself with the queen's thoughts, but concentrates on the bare structure of the plot.) The queen does not let it be known that she has percieved Gyges. In the morning, however, she assures herself of those of her household (*oiketeia*, Hdt. 1.11) who are faithful, and calls the unsuspecting Gyges to her. The queen demands that either the violator (Gyges) or he who enabled such violation to take place (Candaules) be killed: "You must either kill Candaules and take me for your own and the throne of Lydia, or yourself be killed now without more ado. . . . That will prevent you from seeing (*idēs*) what you should not see" (Hdt. 1.11). Only one seer of her naked beauty (*eidos*) and shame (*aidōs*) can live, and that person must be king. The threatened Gyges chooses to kill Candaules, thus ceasing to be the pawn of the king and becoming that of the queen. Now the queen plots to render Gyges invisible to the king, so that he can commit the unlawful murder at the same place (the chamber or *oikēma*) where Gyges saw the naked queen: "You shall come at him from the same place whence he made you see me naked" (Hdt. 1.11). As Gyges wished to be lawful when the king commanded him to spy on the queen, so he again wishes to be lawful when the queen commands him to kill the king. He commits the murder, however, because "he could not get free or by any means escape but either he or Candaules must die" (Hdt. 1.12).

Gyges' murder of Candaules, his marriage to the queen, and his seizure of power mark a change in the *nomos* of the ruling *oikos*: an "economic" revolution. Gyges' power as tyrant is different from that of Candaules. Gyges' violation of the queen's shame and knowledge

---

16. The thoughts of the espied queen may be the subject of a play of the fourth or third century B.C. In this play, the queen first fears for the life of the king when she espies a strange man in the bedroom. Later she guesses the truth. She waits until morning and then orders Gyges to kill her husband (whom she calls *tyrannos*). See D. L. Page, *A Chapter in the History of Greek Tragedy* (Cambridge, 1951), p. 3.

of her beauty depends on sight alone. He will not seek confirmation of her beauty from others (as did the insecure Candaules) but, servant become master, will rule as a tyrant, making even himself invisible.

Herodotus's account of Gyges' rise to power emphasizes reversals of visibility and invisibility. One reason for this emphasis is the Lydian prohibition of nakedness—an extreme form of being visible. Neither a ruler nor his queen may be seen. The emperor must be clothed. A tyrant maintains power by using this *nomos* against being seen to punish enemies who "see," and by ensuring that he himself be invisible when it is prudent to be so. Gyges, for example, uses the law against seeing the ruler in order to trap one of his former enemies, Lixos, who presents a potential threat to Gyges' new regime. According to Xanthos, Gyges commanded Lixos never to look at him, swearing to bury Lixos in the same spot if he did see him.[17] Gyges the servant killed king Candaules in the same place where he had seen the naked queen; Gyges the king now wishes to kill an enemy who has seen him. In order to do this legally, Gyges contrives a meeting with Lixos in a bad part of town, where Lixos would not expect the king to go. Here the king is, so to speak, naked or perfectly visible. Gyges surprises Lixos, who, unable to avert his eyes, commits the capital offense of seeing the king.

One of the foils to Gyges in Herodotus' *Histories* is Deioces the Mede, who became invisible to his subjects by establishing one of the first great bureaucracies in Western civilization. Indeed, Deioces was as successful at being invisible as the neighboring Lydian ruler. The development of a bureaucracy supposes two fundamental social conditions: the development of forms of symbolization, such as money and writing, and the relative invisibility of the ruler. Max Weber argues that money, the invention of which Herodotus discusses in book 1, is the basis of any bureaucracy.[18] In Herodotus's description

---

17. Page (*Greek Tragedy*, pp. 18–19) summarizes the version of Xanthos: "Gyges was sent to fetch the King's bride, a lady named Toudo. On the way home he fell in love with her himself, violently but in vain. The virtuous princess complained to her bridegroom the King, who swore that he would execute Gyges tomorrow. So during the night, Gyges, warned by an amorous maidservant, murdered the King." The version of Xanthos is reported by Nicolas of Damascus (Müller, *F.H.G.*, vol. 3, frag. 49, pt. 2, pp. 383–86).

18. The relationship between money and bureaucracy (suggested by Radet) has been studied by Max Weber, who writes that "the development of the money economy, in so far as a pecuniary compensation of the officials is concerned, is a presupposition of bureaucracy" (Max Weber, *Wirtschaft und Gesellschaft* [Tubingen, 1922], pt. 3, ch. 6; ed. and trans. H. H. Gerth and C. Wright Mills in *From Max Weber* [New York, 1958], p. 204). "Even though the full development of a money economy is not an indispensable precondition for bureaucratization, bureaucracy as a permanent structure is knit to the

of the politics of the Medes, an "invisible hand" (with which money has often been associated) plays a major role.

According to Herodotus, Deioces began his political career as an ordinary judge. By seeming to judge well, he made himself respected among the Medes. When he refused to judge any longer, the people, who had become dependent on his judgments, begged him to be king. Once king, Deioces wished to conceal his unjust motives from the people, and accordingly he built the seven-walled city of Ecbatana. The walls were concentric circles, the innermost of which was made of gold, the medium of exchange (Hdt. 1.98). Inside this wall Deioces lived and reigned.

From within his golden walls Deioces set what Herodotus considers to be precedents in the history of politics: "And when all was built, it was Deioces first who established the rule that no one should come into the presence of the king, but all should be dealt with by the means of messengers; that the king should be seen by no man" (Hdt. 1.99). Deioces established himself as the source of the law, in the same relation to his subjects as money (misunderstood as measure) is to commodities. One interpreter writes: "As the unjust source of all justice, Deioces could not be seen; he was the measure of without being himself measurable by right and wrong."[19] Herodotus explains the attempt to rise above ordinary men: "He was careful to hedge himself with all this state in order that the men of his own age (who had been bred up with him and were as nobly born as he and his equals in manly excellence), instead of seeing him and being thereby vexed and haply moved to plot against him, might by reason of not seeing him deem him to be changed from what he had been (or to be different from themselves)" (Hdt. 1.99). This invisible being (an ancient Wizard of Oz) introduced written communications to protect his position. "When he had established himself in the tyranny, he was very severe in the distribution of justice. And the parties contending were obliged to send him their cases in writing, and he having come to a decision on the cases so laid before him, sent them back again" (Hdt. 1.100). Not only did Deioces thus make himself invisible to others, but he also made others visible to him: "If he received information that any man had injured another, he would presently send for him, and punish him in proportion to his offence; and for this

---

one presupposition of a constant income for maintaining it" (p. 208). Though Weber mentions certain exceptions to this general rule (Egypt is one), the bureaucracies of the Eastern satraps (such as those of Croesus and Deioces) are among his most important examples (p. 205).

19. Benardete, *Herodotean Inquiries*, p. 25.

purpose he had spies and eavesdroppers in every part of his domin-
ions" (Hdt. 1.100).

The employment of money and writing enabled Deioces to establish both bureaucracy and tyranny. The concentric walls of Ecbatana
were "ring-walls," which served to distinguish the invisible, private
realm of the house (*oikos*) or household (*oikia*) from the visible, public
realm of the polis.[20] The dislocating effects of the new media of
exchange—writing and money—helped him to found the kind of
government the Greeks most feared. Aristotle says that the true tyrant has spies (or political Peeping Toms), as powerful as Gyges (the
voyeur), who make others visible to him, and that he makes himself
invisible. Deioces, like Gyges, was a true tyrant.

According to Herodotus's *Histories*, the descendants of Gyges must
pay for his crime.[21] The oracle declares that "the Heraclidae should
have vengeance on Gyges' posterity in the fifth generation" (Hdt.
1.13). Herodotus tells how Croesus, the fifth descendant of Gyges, is
conquered by Cyrus, the fifth descendant of Deioces (Hdt. 1.80 ff.).[22]

20. Hannah Arendt (*The Human Condition* [Chicago, 1958], esp. pp. 63–64) argues
that "the law of the city-state [which distinguishes the visible from the invisible] was
quite literally a ring-wall." Following the Hegelian Fustel de Coulanges (*The Ancient
City* [New York, 1956]; cf. R. B. Onians, *The Origins of European Thought* [Cambridge,
1954], p. 444, n. 1), Arendt notes that words such as *polis, urbs,* town, and *Zaun* express
the notion of a circle. Cf. Heraclitus, frag. 44: "The people should fight for the law
(*nomos*) as for a wall."

21. They must pay as surely as Alberich (in Richard Wagner's *Der Ring des
Nibelungen*) must pay for forging into a ring the gold that he stole from the
Rhinemaidens. The slavish Alberich, like Herodotus's Gyges, has to forswear
Candaules-like love in order to win golden mastery. The Lydian tyrant Gyges (whose
source of power was the gold of the Pactolus River) and the Athenian tyrant Peisis-
tratus (whose source of power was gold mined by slave labor) may have inspired
Wagner's *Das Rheingold*. The latter deals with both the gold of the Rhine River (a
principal source of wealth in medieval Germany, according to Marc Bloch's "The Prob-
lem of Gold in the Middle Ages," in *Land and Work in Medieval Europe* [Berkeley and Los
Angeles, 1967], pp. 186 ff.) and the tyrannical enslavement of the Nibelung people.
George Bernard Shaw (*The Perfect Wagnerite*, in *Selected Prose*, ed. Diarmuid Russel
[London, 1953]), discussing the "sociological aspect of The Ring [of the Nibelung Cyc-
le]" (p. 207), notes that "Fafnir in the real world becomes a capitalist; but Fafnir in
[Wagner's] allegory is a mere hoarder" (p. 289).

22. What is known about Croesus and Cyrus supports the notion that there is more
than historical reason for Herodotus to pit them against each other in book 1. The
ancients told a story about Croesus ("the Midas of Lydia") and Pittacus, in which
Pittacus accepts Croesus's invitation to come to Lydia: "You bid me come to Lydia in
order to see your prosperity; but without seeing it I can well believe that the son of
Alyattes is the most opulent of kings. There will be no advantage to me in a journey to
Sardis, for I am not in want of money, and my possessions are sufficient for my friends
as well as myself. Nevertheless, I will come, to be entertained by you and to make your

After the defeat of Croesus, the oracle speaks: "The god himself even cannot avoid the decrees of fate; and Croesus has atoned the crime of his ancestor in the fifth generation who, being one of the bodyguard of the Heraclidae, was induced by the artifice of woman to murder his master and to usurp his dignity to which he had not right" (Hdt. 1.90).

The oracle's explanation of why Croesus is punished is inadequate. As already explained, the pawn Gyges can hardly be held accountable for his violation of the *nomos*. His rise to power was due not only to the artifice of a woman but also to a power to become invisible (as he was to the king) and to see things that are invisible to other men. It is this frightening power, shared by other rulers of the time, for which Croesus, the richest man in the world, is punished.

To the Herodotean inquiry into how Gyges won the wife and tyranny of Candaules, a commentator added a note mentioning a poem of Archilochus, "who lived in about the same time as Gyges" (Hdt. 1.12). "I care not for the wealth of golden Gyges, nor ever have envied him; I am not jealous of the works of gods, and I have no desire for lofty tyranny; for such things are far beyond my sight."[23] Gyges' wealth, the works of the gods, and lofty tyranny are beyond the sight of most men. Although the wealth of Gyges was proverbial, nothing explicit in Herodotus's tale associates Gyges with wealth. As we shall see in the following section, however, Gygean tyranny may be associated with economic relations between visible and invisible property and with the Lydian invention of coinage about which Herodotus tells us (Hdt. 1.94).

Herodotus's story of Gyges is an "oriental" tale fashioned into a political weapon spying on the workings of tyranny. In his *Histories*, Herodotus himself spies on, or makes naked to the Greek people,

acquaintance" (Diogenes Laertius 1. 81–83). Pittacus is as unwilling to inspect the wealth of Croesus as Gyges was unwilling to inspect the nakedness of the queen. (Diogenes Laertius suggests elsewhere that Alyattes was the inventor of coins.)

Cyrus, who later conquers Croesus, was not afraid of Lydian customs, such as those of retailing, to which Herodotus allies the use of money. Herodotean Cyrus says "I was never yet afraid of those who in the midst of their cities have a place set apart in which they collect and cheat one another by false oaths" (Hdt. 1.152).

23. Archilochus, frag. 25, in *Greek Elegy and Iambus with Anacreontea*, ed. and trans. J. M. Edmonds (Cambridge, Mass., 1968), 2: 111. On the probability that the reference to Archilochus is an interpolation, see the critical note to Hdt. 1.12 in Herodotus, *Histoires*, ed. and trans. Ph.-E. LeGrand (Paris, 1964), bk. 1: *Clio*. Aristotle (*Rhetoric* 1418.42b) suggests that Archilochus makes Charon (a carpenter) speak the lines of the poem, and Plutarch argues that Archilochus speaks *in propria persona*. Archilochus's fragment is the *locus classicus* for similar protests against Gyges. (See Anacreonta 8, in *Greek Elegy and Iambus with Anacreonta*, 2:27–28.)

nomoi different from their own. The Greeks did not have the same pro-
hibitions against nakedness of the human body as did the Lydians.
There is a counterpart in some Greek thought, however, to the *aidōs*
and/or *eidos* of Candaules' queen. In the works of Plato, for example,
the politically crucial sight of the queen is lifted to the level of the *eidos*
(Idea), which most men cannot see, but that Socrates wishes to make
visible to the best men. By most men Socrates' seeing and teaching of
the naked truth is condemned, although, as we shall see, Plato is careful to distinguish the truly damnable tyrant (e.g., Gyges) from the
philosopher (e.g., Socrates).

Plato

Plato's tale of Gyges' rise to power elucidates both Herodotus's
account and various problems raised in the *Republic*. In Plato's dialogue, Gyges is an archetype of one who seems to be but is not good.
His tyrannic power of invisibility is a hypothetical device that neatly
defines one of the extreme positions in the debate about virtue and
justice.

Book 1 of the *Republic* prepares the context within wich the significance of the tale of Gyges must be understood. A preview of the
arguments about the relative desirability of wealth (for which
Cephalus argues) and philosophy (for which Socrates argues), book 1
describes how Socrates and his acquaintances go to the home of
Polemarchus. Cephalus, Polemarchus's rich father, tells the assembly
that he believes money to be good because with it one can act justly
by paying one's debts to men and gods. He gives credence to "tales
told about what is in Hades, that the one who has done unjust deeds
here must pay the penalty there."[24] Like many other Greeks,
Cephalus trusts that his wealth will save him from punishment or
from committing the wrongs that entail punishment. He hopes that it
will make the vengeful Hades (*Haidēs*) unable to see (*idein*) him, and he
believes that his money is in this sense an agent of invisibility.[25]

24. Plato, *Rep.* 330d. Quotations from Plato are adapted from *Plato in Twelve Volumes*,
trans. H. N. Fowler, W. R. M. Lamb, Paul Shorey, and R. G. Bury (Cambridge, Mass.
and London, 1914–37); and *The Republic of Plato*, trans. with an interpretative essay by
Allan Bloom (New York, 1968).

25. In the *Cratylus*, Socrates addresses himself to the error of those men who, like
Cephalus, are good out of fear. He offers an ironic etymology of *Pluto* (who is supposed
to rule over the invisible region below) and *Plutus*: "As for Pluto, he was so named as
the giver of wealth (*ploutos*) because wealth comes up from below out of the earth" (*Cra.*
403a). (Cf. Sophocles' Fragment 273 and Aristophanes' *Plutus* 727). The double meaning
of *aeides* as both "unseen" and "Hades" (the realm over which Pluto is supposed to rule)

Socrates knows that such beliefs, though untrue, are serviceable to the normal functioning of society. Any objection he might make to these beliefs, therefore, might be subversive to the polis. Nevertheless, Socrates does object to Cephalus's assumption that it is just to pay all one's debts: "Everyone would surely say that if a man takes weapons from a friend when the latter is of sound mind, and the friend demands them back when he is mad, one shouldn't give back such things, and moreover, one should not be willing to tell someone in this state of mind the whole truth" (*Rep.* 331c).[26] Socrates' example should convince one who is not mad that justice is not simply paying one's debts. Even if there were a Hades, money (or an ability to pay) would not ensure that one would escape unpunished by just gods. Unable to defend his beliefs, old Cephalus takes his leave of the assembly, saying that he must offer sacrifices to the gods and pay them their due (*Rep.* 331d).

Polemarchus, heir to his father Cephalus's argument as to his wealth (*Rep.* 331d), attempts to defend a version of his father's definition of justice. He quotes the poet Simonides, "It is just to give to each what is owed" (*Rep.* 331e), and interprets this in a purely commercial sense. In disagreeing with Cephalus, Socrates had used the example of the deposit of a weapon. Disagreeing with Polemarchus, he uses the more abstract example of monetary deposits (*Rep.* 332a). Socrates demonstrates that a banker with whom a deposit is left may sometimes justly withhold a deposit from the depositor not only for his own sake but also for the sake of that depositor. Polemarchus, recognizing the problem implicit in a law that demands the return of all deposits, offers a new interpretation of the poet. He states that Simonides meant that justice requires one to help friends and injure enemies (*Rep.* 334b). Polemarchus also argues that one "is most able to help friends and injure enemies" while making war and being an ally in battle (*Rep.* 332e) and, during peacetime, by keeping money deposits (*Rep.* 333bc). Socrates points out, however, that such a definition of justice would make it a neutral art. The artisan of justice (as

---

provides Socrates with the opportunity to expand his consideration of false opinions and etymologies: "And as for Hades, I fancy that most people think that his is a name of the Invisible (*aeides*), so that they are afraid and call him Pluto" (*Cra.* 403a). Socrates, however, objects to this interpretation. He argues that "the name of Hades is not in the least derived from the invisible (*aeides*), but far more probably from knowing (*eidenai*) all noble things" (*Cra.* 404b). Knowledgeable men do not fear going to Hades denuded of their bodies and are good not because they fear but because they know. (See also *Phaedo* 80d.)

26. Aristotle seems to agree with the Socratic argument against simple reciprocity. See *Nicomachean Ethics* 1133a.

defined by Polemarchus) would be as clever at guarding money as at stealing it (*Rep.* 334c). One interpreter writes that "instead of being the model of reliability, the just man becomes the archetype of untrustworthiness, the possessor of power without guiding principle. He is a thief and a liar, the contrary of the debt-paying, truth-telling (seemingly) just man defined by Polemarchus' father."[27] True justice, then, must also inform us about who are friends and who (if any) are enemies and about what is the meaning of benefiting friends. Socrates' argument focuses not only on (the friendliness of) the transactors but also on the nature of what is owed. He suggests throughout that Simonides "meant that the owed is the fitting" (*Rep.* 332c) and that the deposition itself is finally unimportant.

Polemarchus, however, maintains his definition of justice as loyalty to friends and taking advantage of enemies. In order to show his mistake, or at least mock his position, Socrates takes this definition to an extreme by extending Polemarchus's argument to the individual who believes that he has no friends and is loyal only to himself. Such an individual is or would be a tyrant. Socrates implies that Polemarchus's definition of justice, even though it seems gentlemanly, is that of a tyrannical rich man (*Rep.* 336a). Polemarchus is an unwitting ideologue for rich men like his father Cephalus. Socrates thus exposes the contradictions in Polemarchus's love of property. Moreover, the youth's heretofore facile acceptance of the law is undermined, as that of Cephalus was not. The company finally agrees that Polemarchus's interpretation of Simonides' sentence was unwise (*Rep.* 335e), and Socrates even suggests that the doctrine Polemarchus had been expounding was merely that of some "rich man who has a high opinion of what he can do" (*Rep.* 336a).

At this point in the dialogue, the maddened Thrasymachus interrupts (*Rep.* 336b). He tries to "capitalize" on Polemarchus's love of property and Socrates' proof of the potential injustice of conventional law. Thrasymachus dismisses the Polemarchean conception of justice as an art or technique for harming one's enemies and helping one's friends. He tries, moreover, to destroy the Socratic hypothesis of the existence of true justice by arguing that the law lends an appearance of justice to whatever is done, and by arguing that appearance is all. He states that justice is "the advantage of the stronger" or "the advantage of the established ruling body," which, whether democratic or tyrannical, rules by threatening to punish lawbreakers (*Rep.* 338c–d). This position is taken to one extreme in Clitophon's argument that

---

27. Allan Bloom, "An Interpretative Essay," in *The Republic of Plato*, trans. Allan Bloom (New York, 1968), p. 320.

justice is what appears to the stronger man to be his own advantage (*Rep.* 340b). Thrasymachus himself does not understand any other reasons why a man would want to be a ruler than for selfish gain or money-making. He believes that a ruler is like a shepherd who serves not as protector of sheep but as their exploiter. Thrasymachus attacks the naïve position (which he believes Socrates to have adopted) that rulers rule for the sake of the ruled. "You do not even recognize sheep or shepherd. . . . You suppose shepherds consider the good of the sheep and take care of them looking to something other than their master's good or their own. You also believe that the rulers in the cities, those who truly rule, think about the ruled differently from the way a man would regard sheep" (*Rep.* 343b). Socrates points out, significantly, that Thrasymachus's shepherd is not essentially a shepherd but a moneymaker. "[Thrasymachus's shepherd], insofar as he is a shepherd, fattens the sheep, not looking to what is best for the sheep, but, like a guest who is going to be feasted, to good cheer, or in turn, to the sale, like a money-maker and not a shepherd. The art of the shepherd, as shepherd, surely cares for nothing but providing the best for what it has been set over" (*Rep.* 345d).[28] The distinction between "looking to what is best for the sheep" and "looking to the sale of the sheep" arises from the important distinction in Platonic thought between economics and chrematistics,[29] or between the various crafts and money-making. "Every artisan practices two arts—the one from which he gets his title, and the wage-earner's art. With the latter art he cares for himself; with the former, for others."[30] The architectonic and ubiquitous principle of wage-earning is exchange value or money. Seen from Thrasymachus's point of view, money seems to provide an architectonic principle for all the arts.

By exposing how money informs Thrasymachus's argument, Socrates offers an ideological critique of its sophistry, laced with suggestions that Thrasymachus seeks not wisdom but gold.[31] That to which Thrasymachus appeals is pure chrematistics, the tyrannical art *par excellence*.

Money is one of two competing architectonic principles in the *Re-*

28. Socrates also considers the relationships between shepherd and master and between shepherd and dog.

29. The distinction between shepherd and wage earner is like that between chrematist and economist (i.e., steward) in the economics of Aristotle (*Pol.*, bk. 1). See below, Chapter 3.

30. Bloom, "An Interpretative Essay," p. 332.

31. See *Rep.* 336d, and also Glaucon's suggestion that Thrasymachus speaks "for money's sake" (337d).

public; the other such principle is philosophy.[32] Philosophy and money both order the "other" arts and are about "worth" (although in different senses). Wage-earning is the tyrant's substitute for philosophy. A man cannot be both philosopher and wage earner. Cephalus, Polemarchus, and Thrasymachus cannot become philosophers and continue to believe in conventional debts and credits.

Book 1 of the *Republic* ends with Thrasymachean economics, the extreme form of Cephalean economics, "liberated" (with the help of Socrates himself) from inhibitions about friendship, punishment in Hades, and erroneous ideas about the *nomoi*. Socrates himself has presented no adequate definition of justice but has thoroughly and subversively debunked the convention of returning deposits or *parathēkai*. Moreover, he has not yet explained why, when, or if it is just to keep deposits belonging to another man, or why men should not become Thrasymachean tyrants. Book 1 is a politically subversive book: belief in the old Cephalean gods has been removed and nothing has replaced it. In the following books of the *Republic*, Socrates hopes to teach Adeimantus and Glaucon (Plato's brothers, who have been disturbed by Thrasymachus's argument) that it is better to be than to seem good, that is, it is better to be a philosopher than a clever and wealthy tyrant.

Book 1 of the *Republic* began with Cephalus's (mistaken but serviceable) argument that men should be "just." His argument was based on tales about punishment in Hades. Book 2 begins with a tale intended not to make men just but rather to demonstrate (as would Thrasymachus) that men are and should be unjust. This tale has the effect of removing ("in thought" only, *Rep.* 359 b) the threat that men will be punished for wrong-doing. The tale gives to, or deposits with, a man a hypothetical power almost as great as that of the Helmet of Hades (*Rep.* 612b). This helmet renders the wearer invisible to the

---

32. Philosophy and money-getting confront each other throughout Plato's works. Plato writes typically: "From the moral standpoint, it is not the right method to exchange one degree of pleasure or pain or fear for another, like coins of different values. There is only one currency for which all these tokens of ours should be exchanged, and that is wisdom" (*Phd.* 69a). In the *Laws* (913 ff.), he compares justice in the soul to money in the purse. Thomas Aquinas, interpreting Aristotle's *Politics*, suggests that the Platonic and Aristotelian argument about the architectonic characters of money and philosophy holds true in the Judaeo-Christian religion. "Money," he reads in Ecclesiastes (10:19), "answers for everything" (Thomas Aquinas, "Commentary on the Politics of Aristotle," trans. Ernest L. Fortin, para. 86). The preacher also said, "The protection of wisdom is like the protection of money" (Ecclesiastes 7:12).

gods and so ensures him protection from punishment in Hades similar to the protection that Cephalus believed money made available to
him. The Helmet of Hades, like money, can make wrong-doers invisible to a vengeful Hades. Glaucon wonders whether or not such a
power, if it did exist, might justify or make inevitable a decision to
become tyrannical. Fence-sitting between the love of wisdom
(philosophia) and the love of profit (philokerdeia), he tells the tale of
Gyges (for which he disclaims authorship).[33] This tale provides the
stimulus needed for further exploration of problems introduced in
book 1.

Glaucon beings the tale with a hypothesis:

> That those who practice [justice] do so unwillingly and from want of
> power to commit injustice—we shall be most likely to apprehend that if
> we entertain some such supposition as this in thought: if we grant to
> each, the just and the unjust, license and power to do whatever he
> pleases, and then accompany them in imagination and see whither his
> desire will conduct each, we should then catch the just man in the very
> act of resorting to the same conduct as the unjust man because of the
> self-advantage which every creature by its nature (physis) pursues as a
> good, while by the convention of laws (nomos) it is forcibly diverted to
> paying honour to "equality." (Rep. 359b–c)

The hypothetical grant of such a power has the limited purpose of
catching men and enabling us to see them as they truly are, or at least
as they would be if all restraints from the nomoi were removed. In this
sense, we see men morally naked. The tale gives us the same power,
in relation to those who have the power of which Glaucon speaks,
that Herodotus's Gyges had in relation to the king and queen of
Lydia. Glaucon grants the license to the supposedly historical per-
sonality Gyges. Such a license, he says, "would be most nearly such
as would result from supposing a man to have the power which men
say once came to (the ancestor of) Gyges the Lydian" (Rep. 359c–d).[34]
The power is that of invisibility. By being granted the power of invisibility, and hence the power to do evil without harm to his own
person and/or reputation, a man is supposedly made free of all social
restraints and able to do (without fear of punishment) anything he
wants. This makes him morally visible to those who hypothesize his
existence. He is on the same level as the souls, stripped and naked,

33. The Hipparchus (which was probably not written by Plato) is about the tension
between philosophia and philokerdeia.

34. Glaucon refers to an ancestor of Gyges rather than to Gyges himself. There may
be an error in the text (as some have argued) or there may have been an ancient
controversy about the name that has been lost to us.

brought before Zeus on the day of judgment. In this tale, Gyges, invisible to his fellow Lydians, will be morally naked (or perfectly visible) to us, who see him acting out his intentions.[35] We will be able to judge his justice and his happiness.

Gyges in Glaucon's tale is not an aristocrat (as in the versions of Herodotus and Xanthos), but a shepherd: "They relate that he was a shepherd in the service of the ruler at that time in Lydia. . . ." (*Rep.* 359d). Why does Plato make Gyges a shepherd? In book 1 of the *Republic*, the shepherd is an archetype of the ruler as well as the ruled. A shepherd "rules" his sheep and is "ruled" by his king. He is a king-in-training, who serves a king. A shepherd who is essentially a wage earner, said Socrates, will serve neither his sheep nor his master, but only himself. We wonder whether Gyges, if given the opportunity, will remain a shepherd or become a pure wage earner.

The rise to power of Plato's Gyges begins when he sees something.

> After a great deluge of rain and an earthquake, the ground opened and a chasm appeared in the place where he was pasturing; and they say that he went down and wandered into the chasm; and the story goes that he beheld other marvels there and a hollow bronze horse with little doors, and that he peeped in and saw a corpse within, as it seemed, of more than mortal stature, and that there was nothing else (*allo men ouden*) but a gold ring on its hand, which he took off and went forth. (*Rep.* 359d–e)

Gyges is said to see (*idein*) several things in the cave, including a corpse, apparently larger than an ordinary man, wearing a ring.[36] *Allo men ouden* implies both that Gyges saw nothing else, and that there was nothing else upon the corpse, so that Gyges saw the corpse naked. Seeing naked a man who is larger than life is (as the Lydians might say about seeing a naked queen) a hubristic step toward becoming an *isotheos*.[37] Gyges takes the initiative to steal the ring from the finger of the corpse.[38] He is no apparently fearful pawn, as was Herodotus's Gyges, who acted almost unwillingly. Plato's Gyges de-

---

35. Eva Brann, *Agōn* 1, no. 1, p. 6. Cf. *Gorgias* 523c.

36. Some things seen, which I do not here discuss, include the horse, which Pierre Maxime Schuhl (*La Fabulation platonicienne* [Paris, 1968], pp. 66 ff.) links to the story of the Trojan horse in Homer. The art of hollow-casting (by which alone such a statue could have been constructed) was founded in Samos, an island neighbor of Lydia and home of Polycrates (who tried unsuccessfully to rid himself of a ring).

37. The concept of *isotheos* (the one who is equal to the gods or godlike) plays an important role in the *Republic* (e.g., 568a–b). Compare *Gorgias* (509a) to Glaucon's description of Gyges.

38. This ring of Gyges was famous throughout antiquity. See *Suidas' Lexicon* (ed. G. Bernhardy [Halle, 1853]) on Gyges' ring.

cides of his own accord to take the illegal step that changes the course of Lydian history. Herodotean Gyges' violation of the law began with stealing a sight of Candaules' queen. Platonic Gyges' violation begins with stealing the ring from the king. (According to Greek and other law, all buried treasure belongs to the king of the land and not to him who may discover it.)[39]

Some time after this theft, Gyges and the other shepherds met to consider their monthly reports to the king about the flocks. Gyges comes wearing the ring.

> As he sat there it chanced that he turned the collet of the ring towards himself, towards the inner part of his hand, and when this took place they say that he became invisible (*aphanēs*) to those who sat by him and spoke of him as absent; and that he was amazed, and again fumbling with the ring, turned the collet outwards and so became visible (*phaneros*). On noting this he experimented with the ring to see if it possessed this virtue and he found the result to be that when he turned the collet inwards he became invisible and when outwards visible. (*Rep.* 359e–360a)

The ring makes the wearer visible or invisible. Invisibility enables the wearer to become a perfect spy, making others visible and thus vulnerable to him. This power and the description of it in terms of the opposition between the *aphanēs* and the *phaneron* provide us (as we shall see in the following section) with important clues to the social character of the license that Glaucon's tale grants to Gyges.[40]

Herodotean Gyges became unjust when he saw that which should have remained invisible.[41] Platonic Gyges, after his theft of the ring, is enabled by its powers to act even more unjustly. The ring helps Gyges to precipitate a revolution in the state and in the household of the king. "Learning that the ring made him invisible, he immediately contrived to be one of the messengers of the king. When he arrived, he committed adultery with the king's wife and, along with her, set upon the king and killed him. And so he took over the rule" (*Rep.*

---

39. *Blackstone's Commentaries*, W. D. L. Lewis, ed. (Philadelphia, 1898), bk. 1, ch. 8, pt. 3, sect. 9, "[Treasure] found hidden *in* the earth ... belongs to the king." Cf. Plato (*Leg.*, 913a ff.): "Take not up what you laid not down." Plato would guard against men stealing treasures that neither they nor their ancestors deposited. Wardens in the agora guard against such Gygean thieves.

40. Herodotus does not use the words *aphanēs* and *phaneros* in his tale of Gyges. As we shall see, Plato is pursuing a different tack in the exploration of visibility and invisibility.

41. Benardete, *Herodotean Inquiries*, p. 26.

360a). Gyges the "ringleader"[42] overcomes or seizes control of the
nomos. He even has the economic power "to take what he wishes
from the market-place," "to enter into houses (*oikiai*) and lie with
whomsoever he chooses," and "to slay and loose from bonds whomsoever he would" (*Rep.* 360b). He has the power to seem to be good and
to keep his wickedness hidden.

Why not become a Gygean tyrant? Herodotus's account gives an
answer in the form of an oracular history whereby Croesus is
punished for the crime of his ancestor. This punishment is paralleled
in Plato's account by the fine philosophic argument of Socrates in
which it is almost proven that the tyrant Gyges is neither enviable nor
happy. In this argument (which we shall interpret in the section entitled "Plato and the Money Form"), Socrates opposes tyranny (which
motivated Gyges) to the love of wisdom (which motivates the
philosopher) and concludes that Gyges, even if he had not only a ring
to make him invisible to men but also a Helmet of Hades (*Haidēs*) to
make him invisible to the gods, could not be happy or enviable: "We
have met all the . . . demands of the argument and we have not in-
voked the rewards and reputes of justice as you said [the poets] do,
but we have proved that justice in itself is the best thing for the soul in
itself, and that the soul ought to do justice whether it possess the ring
of Gyges or not, or the Helmet of Hades to boot" (*Rep.* 612b). Here
Socrates answers Glaucon's questions about whether any man would
be happy to have the ring of Gyges and whether all men would
inevitably be corrupted by it. The philosophical trial of Gyges, during
which he has been made truly visible to us, is supposed to be
ended.[43]

The conclusion that the ring of Gyges is finally a bad thing and
ought (if found) to be thrown away influenced many political
philosophers after Plato.[44] The ring of Gyges is a hypothesis that is

---

42. "Ringleader" is the Anglo-Saxon term for kings who ruled by virtue of rings.
Rings have often been associated with seizures of power. See William Jones, *Finger-
Ring Lore* (London, 1877); and Carl Heinz Klosterhalfen, *Ringe und Kreise; Macht und
Magie* (Emsdetten, 1967).

43. In a court case (significantly, about bank deposits), Isocrates writes: "Judges, pay
attention to my arguments! I shall render the dishonesty of the defendant visible
(*phanera*) to you" (*Discours*, ed. and trans. G. Mathieu and Emile Bremond [Paris, 1928],
no. 17). It is the goal of thought to make men such as Gyges visible to mankind.

44. In *Les Rêveries du promeneur solitaire* (in *Oeuvres complètes de Jean-Jacques Rousseau*, 4
vols. [Paris, 1959-]) Rousseau hypothesizes that he is offered the ring of Gyges, which
makes a man invisible as a god: "Si j'eusse été invisible et tout-puissant comme Dieu,
j'aurois été bienfaisant et bon comme lui. C'est la force et la liberté qui font les

discarded in the philosophical course of the *Republic*. Though philosophy seems thus to escape the power of the ring, we shall see that particular powers of the ring are actually internalized in Socratic thought and philosophy itself.

VISIBILITY AND INVISIBILITY

The Herodotean and Platonic versions of Gyges' rise to power both assign the ability to make things visible or invisible a crucial role. In Greek thought in general, the concepts of visibility and invisibility involve definitions of political orders (tyranny, for example) and of economic forms (money and real estate, for example) upon which political orders are often founded. We shall see that in the Platonic account of the accession of Gyges, the particular opposition of the invisible (*to aphanes*) to the visible (*to phaneron*) (Rep. 359e–360a) suggests an interpretation of the story and of the *Republic* itself in political and economic terms.

Invisibility and Tyranny

Several ancient critics tried to interpret the tales of Gyges by focusing on the problem of vision. Tzetzes notes that the queen (in the version by Herodotus) was successful in making Gyges invisible. He suggests that she was actually the owner of the magic ring (which appears only in Plato) and that she gave it to Gyges.[45] That the queen could see Gyges in the bedroom indicates that she possessed not only a power to make things invisible but also a corresponding power (as invisible spy) to make visible to herself things that were invisible to other people. Ptolemaeus Chennus writes that the eyes of "the wife of [C]andaules... had double pupils, and she was extremely sharp-

---

excellens hommes. . . . si j'eusse été possesseur de l'anneau de Gygès, il m'eut tiré de la dépendance des hommes et les eut mis dans la mienne" (1: 1057). Rousseau pretends for a moment that such a power would enable him to see men as they are—"[voir] les hommes tels qu'ils sont." The ring, in fact, would seem to grant him the power to accomplish the goal that he sets himself (1: 1047). Rousseau recognizes, however, that the ring is necessarily corrupting, even to a social utopian. "Celui que sa puissance met au dessus de l'homme doit être au dessus des foiblesses de l'humanité, sans quoi cet excés de force ne servira qu'à le mettre en effet au dessous des autres et de ce qu'il eut été lui-même s'il fut resté leur égal." Rousseau would throw away the ring of Gyges: "Tout bien considéré, je crois que je ferai mieux de jetter mon anneau magique avant qu'il m'ait fait faire quelque sotise" (1: 1058).

45. Johannes Tzetzes, *Chiliades* 1: 162 ff. and 7: 195 ff. (cited by Page, *Greek Tragedy*, p. 40).

sighted, being the possessor of the dragon-stone. This is how she came to see Gyges as he passed through the door."[46] The dragon-stone has an opposite effect from the magic ring. In one case the talisman makes people invisible; in the other case, it makes people visible: taken together, their power makes things visible or invisible. This is the power of Platonic Gyges. It is also the power of the archetypal tyrant.

Aristotle describes two methods, in polar opposition to each other, by which a tyrant seizes and maintains power. The first method is to ensure that the people of his city always be visible (*phaneroi*, *Pol.* 1313b7) to him, by the use of spies and rules against secret meetings. (This is the method employed by the bureaucratic Deioces and by Candaules' queen in the account of Ptolemaeus.) The second method of gaining tyrannical sway is for the tyrant to make himself invisible to the people. They are thus unable to see his true nature, and think (like Deioces' former associates) that the tyrant is something other than what he really is. The tyrant acts the part of a good king (*Pol.* 1314b):[47] he pretends that he is an honest businessman (like the albeit sincere Cephalus of Plato's tale) or an economic steward of the state. To this end the tyrant renders accounts of receipts and expenditures, adorns the city as if he were a trustee and not a tyrant, and behaves "as if he were a guardian of a public fund and not a private estate" (*Pol.* 1314b). "It is necessary to appear (*phainesthai*) to the subjects to be not a tyrannical ruler but a steward and royal governor" (*Pol.* 1314b42). The tyrant makes others visible to him and is himself invisible to them.

Invisibility and Economic Transactions

Visibility and invisibility are associated by some Greek thinkers with something at times believed to be more insidious than tyranny—namely, money. The tyrant depends upon money for his material or economic base, and it is money that precipitated in the Greek world changes in the organization and understanding of visible and invisible estates. The distinction between visible and invisible things in Greek thought includes the opposition of *ousia phanera* (visible substance) to *ouisa aphanēs* (invisible substance). Greek economic theory and practice suggests two meanings of this opposition. One meaning involves wit-

46. Ptolemaeus Chennus, *New History*, cited by Page (*Greek Tragedy*, p. 19), who refers to Photius, *Bibliotheca* 150 B 19.
47. For Aristotle, tyranny is a deviation from, or perversion of, monarchy (*Pol.* 3.5.4 and 5.8.3).

nesses: *ousia phanera* is property whose transfer was seen by others, and *ousia aphanēs* is property whose transfer was not seen. (In a visible transfer, the buyer and seller might exchange a symbolic deposit not as part of the purchase price but as a visible sign of their agreement.) The second meaning of the opposition involves money: *ousia phanera* is a nonmonetary commodity (such as land or "real" estate) and *ousia aphanēs* is money (such as a coin). These two meanings of *ousia phanera* and *ousia aphanēs* are not mutually exclusive. For the sake of a simple exposition, however, we shall discuss them separately.

Ousia Aphanēs *as Money*

The argument that *ousia aphanēs* is coined money has been put forward by P. M. Schuhl: "La langue grecque... oppose la fortune visible, c'est-à-dire mobilière (*ousia aphanēs*) aux richesses manifestes, c'est-à-dire immobilières (*ousia phanera*) aux biens fonds."[48] Louis Gernet also argues that money is usually "le type des biens 'non-visibles.'"[49] Although he recognizes certain problems with this interpretation, he concludes nevertheless that the distinction is one between fiduciary and real estate values. "Entre une propriété au sens vraiment 'patrimonial' et une propriété au sens purement économique, il n'y a pas commune mesure.... Il y a... une antithèse majeure... entre les biens qu'on appréhende matériellement et les créances de tous ordres."[50] This distinction between *ousia aphanēs* and *ousia phanera* suggests that the ring of invisibility in Plato's tale grants to its possessor a monetary science or license. Though the distinction is overly simple, it does help to explain why certain thinkers have intuited that the real source of the Platonic Gyges' power was a "science économique."[51]

Ousia Aphanēs *as Property Transferred without Witnesses*

Before the invention of money in archaic Greece, contracts of exchange required witnesses and/or visible *symbola*. *Symbola* were pledges, pawns, or covenants from an earlier understanding to bring

48. P. M. Schuhl, "Adèla," *Annales publiées par la Faculté des Lettres de Toulouse. Homo, Études philosophiques*, 1: 86–93, esp. n. 2.
49. Louis Gernet, "Choses visibles et choses invisibles," in *Anthropologie de la Grèce antique* (Paris, 1968), p. 408.
50. Gernet, "Choses visibles," p. 411.
51. Radet, *Lydie*, pp. 155 ff. Cf. Ure, *Origin of Tyranny*, p. 26. On money as *ousia aphanēs*, see also A. R. W. Harrison, *The Law of Athens* (Oxford, 1968), vol. 1; and J. Walter Jones, *The Law and Legal Theory of the Greeks* (Oxford, 1956), esp. pp. 217, 219, 230. For "money in the bank" as *ousia phanera*, see Isocrates, Discourse no. 17, para. 7 n.

together a part of something that had been divided specifically for the purpose of later comparison.[52] "Some small article, such as a ring (*sphragis*), sufficiently specific to relate back to the original pact," was exchanged as a token of the agreement.[53] In many Greek contracts, such as that of bank deposition, the *symbolon* was essential:

> The deposit was shown to the depositor only or to his agents, if they expressed this wish, and to nobody else. The agents had to show a *symbolon*, a means of recognition. . . . The most usual *symbolon* was the signet ring which had been used to seal the deposit. However, the depositor could instead take one half of a broken coin or of a clay token with him while the other half was kept in the temple or the bank to prove his identity by joining the two fragments.[54]

A coin could be a *symbolon*. Indeed, *symbola* were often "halves or corresponding pieces of [a bone or] a coin, which the contracting parties broke between them, each keeping one piece."[55] As a *symbolon*, the broken coin did not function as money, which derives its worth from the material of which it is made or which transactors suppose that it represents. Not itself one of the goods transferred, the coin as *symbolon* merely provided a necessary symbol of credit or trust. After the widespread development of coinage, the *symbolon* might amount to a substantial portion of the price, but it was never legally a part of that price.[56] It was not a deposit (or down-payment) in our modern (Roman) sense of the word, but only a symbol of a contract.[57]

In Roman law, cash exchange and transfer of ownership of prop-

---

52. *Symbola* means *arrae* or *tesserae hospitales*. The etymology of the Greek *arrabōn* is the Semitic word *eravon*. The *eravon* exchanged between Judah and Tamar is a signet ring that is both pledge and token of recognition (Genesis 39). See E. Cassin, "Symboles de cession immobilière dans l'ancien droit mésopotamien," *L'Année sociologique* (1952), pp. 107–61. Ludovic Beauchet (*Histoire du droit privé de la république athénienne* [Paris, 1897; reprint ed., Amsterdam, 1969], pp. 12 ff.) discusses two ancient treatises on the *symbolon* or contract: Lysias, *Peri symbolōn*; and Philocrates, *Symbolaiou apologia*. On contract in general, see Aristotle (*Rhetoric*, 1.15.21), who conceives contract in the widest sense.

53. Jones, *Law and Legal Theory*, p. 217. *Symbola* were often rings, but other objects were also used. Lysias (19, 25) refers to a gold cup.

54. F. M. Heichelheim, *An Ancient Economic History*, trans. Joyce Stevens (Leyden, 1964), 2: 76.

55. Adapted from "*symbolon*," H. G. Liddell and Robert Scott, *A Greek-English Lexicon* (Oxford, 1940). On bones and coins, see note 85.

56. Jones, *Law and Legal Theory*, p. 230.

57. The accord of two contractors was not sufficient to establish a contract. *Nuda pactio obligationem non parit* (Beauchet, *Histoire du droit privé*, p. 17). For this reason and others the words *contract* and *pact* are not sufficient to translate the Greek *symbolon* (Beauchet, *Histoire du droit privé*, pp. 15–16).

erty are separated. Ownership can be transferred by means of a "contractual" obligation or credit without exchange of cash or symbol. In Greek law, on the other hand, cash sales and *sumbola* are the only proofs of exchange or ownership. "Sale is for the Greeks identical with exchange of money against goods. They cannot imagine sale without payment of the price.... Transfer depended on payment, not on delivery."[58] In archaic Greek law, barter necessitated payment in the sight of witnesses: "Visibility of the act is the decisive element, real and formal at the same time."[59] The *symbolon* is a kind of "witness" to a transaction.[60]

Ousia phanera refers, then, to "property which is in sight of everybody and cannot be concealed" or be made invisible.[61] In a monetary economy, invisible exchanges (of *ousia aphanēs*) are easily effected. Not the presence of money but rather the absence of witness or *symbolon* makes such transactions "invisible."[62] Money, certainly, does facilitate contract without witness (or *symbolon*) and hence contributes to the development of the importance of invisible property (*ousia aphanēs*, second definition), of which money (*ousia aphanēs*, first definition) is also one possible example. As money became increasingly important, all *symbola* became down-payments; the visible *symbolon* seemed to become part of the invisible price.[63] Replacing the archaic

58. Fritz Pringsheim, *The Greek Law of Sale* (Weimar, 1950), pp. 90–91.

59. Pringsheim, *Greek Law of Sale*, p. 68. Cf. Pringsheim's remark that "sale in Greece means cash sale. Cash sale is not a contract, but barter" (p. 98).

60. Disputes about whether an exchange has taken place are often resolved by reference to a witness or a *symbolon*. Pringsheim (*Greek Law of Sale*, p. 190) reminds us that "in the Choephori of Aeschylos Electra says that her mother has sold her and her brother and ... that she has exchanged Aigisthos for them [v. 132 ff.]." The theme recurs in a speech of Orestes (v. 915). "The popular feeling in Athens," writes Pringsheim, "was that without the receipt of the price sale is out of the question" (pp. 190–91).

61. "The *phaneron* reminds us of the distinction between *phanera ousia* and *aphanēs ousia*, property which is in sight of everybody and can therefore not be concealed, and invisible property. If the second category contains in the main debts the parallel would be complete: in both cases there is a contrast between visible things and mere obligations" (Pringsheim, *Greek Law of Sale*, p. 69).

62. "It is not wrong to translate *phaneron* with 'in cash' or with 'il reçoit de bel et bon argent.' But the main and most simple meaning 'visible, manifest' is better. Visible money is given and taken. Of course it is given in cash. But above all it is visibly given and taken, i.e. publicly, in the presence of witnesses" (Pringsheim, *Greek Law of Sale*, p. 68).

63. As money transactions became more common in Greece, so too did written contracts. Neither money nor writing require witnesses. Both are "invisible." Written contracts (like those probably issued by Deioces) could not easily replace the Greek preference for witnesses. Pringsheim (*Greek Law of Sale*, p. 43) writes: "The Greeks had been a writing people since the 9th century. Nevertheless for a long time they preferred

symbolon, money (like writing) changed Greek economy and culture in ways difficult for us (who are now accustomed to Roman law and "symbolization") to understand.[64] It is certain, however, that the Greeks (and especially the landed aristocracy) feared the *ousia aphanēs.* To them, the development of money seemed to threaten not only the material basis of their wealth but also their mode of thought.

Invisibility and the Ring

The ring of Gyges controls the opposition of visibility to invisibility, which concerns the definitions of tyranny and economic exchange, especially during the transition from barter to money. Why did Plato choose a ring as the talisman of the person whose way of life he tries in the *Republic?* If Plato did adopt the ring from previous accounts of the reign of Gyges, he did so with reason. Rings played several roles in the economic development of money and in the opposition of *ousia phanera* to *ousia aphanēs.* First, rings were among the most common *symbola* before the introduction of coinage. Second, some of the first coins were ring-coins.[65] Third, the die by which coins were minted was originally the seal of the ring of the king (or *symbolon,* as Pliny calls the royal seal).[66] To some Greeks, a coin (as money) may have appeared to play the same role as a *symbolon.*[67] In fact, however, coins

---

witnessed oral transactions to documents. . . . The preponderance of witnesses, especially in Athens, may be attributed to a predilection for publicity which is congenial to the ideas of the *polis.* Even private agreements have to be made publicly." In Athens it became common to commit the terms of a contract to a *syngraphē* only in the second half of the fourth century B.C. (Jones, *Law and Legal Theory,* p. 219). Sometimes written contract and witness were combined (Pringsheim, *Greek Law of Sale,* pp. 43–44). The general relation of visible to invisible changed with the introduction of written contracts as with the introduction of money.

64. Even the symbolical or contractual significance of dividing a ring is foreign to us. Hegel writes that "when friends part and break a ring and each keeps one piece, a spectator sees nothing but the breaking of a useful thing and its division into useless and valueless pieces; the mystical aspect of the pieces he has failed to grasp" (G. W. F. Hegel, "The Spirit of Christianity," in *Early Theological Writings,* trans. T. M. Knox, intro. and frags. trans. Richard Kroner [Chicago, 1948; reprint ed., Philadelphia, 1971], p. 249). There is more to the ring than the spectator sees.

65. Cf. Charles Seltmann, *Greek Coins: A History of Metallic Currency and Coinage down to the Fall of the Hellenistic Kingdoms,* 2nd ed. (London, 1955), pp. 4–5. There is disagreement about whether the first "coins" were ring-coins; we can at least be certain that some rings were also pieces of money.

66. Pliny, *Naturalis Historia,* 33.10.

67. Some ancient coins were impressed with legends that suggest the artist mistakenly believed that coins were identical to the older *symbola.* See, for example, "Tessera Fati," cited by Stuart Mosher, "Coin Mottoes and Their Translation," *Numismatist,* December 1948, p. 818.

and *symbola* (and the economic classes whose interests they served) were quite different. Plato knew that the ring which once had served to symbolize a peaceful pact had become a great and dangerous power affecting both economic and verbal symbolization and logic.[68] We should not underestimate the significance of the development of money for the study of other media of symbolization and transfer, such as verbal metaphor. *Symbolon*, in fact, meant not only pactual token but also word;[69] and, as Plato knew, the development of money corresponds to the development of a new way of speaking.

PLATO AND THE MONEY FORM

Logic is the money of mind, the speculative or thought-value of man and nature—their essence grown totally indifferent to all real determinateness, and hence their real essence; logic is alienated thinking, and therefore thinking which abstracts from nature and from real man: abstract thinking. -Marx, "Critique of the Hegelian Dialectic and Philosophy as a Whole"[70]

The Sophists

There is a ring of Gyges secretly at work within the minds of men: it is the money of the mind. Sometimes Plato studies that money by considering his original metaphor that the seal of a ring impresses the waxen or metallic minds of men.[71] More often he studies the money of the mind directly, by considering the thought of the sophists. Plato

68. Another reason for Plato's choice of a ring as Gyges' talisman is that Plato means to compare justice itself with a ring. In The *Republic*, Socrates calls justice "a thing which rolls" (*Rep.* 432d; cf. *Rep.* 479d), and those who seek justice stand in a circle (*Rep.* 432b).

69. *Symbolon* means "watch-word" in Euripides; it means "coin" in *Onom.* 9. 48 ff. (on Aristotle's frag. 44) and Hermippus. Plato's Aristophanes says that we are tallies (*symbola*) of men (*Symposium* 191d and 193a) and that it is a priceless boon (*Symp.* 193d) we ask of the gods when we ask them to hold us together again. On *symbolon* as a metaphor in ancient Greek, see J. Hangard, *Monetaire en daarmee verwante metaforen* (Groningen, 1963), pp. 48 ff. and 73.

70. In this sentence Marx is referring directly to the first part of Hegel's *Enzyklopädie der philosophischen Wissenschaften im Grundrisse*, which is devoted to the study of logic. Marx's suggestion that Hegel's logic, as it appears there, is the money of the mind refers indirectly to the thought of Plato and Heraclitus, although the ancient philosophers lacked the Hegelian perspective of "Absolute Knowledge," which Marx (and in another sense Feuerbach) attacked.

71. Cf. *Theaetetus* (191–94), where the metaphor is finally discarded as an unsatisfactory explanation of memory and false belief; Aristotle, *Interpretation* 16a; and below notes 80, 95, and 146.

attacked sophists (like Thrasymachus) because they changed money for wisdom (selling their wares and altering them according to the conditions of the market) and because, like the rhetoricians, they made convention, as exemplified in language and money, their universal measure.[72] Gyges the tyrant had the power to make the unreal appear real. The sophist, according to Aristotle, is "one who makes money out of an apparent but unreal wisdom."[73] The words "make money" and "unreal" define the special art of the sophist in Greece. Like the tyrant, the sophist is purely a wage earner.[74] "Sophists are those who sell their wisdom for money to anyone who wants it."[75] With irony Plato praised Protagoras, the first to accept money for teaching, because Protagoras taught virtue (aretē) for money, thus making money an architectonic measure.[76] Sophists made it appear that wisdom could be bought and sold or measured by money. While the Good is the architectonic principle of the true philosopher, money is that of the wage-earning sophist who would rule the world as a Gygean tyrant.

The sophist subordinates wisdom to money either by persuading others that persuasion is the only important political art or by arguing that rhetoric or language, which he teaches, is the master art.[77] The cleverest sophists, such as Gorgias, "refused to be included among

72. *Rep.* 337d; cf. 336d ff. Plato often suggests that the philospher alone is the architectonic knower and that sophists are only apparent jacks-of-all-trades, who set forth their wisdom just as moneychangers set forth their gold and who brag about works of their own manufacture. In the Platonic *Lesser Hippias* (286b), Socrates offers as one example of such works the ring(s) of Hippias: "I know in most arts you are the wisest (*sophōtatos*) of men, as I have heard you boasting in the *agora* at the tables of the moneychangers, when you were setting forth the great and enviable stores of your wisdom, and you said upon one occasion all that you had on your person was made by yourself. You began with your ring, which was of your own workmanship, and you said you could engrave rings, and you had another seal that was also of your own workmanship. . . ."

73. Aristotle, *Nicomachean Ethics* 1164a30.

74. The sophists were among the most highly paid of all professional workers in Greece. See Plato, *Meno* 91d, and W. Drumann, *Die Arbeiter und Communisten in Griechenland und Rom* (Konigsberg, 1860), esp. pp. 86 ff. Cf. Marcel Detienne, *Les Maîtres de vérité dans la Grèce archaïque* (Paris, 1973), esp. p. 106, n. 4–6.

75. Xenophon, *Memorabilia* 1.6.13. Cf. similar statements of Aristophanes (*The Clouds*, where Socrates seems to be a sophist) and Lucian (*The Sale of Philosophers*, in which philosophers are put on the auction block).

76. Plato, *Protagoras* (349a et passim). See also *Meno* (91b). "Money," says Lysias, "is the glue of society" (K. J. Dover, *Lysias and the Corpus Lysiacum* [Berkeley and Los Angeles, 1968], pp. 28 ff.). Lysias is said to have been the brother of Polemarchus and Cephalus.

77. See W.K.C. Guthrie, *A History of Greek Philosophy*, 4 vols. (Cambridge, 1969), 3:35 ff.

the teachers of *aretē*, [holding] that rhetoric is the master-art to which all others must defer."[78] Plato (and to a lesser extent Aristotle) doubted that language could be architectonic or even truthful.[79] Plato called the sophists imitators of those who know.[80] The sophist, like Theuth, the inventor of writing,[81] is interested not in the original but only in its tokens. Critics of the sophists often seized on their apparent belief in the architectonic nature and interchangeability of verbal and economic tokens, and made clever statements and jokes about their attitude toward language and money: "It is possible to stop the sophist's tongue with a coin in his mouth;"[82] "Gold weighs more with men than countless words;"[83] "Sophists are money-coiners of words."[84] The metaphorical association of money and words is as old as Zeno, to whom, however, it seems to have posed no threat.[85] To Plato, on the other hand, the sophists or "philosophical tyrants of the

78. Ibid., 3:39.

79. On the debate between the sophists and Plato about the nature of language, see E. L. Harrison (*Phoenix* [1964], pp. 271 ff. on *Gorgias*); and Jacob Klein ("Speech, Its Strength and Its Weaknesses," *College* [July 1973]), who discusses (p. 4) the five kinds of word merchantry that play an important role in the *Sophist* (for example, 231d). See *Meno* 95c and *Grg.* 456c–e, 460a.

80. *mimētēs tou sophou*, *Soph.* 268c. The mind of the sophist is like a lump of wax or metal ingot into which original impressions are poorly stamped. Jacques Derrida writes (*La Dissémination* [Paris, 1972], p. 121) that "le sophiste vend donc les signes et les insignes de la science: non pas la mémoire elle-même (*mnēmē*), seulement les monuments (*hypomnēmata*). . . ." Socrates accuses Hippias of not employing his memory (368a–d).

81. On Theuth and writing, see *Phdr.* 274.

82. Cf. Aristophanes, *Plutus* 379, *Peace* 645. Victor Ehrenberg (*The People of Aristophanes* [New York, 1962], p. 226) notes that it was customary to walk with coins in one's mouth.

83. Euripides, *Medea* 965. Cf. frag. 44. (See Ehrenberg, *People of Aristophanes*, p. 226).

84. Cratinus 226. The phrase is a comic counterpart to *Agamemnon* 437. (See Ehrenberg, *People of Aristophanes*, p. 234).

85. "To those who reproached his [Zeno's] incorrect elocution he answered that well-ordered discourses resembled the coins of Alexander which, although beautiful and well stamped, were nevertheless made of a bad alloy, and that propositions badly expressed but full of reason resembled the Attic coins of four drachmas" (Diogenes Laertius 7. 18). Cf. Diogenes Laertius 7. 33, where it is reported that Zeno said that there should be a coinage of bones or stones. (See *The Fragments of Zeno and Cleanthes*, ed. A. C. Pearson [London, 1891], esp. frags. 81 and 202.) Zeno of Elea was a compatriot of Parmenides and, like him, originally a follower of Pythagoras (who minted coins in Southern Italy). Zeno's comparison between words and coins is the first of many similar descriptions of language. Lucian, for example, speaks of debasing the established "currency" (*nomisma*) (*Lexiphanes*, para. 20); Horace insists it is permitted to issue "current" words (*licuit semperque licebit signatum praesente nota producere nomen*, *Ars Poetica* 58); Juvenal speaks at length of the poet as "minter" of money (*moneta*) (*Satire* 7: 54 ff.). See J.E.B. Mayor's note to *Satire* 7: 54 ff., in his edition of Juvenal (*Thirteen Satires of Juvenal* [Cambridge, 1853]).

world" did pose a profound threat. For him, money (wage-earning) and language (sophistry) were finally in necessary opposition to the Good (philosophy), which must overcome them. In his critique of the sophists and in his own thought, therefore, Plato purposefully and critically internalized the money form. Indeed, Plato's critique of political, verbal, and economic tyranny probes even into the theory of the Ideas and into the hypotheses of the dialectic.

The Ideas

One precondition for the development of philosophy may be the existence of an economic surplus and a leisure class.[86] Another may be a supposedly natural tendency in the human mind (for example, the inclination to simplify and reduce the world to unity). In themselves, these preconditions cannot explain the genesis of philosophy, since they existed or are supposed to have existed both in Greece before the development of philosophy and in other geographic areas where that development did not occur. The student of the origin of philosophy, then, must study not only its preconditions but also the actual conditions under which it did develop.

In an ingenious variation of class analysis, George Thomson suggests that philosophy depends on the growth of a new class of merchants for whom objects were divested of their qualitative use-value and retained only an abstract exchange-value. That all goods could be measured (so to speak) by one good he supposes to be not only a precondition for the development of philosophic modes of thought but also a direct link between Being and Money, both of which seem to define things. Thomson argues that the development of a concept of oneness (*to on*) from multiplicity (*ta onta*) is a direct reflection of changes in the symbolization of the economic system: "The ... One, together with the later idea of 'substance,' may ... be described as a reflex or projection of the substance of exchange value."[87] Thomson's thesis only appears to satisfy the requirements of ideological analysis, which sometimes demonstrates relations between material and intellectual conditions. For many ancient Greeks,

86. Aristotle himself argues that one of the social preconditions for the development of philosophy is an economic surplus. See George Thomson, *Studies in Ancient Greek Society*, 2 vols. (London, 1949–55), 2: 175–79; and Vernant, "La formation de la pensée positive dans la Grèce archaïque," p. 297.

87. Thomson, *Ancient Greek Society*, p. 300–301. Cf. Kenneth Burke, who discusses money as an agent of reduction (*A Grammar of Motives* [Berkeley and Los Angeles, 1969], pp. 91–96; cf. pp. 503 ff. on metonymy as reduction) and as a substitute for God (pp. 108–13; cf. pp. 4, 355–56).

money may indeed have seemed to be a logical category (like an Idea) embracing all commodities within its scope. Thomson's easy metaphor between One and Money, however, confuses philosophy with ordinary "false consciousness," and ignores the dialectical relationship between philosophy and that from which it may be said to arise.[88] Indeed, Thomson unwittingly pursues one of the directions suggested by Plato, who had recognized and feared the ideological perceptions or misperceptions of monied man. For Plato, money can appear to some men to be as lofty as the Idea is, but money is not the Idea. The good that is money is not the Good.

Plato studied the "false consciousness" in which money appears to be that which it is not. In the monetary theories of many idealist philosophers, value is as radically separated from the material (for example, gold) of money (a supposed "symbol") as ideas are radically separated from sensible things. Jean-Joseph Goux notes this partial error of idealist thought. "L'illusion d'optique idéaliste consiste à considérer le monde visible et matériel comme le reflet des équivalents généraux, tandis que ce sont les équivalents généraux qui forment le reflet achevé, la spéculation focalisée, de ce monde visible multiple et différencié."[89] Goux confuses simplistic "optics" with

88. Thomson writes that "the Parmenidean One represents the earliest attempt to formulate the idea of 'substance'. . . . What was the origin of this conception? . . . Civilised thought has been dominated from the earliest times down to the present day by what Marx called the fetishism of commodities, that is, the 'false consciousness' generated by the social relations of commodity production. In early Greek philosophy we see this 'false consciousness' gradually emerging and imposing on the world categories of thought derived from commodity production, as though these categories belonged, not to society, but to nature" (Thomson, *Ancient Greek Society*, pp. 300–301; see also p. 315).

Thomson's ignoring the possibility of a dialectical relationship between philosophy and political economy is merely the reflection of Engels' claim that "when men created money they did not realize that they were . . . creating a new social power . . . before which the whole of society must bow" (F. Engels, *Origin of the Family, Private Property, and the State* [London, 1920], quoted by Thomson, *ibid.*, p. 196). Vernant (*Mythe et pensée*, esp. pp. 296–97, 307–8, 311, on money) criticizes Thomson, but is not himself able to offer a rigorous analysis of the relationship between money and thought.

89. Jean-Joseph Goux, *Economie et symbolique* (Paris, 1973), p. 182. Goux argues that all idealists (he believes Plato to be one) share a theory of the arbitrariness of the sign. "Pour Platon, la valeur est donc radicalement séparée de la matière monétaire—et le philosophe défend la notion d'un arbitraire de la monnaie, qui restera caractéristique, à travers Berkeley et Steuart, de la tendance idéaliste en philosophie et en économie politique,—tandis que Aristote, tout en maintenant le caractère législatif, 'numismatique,' de la valeur monétaire, attribue cependant une valeur intrinsèque à sa matière métallique. On voit comment le reproche qu'Aristote fait à Platon, d'avoir

Plato's theory of Ideas: Plato consciously incorporated such "optics" into his economics and tried to overcome the mistaken illusions of idealism. In the thought of Plato, the Idea (especially that of the Good) plays a role at once visible and invisible, unreal and real. Aware of the chimera of the money form and of the power of the Gygean ring to affect even his own thought, Plato responds to the terrifying talisman not with a simple wish that it return whence it came,[90] but rather with an attempt to explain and overcome its power to misinform the mind.

The talismanic ring of Gyges, which transforms invisibles into visibles and visibles into invisibles, must have appeared to many (for instance, Thrasymachus or even Glaucon at the beginning of book 2) to be the only reality in the world. Friedrich Engels suggests that metallic money must have appeared to the Greeks to be "a talisman, which could at will transform itself into any desirable or desired object" and in comparison with which "all other forms of wealth were only simple appearances."[91] Like Thomson, Engels considers the power of money only at the most superficial level of ideological analysis. There is, however, a sense in which money not only appears to transform but actually does transform the world. This more subversive aspect of the money form is considered by Karl Marx.

Being the external, common medium and faculty for turning an image into reality and reality into a mere image (a faculty not springing from man as man or from human society as society), money transforms the real essential powers of man and nature into what are merely abstract conceits and therefore imperfections—into tormenting chimeras—just as it transforms real imperfections and chimeras—essential powers

---

'séparé les idées,' s'expose fidèlement dans les conceptions monétaires respectives des deux philosophes" (Goux, *Economie et symbolique*, p. 183).

Goux is mistaken in believing that the Platonic Idea is an arbitrary sign with no value as commodity. Nevertheless, he does suggest interesting correspondences between the verbal and economic representations of later thinkers. Even Ezra Pound realized the correspondence between economics and Berkeleyan linguistics. He wrote that "the moment a man realizes that the guinea stamp, not the metal, is the essential component of the coin, he has broken with all materialist philosophies" (Hugh Kenner, *The Pound Era* [Berkeley and Los Angeles, 1971], p. 412).

90. See above, n. 44. Polycrates, tyrant of Samos, threw his royal signet ring (the work of the famous sculptor Theodorus) into the sea (Hdt. 3: 39 ff.). C. H. V. Sutherland (*Art in Coinage* [New York, 1956], pp. 21–23) interprets this ring as the seal or die of coins.

91. Quoted by Goux, *Economie et symbolique*, p. 181.

which are really impotent, which exist only in the mind of the individual—into real powers and faculties.[92]

Marx's insight is crucial to any understanding of the ring of Gyges. Lead, touched by Midas, is changed alchemically to gold. Thought and art, touched by Gyges' *lapis invisibilitatis*, are changed into tormenting chimeras supporting that which their uncomprehending creators would destroy. It is this deeper power of money to affect the human mind that Plato addresses in his philosophy.

In the *Republic*, Plato tries to lift the debate about visibles and invisibles onto a supposedly higher level at which not the tyrant but rather the philosopher is master. Between the telling of Glaucon's version of the tale of Gyges (*Rep.* 359) and Socrates' verdict on or rejection of the life of the tyrant (*Rep.* 612b) occur arguments in which Cephalean, Polemarchean, and Thrasymachean economic theories are subjected to careful (if indirect) analysis. Socrates, who has attacked the traditional, but mistaken, beliefs that make men act justly (such as the belief in punishment in Hades), wishes to convince his listeners that they should be just men. At one stage in his argument, Socrates presents a metaphysics that purports to explain the doctrine of the Ideas. The pedagogic devices that he uses to explain this doctrine include the epistemological divided line and the political allegory of the cave.

The Ideas cannot be separated from problems of visibility. *Eidē*, in fact, is cognate with *idein* (to see). Socrates' opinion is that Ideas are invisible, whereas things themselves are visible: "And we say that things are seen (*horasthai*) but not intellected (*noeisthai*), while the Ideas (*eidē*) are intellected but not seen" (*Rep.* 507b). The impossibility of seeing (*idein*) Ideas is the tropic center of the doctrine of the Ideas.

Socrates introduces the illustrative metaphor of the divided line in order to explain what he means by the invisible Idea. In the divided line the Ideas are the highest objects of contemplation.[93] The relation between *eidē* and *horaton* is significant. Although the two words are grammatically related,[94] the *eidē* (the object of the philosopher's sight or intellection) are opposed to *to horaton* (the object of the sharp-

---

92. Karl Marx, *The Economic and Philosophic Manuscripts of 1844*, ed. Dirk J. Struick, trans. Martin Milligan (New York, 1964), p. 169.

93. The diagram is adapted from Bloom ("An Interpretative Essay," p. 464) and describes *Rep.* 509 and 534.

94. Cf. *horaō, opsomai, eidon, heōraka, ōpthēn*.

The intelligible (*to noēton*)	Ideas (*eidē*)	Intellection (*noēsis*)
	Mathematical objects (*ta mathēmatika*)	Thought (*dianoia*)
The visible (*to horaton*)	Things	Trust (*pistis*)
	Images (*eikones*)	Imagination (*eikasia*)

Figure 1.   Diagram of the Divided Line

eyed tyrant's sight).[95] The tyrant can see *to horaton*, but he cannot see the *eidē*. Only the intellect, the philosophical faculty or power of sight, can make the *eidē* visible. The intellectual philosopher, therefore, has a power like, but superior to, that of the ring of the spying, tyrannical Gyges. The divided line is a "put-down" of Gygean tyranny.[96]

Philosophy seeks to make the Idea visible. As the Herodotean Gyges is said to see (*idein*) the beauty (*eidos*) and shame (*aidōs*) of the queen, or as Cephalus's Hades (*Haidēs*) is said to see the corrupt souls of the damned, so, at a higher level, the philosopher sees the Idea (*eidos*). The story of Gyges, as reported by Herodotus, depends on the

95. The distinction between visible and invisible is similar in other works of Plato. In the *Timaeus* (52 a–c), Plato writes that "we must acknowledge that one kind of being is the form which is always the same, uncreated and indestructible, never receiving anything into itself from without, nor itself going out into any other, but invisible and imperceptible by any sense, and of which contemplation is granted to intelligence only." Plato divorces the things of the world from the invisibles. "The reality after which an image is *moulded* does not belong to it" (*Ti.* 52c) any more than the die from which a coin is cast belongs to it. In the *Phaedo* (79a), Plato again addresses the two classes of things: "So you think that we should assume two classes of things, one visible and the other invisible . . . the invisible being invariable and the visible never being the same." See also *Parmenides* (133c ff.) on visibles and invisibles.

96. At the same time, Plato derogates or puts way down on the divided line all Greek "science" (*dianoia*) that attempts to make the invisible visible. As Schuhl ("Adèla," p. 89) writes, "Toute la méthodologie scientifique est en cause dans la manière d'aller du visible à l'invisible."

unnatural Lydian *nomos* against nakedness. Cephalus's morality depends in part on an equally conventional belief about Hades. Plato had contempt for the (Lydian) prohibition against nakedness[97] and for Cephalus's fear, examples of the delusions from which men suffer who are bound to the lower part of the divided line. Despite their serviceable political functions, such *nomoi* are those of blind men living in the "cave" of shadowy images and mistaking those images (*to horaton*) for reality (*eidē*).

Like the divided line, the allegory of the cave elucidates the doctrine of the Ideas, setting that doctrine within a political context. The cave is like human society, and the sun (in the visible world) is like the Idea of the Good (in the intelligible world). The men who sit in the cave mistake images for reality. They are men, like Herodotus's Lydians or Plato's Cephalus, who do not see things (even *to horaton*) the way they are. In Socrates' story about the cave, one man ascends from the cave and concludes "that the sun is the source of the seasons and the years, and is the steward of all things in the visible place, and is in a certain way the cause of all those things he and his companions had been seeing."[98] The man descends back into the cave and imprudently reports what he has seen. His former associates judge that he is a lunatic or a dangerous subverter of the *nomoi*. They would silence or even kill him (as the Athenians killed Socrates). Such is the fate of a potential philosopher-king.

The allegory of the cave repeats at the level of *to horaton* the tale of Gyges. Gyges ascends from the chasm where he found the ring and comes to the court of Candaules. This court, in which men are blind not only to the *eidē* but even to Gyges, is like the allegorical cave. Gyges does not see the *eidē*, but as perfect spy, he can see and kill what his former associates cannot see and kill. He is their epistemological and political superior. Not telling the people about what he has seen, he conquers them and establishes a tyranny. The tyrant, then, may seem to rise a little from the cave of conventional opinion and to see more than his fellows. He lacks the intellect, however, to see the sunny *eidē*. Although the tyrant (as perfect spy) has a power to

97. Socrates suggests that both men and women ought to be naked (*Rep.* 457a–b). Benardete (*Herodotean Inquiries*, p. 12) suggests that clothes are like the *nomoi*, since they conceal from us the way we are. Plato writes: "The women guardians must strip, since they'll clothe themselves in virtue instead of robes." See above, n. 14.

98. Socrates says that "in the knowable the last thing to be seen, and with considerable effort, is the Idea of the Good; but once seen it must be concluded that this is in fact the cause of all that is right and fair in everything—in the visible (*horatōi*) it gave birth to light and its sovereign; in the intelligible (*noētōi*), itself sovereign, it provided truth and intelligence" (*Rep.* 517c).

see invisibles, only the philosopher has the similar but loftier power to see the sunny *ousia aphanēs* itself.[99]

Plato's *Republic* is a trial intended in part to prove the superiority of the life of the philosopher to that of the tyrant. In the *Sophist*, Plato seems to recall a fragment of Heraclitus: "The hidden (*aphanēs*) harmony is superior to that which is not hidden (*phanerē*)."[100] Plato probably does not mean to imply that *ousia aphanēs* (as money or as transaction without witnesses) is better than *ousia phanera* (as land, or as property transferred with witnesses), although he might have considered this meaning. He means only that the *eidos* (the Idea that is invisible to all except the perfect philosopher who is its witness) is better than *to horaton*. In the *Republic* he describes philosophy in apparent opposition to economic tyranny. The economics of visibility and symbolization, however, play a formal role within the dialectic itself.

Hypothesis and Hypothecation

Several critics have noted and most have misunderstood Plato's comparison between the money form and the Idea. None has noted another comparison between economic and intellectual life to which Plato also tries to direct the reader's attention. Plato suggests that the dialectic is informed by the act of depositing money and drawing interest on the principal. A hypothesis is a logical correspondent to a hypothec.[101] Not itself subject to questioning, it is that principle from which knowledge can be drawn. The problem of deposition in the military and economic world, with which the *Republic* begins, is thus an internal problem for philosophy itself. The deposit or hypothec

99. On the word *ousia* in Plato, see H. H. Berger, *Ousia in de dialogen van Plato*, (Leiden, 1961).

100. Heraclitus, frag. 54, in Diels, *Fragmente der Vorsokratiker*. In the *Sophist* (232c), Plato opposes divine invisible things (*aphanē*) to mere appearances (*phanera*). Cf. *Ti.* 52a,c. In Ephesian law "credit" means "invisible." (See the laws of Ephesus in *Inscr. juv. gr.*, no. 5, 1.42; Gernet, "Choses visibles," p. 411).

101. Hypothecation is the act of making a hypothec. "Hypothec" derives from *hypothēkē* ("deposit," "pledge," or "mortgage;" literally "a putting down"). According to some theorists of Roman law, a hypothec is "an improper pledge . . . of a thing not delivered, which is made and perfected by covenant onelie" (William West, *Symbolaeography, which may be termed the Act, Description, or Image of Instruments, Extraiudicial, as Covenants, Contracts . . . Wills, etc.* [London, 1592], para. 18c). Hence, a hypothec is directly related to the problem of symbolization and deposition. The association of the single word *hypothēkē* with both economic and intellectual deposition is not unlike the similar associations of *anaireō* (in Platonic and Aristotelian logic) and *aufheben* (its Hegelian translation into German).

about which Socrates spoke with Cephalus and Polemarchus in book 1 (e.g., *Rep.* 332a–b) is an original basis for the hypothesis about which he speaks in book 6.

Before he begins his crucial discussion of the Ideas in book 6, Socrates suggests that the Idea of the Good has been deposited with him. "I could wish that I were able to pay and you were able to receive [the Good] itself, and not just the interest (*tokos*), as is the case now. Anyhow, receive this interest and child of the Good itself. But be careful that I don't in some way unwillingly deceive you in rendering the account of the interest fraudulent" (*Rep.* 507a). Socrates indicates that he is a banker-philosopher, distributing *tokos* (interest or offspring). In book 1 Socrates had argued that deposits of weaponry and money should only be dispensed with care. In the allegory of the cave he suggested that those who have seen the sun should only tell their companions about it with prudence, lest they be convicted of lunacy or treason. In this preface to his telling about the divided line and the allegory of the cave, Socrates hints that he will carefully suit his ability to give the truth to his companions' ability to receive it.[102] Socrates dispenses the interest (*tokos*) of the principal that is the Good. He trusts that the effect of the interest will be homogeneous with the Good in the same way that a child (*tokos*) is homogeneous with its parent.[103] The divided line and the allegory of the cave are such *tokoi* of the good.

Dialectic, the art of Socrates, depends initially on hypothesis (for example, the ring of Gyges). The dialectician ultimately sheds

---

102. The problem arises for the philosopher as for the banker that it is not always "just" to return "deposits." Properly dispensing to others the truth that has been deposited with oneself is the principal concern of the doctrine of the "economy of truth." The lies of the philosopher are partial of and partial to the truth. The lies of the philosopher-king serve the public good. The lies of the tyrant, who may know a little more than some other men and who wishes to keep even this little hidden from them, serve what he believes to be his private good. Voltaire and Cardinal Newman consider Plato to have been a good *économiste* or economist (steward) of the truth. (See below, Chapter 3.)

103. On *tokos* (as interest and offspring) see below. The concept of offspring plays an important role in the description of the sun (the counterpart to the Idea of the Good in the allegory of the cave). Socrates speaks: "The sun is the offspring of the good I mean—an offspring of the good begot in proportion with itself: as the good is in the intelligible region with respect to intelligence and what is intellected, so the sun is in the visible region with respect to sight and what is seen" (*Rep.* 508c). Sight, as Socrates argues, depends on light: "The sun not only provides what is seen with the power of being seen, but also with generation, growth, and nourishment although it itself isn't generation" (*Rep.* 509b). The sun, like the Good, is a kind of principal from which interest may be drawn. Glaucon reminds Socrates later in the dialogue that he still owes him what is due on the father's narrative.

hypotheses, which belong to the second-to-highest level (*dianoia*) in the divided line. As the interlocutors in book 1 question the justice of economic deposition, so the dialectician must question, or rather rise above, the (visible) hypotheses that initially inform and generate his own arguments.[104] In ridding the dialectician of hypotheses, Plato institutes a new kind of symbolization, or relation between things and that which represents them (language or money, for example). This idealist symbolization operates without the supposed "material" guarantees (or hypothecs) in the bank, like those the ironic (and often too-much-credited) banker Socrates tells his interlocutors the gods have deposited invisibly with him.[105]

Plato indicates that Socrates disliked wage-earning. His Socrates does engage, however, in philosophical chrematistics in which deposit and interest are important. Certain writers of the ancient world actually accused him of engaging in profiteering. "Aristoxenus, the son of Spintharus, says... that he made money; he would at all events invest sums, collect the interest accruing, and then, when this was expended, put out the principal again."[106] Aristoxenus's statement may be historically inaccurate; it is not likely that Socrates was a wage earner. However, he did incorporate into his philosophical method the investment of sums, the collection of interest, and the reinvestment of funds. Socrates, who attacked the sophists, purposefully internalized the money form into his thought as a dialectic of hypothecations.

Plato felt the possible contradiction between Socrates' reliance on hypothesization and his attack on money-making. For this reason Plato's Socrates appeals powerfully from hypothesis and dialectic to the Ideas, which are supposed to rise above hypotheses. Socrates knows, however, that the ideas of most men are pervaded by money-thinking. He often remarks that men divide wholes into parts or the Idea into its genuses and species as if they were traders changing a coin of large denomination into coins of smaller denominations.

---

104. Among those who use hypotheses or visible forms (*eidē*, *Rep.* 510d) are the mathematicians.

105. Just as Socrates seems to hope that some men (for instance, Cephalus) will continue to believe in the customary laws of deposition, so he seems to hope that some men will continue to believe in (what the Greek rhetoricians call) "the hypothetical gods." Cf. Isocrates, Discourse no. 17.

106. Diogenes Laertius 2. 19–21. Aristoxenus was a scandalmonger. Critics of philosophers, however, have long noted that the operations of the philosophic mind are not unlike those of money. Thales, for example, is often credited with being both the first philosopher (manipulating language in a new way) and a clever employer of the power of the economic *arra* or *symbolon* (manipulating capital in a way profitable to himself and new to the Greeks of his native city). (See Aristotle, *Pol.* 1259a.)

In the Platonic dialogues, *kermatidzein* means both "to make small change" and "to divide by dialectically improper (and in the later dialogues, perhaps, proper) *diairesis*."[107] One commentator notes that in Platonic dialectic "the *eidos* puts a seal [-ring] on a class (*episphragidzesthai*), classes are divided into small change (*katakermatidzesthai*), and each class must take a certain impression. . . . Because money is still money no matter what its value may be, it resembles the set of *eidē* in their all being *eidē*, no matter how they may differ in rank."[108] Even the way of the Ideas does not always lead away from the money of the mind. The internalization of money-thinking into Plato's thought finally takes the form of a desperate attempt to rise above monetary hypothecation and Gygean chrematistics. In the last analysis, however, the vehemence with which Plato attacked the sophists cannot be separated from his awesome critique of Socrates and his pupils, of whom Plato himself was one. Socratic thought, feared Plato, is the money of the mind.

---

107. In the *Republic* (395b, 525) and *Meno* (78b–d, 79a–c), for example, Socrates warns his interlocuters not to divide the One as though it were a coin. Jakob Klein (*A Commentary on Plato's Meno* [Chapel Hill, 1965], p. 81) discusses Socrates' objection that "all that Meno has done is to break virtue into parts, as if he were changing a big piece of money into small coins." In the later dialogues (*Prm.* 142e, 144b, 144e; *Statesman* 266a; etc.), however, Socrates is silent about and perhaps resigned to the conflation of moneychanging and dialectical division. In the *Sophist* (257c), the Stranger states that "the nature of the other seems to me to be all broken up (*katakermatisthai*) just like knowledge (itself)." In the *Timaeus* (62 a; cf. 58b), Heraclitean fire, or *pyr* (which Heraclitus's Fragment 90 allies with golden money or *chrysos*), is discussed in terms of the power to divide (*kermatidzein*), which is essential to Platonic *diairesis*.

The relationship between change-making and mathematical division and unity is noted by Greek mathematicians. They write, for example, that one can understand units (or monads) by understanding how one can hypothesize a drachma as being indivisible (i.e., as a single member of the multitude of drachmas) and as being divisible (i.e., as a coin [*nomisma*]) (Hero of Alexander, *Opera*, W. Schmidt, L. Nix, H. Schöne, and J. L. Heiberg, eds. [Leipzig, 1899–1914], 4: 98, 24–100, 3; discussed by Jakob Klein, *Greek Mathematical Thought and the Origin of Algebra*, trans. Eva Brann [Cambridge, Mass., 1968], p. 41). On the relationship between money theory and number theory, see below, Chapter 2, note 11.

108. Seth Benardete, "Eidos and diairesis in Plato's *Statesman*," *Philologus* 108 (1963): 212. Kenneth Burke (*Grammar of Motives*, p. 94) argues that "dialectically, [money] is the 'homogenizing' principle that, in compensating for heterogeneity, so permits much heterogeneity to arise without disaster." Plato, however, does not allow for any easy substitution of the money form for the Idea, and Sophocles and Aristotle (as we shall see in Chapter 3) consider monetary homogenization to be disastrous and disintegrative. Cf. Burke's consideration (*Rhetoric of Motives*, pp. 244 ff.) of "the Kierkegaardian dialectic" as "changing finite species into the currency of the infinite."

HERACLITUS AND THE MONEY FORM

We have . . . to consider exchange from a formal point of view; to investigate the change of form or metamorphosis of commodities which effectuates the . . . circulation of matter. -Marx, Capital

Nietzsche's argument that the thinking of early man constituted his price-making derives some support from the infinite generalizability of the concept of exchange. In ancient Greek, for example, *ameibō* and *allassō* apply not only to "the closure of a commercial transaction, like barter, sale, or loan and to the satisfaction of justice" but also to "physical sequences where one event was regularly followed by (and thus 'exchanged for') its reciprocal. . . . The uniformity of nature as a whole could be construed as a reciprocity among its basic components."[109] Such a universal concept of exchange informed Anaximander's theory of justice, in which "the underlying principle is that of an exchange: equal value rendered for value taken."[110]

Plato questioned the various presocratic theories of exchange and also the relevance of theories of *physis* to social theory about justice. For instance, in the *Republic* Socrates tries to show that indiscriminate exchange of equal deposits is not truly just. He implies that much early thought was like the thought of Cephalus (which he condemns), except that Cephalus considered only the commercial aspect of the theories of universal exchange and justice. Plato sought an Idea above these physical theories and tried to show the unimportance of barter-equality in an age in which monetary exchange was secretly

109. Gregory Vlastos, "Equality and Justice in Early Greek Cosmologies," *Classical Philology* 42 (July 1947): 173-74. Vlastos includes several examples of these sequences: "the cycle of birth and death . . . waking and sleeping . . . the succession of day and night . . . the cycle of the seasons . . . hoofs that strike the ground in turn . . . land plowed and left fallow in turn. . . . Scientific thought used this pattern to join events which had either been left unconnected (like evaporation and precipitation . . .) or else had not been clearly grasped as strict equations by the popular mind (like breathing in and breathing out . . . or the stretching of a lyre string and the vibration when released. . . .)."

110. Ibid. Simplicius's version of Theophrastus's account of Anaximander's originative substance includes this statement: "And the source of coming-to-be for existing things is that into which destruction, too, happens, 'according to necessity (*kata to chreōn*);' for they pay penalty and retribution (*dikēn kai tisin*) to each other for their injustice (*adikias*) 'according to the assessment of Time (*kata tēn tou chronou taxin*),' as he [Anaximander] describes it in these rather poetical terms" (Simplicius, *Phys.* 24.13, trans. G. S. Kirk and J. E. Raven, *The Presocratic Philosophers* [Cambridge, 1971], pp. 106-7).

invading language and thought itself. The Greek concept of exchange includes not only commercial transactions and physical sequences but also such transfers as metaphor and dialectic. *Antamoibē,* for example, refers to verbal or logical as well as economic exchanges. Plato himself calls the dialectic an *antamoibē.* A conflict about economic exchange usually produces (at least implicitly) a corresponding discussion about linguistic exchanges.

The importance of metaphorization, therefore, must not be underestimated when we study those philosophers of exchange who are also poetic seers (or see-ers). Metaphor enables them to see.[111] The eye, says Plato, must be turned tropically in order to see that which is: "The eye must be turned around from that which is coming into being (*ta gignomena*) together with the whole soul until it is able to endure looking at that which is (*to on*) and the brightest part of that which is (*to on*)" (*Rep.* 518c). The correct mode of metaphorization or tropic turning, like the correct mode of physical and commercial exchange, was a key problem for early philosophers.[112]

In Plato's writings, Heraclitus is as much the target of philosophical diatribe as Gyges is the target of political diatribe. Gyges was a master of monetary exchange and Heraclitus was a master of the kind of linguistic exchange Plato most disliked. The Platonic attack on Heraclitus usually takes the form of mocking the Heraclitean doctrine of motion and exchange. For Plato, all motion "culminates in the ... *idea,* which is the highest object of knowledge." In grammatical terms, "this means that the 'ideality' peculiar to the verb is hardened [by Plato] into a concrete substantial concept, whence it is expected to satisfy more exacting tests of intelligibility."[113] Plato makes *ousia* into a substantial concept that, he hopes, will lift the philosopher out of the mire of economic exchange. What Plato dislikes in Heraclitus's philosophy is the lack of a concept of metaphysical stillness and of a concept of justice above the supposedly escapable movements of commodities.[114] Heraclitus studies those changes that never "hard-

111. Bruno Snell (*The Discovery of the Mind* [New York, 1960], pp. 218–9) maintains that the Greeks "discovered" the human mind by reading it comparatively into their myths. Thales' teaching that "the earth floats on water like a log of wood" is the beginning of this comparative, scientific thinking. The form of such thought is its true content.

112. Aristotle (*Rh.* 1411b) refers to "smart sayings derived from proportional metaphor and expressions which set things before the eyes" and argues that "things are set before the eyes by words that signify actuality."

113. Snell, *Discovery of the Mind,* p. 222.

114. See *Cra.* (439–40) and *Phd.* (79 ff.). The Platonic fear that wisdom itself might come to be measured by commerce is dramatized in Lucian's satiric dialogue *Sale of*

en." His medium is the copulative verb rather than the substantial noun *ousia*. Although he was as much the enemy of money and the monied classes as was Plato,[115] Heraclitus internalized the money form into his thought differently, focusing on metaphorization and symbolization themselves. If Plato studies the metaphor of still Being, Heraclitus studies the activity of metaphorization itself. Into the energetic metaphorization of Heraclitus (and into his particular metaphors) are internalized formal metamorphoses of thought associated (by him) with the money form.[116] Heraclitus's thought is that critical money of the mind that Plato incorporated into his own thought and over which he tried, unsuccessfully if not unwisely, to leap.

Heraclitus was a student of both economic exchange and language. In Fragment 90 he speaks of the money form and its significance as a new kind of metaphorization or exchange.

Philosophers, in which Heraclitus is set on the auction block. No one, however, is willing to exchange property for him, so he remains unsold. (See *ameibomena* in *Sale,* sect. 14.)

115. "May you have plenty of wealth (*ploutos*), you men of Ephesus, in order that you may be punished for your evil ways" (Heraclitus, frag. 125).

116. In the *Cratylus,* Plato offers a subtle critique of the thought of Cratylus (an epigone of Heraclitus), in which money and language are compared implicitly. Cratylus insists that "*Hermogenes* is not the name of the man called Hermogenes even if all mankind call [him] so" (*Cra.* 383b). Socrates responds by hinting ironically that his own knowledge of naming is inadequate because he could not purchase enough knowledge from a series of lectures (given by Prodicus who charged fifty drachmas for his course). Nevertheless, he suggests that one reason for Cratylus's insistence is that Hermogenes seems unable to make money: Hermogenes is no son (*genos*) of Hermes, the patron deity of traders and bankers.

Later in the dialogue Socrates suggests ironically another reason for Cratylus' strange insistence: "Hermes seems to me to have to do with speech; he is an interpreter (*hermēneus*) and a messenger, is wily and deceptive in speech, and is oratorical" (*Cra.* 408b). Hermogenes is compared first with a hermetic banker and then with a hermetic speaker. Socrates implies that both money and language must be considered from the points of view of nature and convention. The serious question of the possibility of true and false names arises principally in connection with Hermogenes: "And when anyone says that our friend is Hermogenes, is he not even speaking falsely?" (*Cra.* 429c). The apparent possibility of speaking that-which-is-not presents Socrates with an opportunity to criticize the Heraclitean theory of flux and to seem to praise his own theory of still Ideas. (On Hermes and his relation to money and language, see H. V. Prott and W. Kölbe, *Mitteilungen des Kaiserlich Deutschen Archäologischen Instituts, Athenische Abteilung,* Band 27 [1902], esp. pp. 86 ff.; N. O. Brown, *Hermes the Thief* [New York, 1947]; and R. Raingeard, *Hermès psychagogue* [Rennes, 1934], esp. pp. 217 ff.).

All things are an equal exchange (*antamoibē*) for fire and fire for all
things, as goods (*chrēmata*) are for gold (*chrysou*) and gold for goods.[117]

The metaphors (or content) of the fragment are commercial. More
significantly, its metaphorization (or form) is also commercial. The
fragment is not only about the exchanges of fire or gold but also about
its own exchanges of meanings or metaphorization. The interpreter
must consider the tropes of the language of this fragment, as Heraclitus elsewhere considers the "tropes" of fire (*pyros tropai*).[118] To
understand Heraclitean exchange is to understand Fragment 90 as a
series of formal exchanges.

The fragment comprises four metaphors, two statements, and one
simile. The metaphors are:
  (a) all things are an exchange for fire
  (b) fire is an exchange for all things
  (c) goods are an exchange for gold
  (d) gold is an exchange for goods.
Metaphor is itself an exchange. In each of the four metaphors, the
relation between the two terms is defined as an exchange. "Exchange" not only expresses the relation between the terms of each
metaphor but also names the metaphorization itself. As we shall see,
the fragment defines a kind of exchange (or metaphor) that did not
exist in the world much before the time of Heraclitus.

There are two statements in the fragment:
  (1) there is an exchange of all things for fire and fire for all
      things
  (2) there is an exchange of goods for gold and gold for goods.
The metaphors within each statement cannot be separated from each
other without destroying the meaning of the statement or of either one
of its metaphors. Each statement is composed of two metaphors that
are in polar opposition to each other. In statement (1), for example,
metaphor (a) and metaphor (b) are polar opposites like the North and
South Poles and like sale and purchase. The relation between the terms
of each metaphor, moreover, is similar to the relation between that
metaphor and its polar opposite. In metaphor (a), for instance, "all
things" and "fire" depend on each other in the same way as do meta-

117. Heraclitus, frag. 90, in *Heraclitus, the Cosmic Fragments*, trans. G. S. Kirk (Cambridge, 1952), p. 345. There is some dispute about whether *exchange* is a noun or verb. I
think that it does not make any difference for my analysis. Most critics (including Kirk)
argue that it is a noun.
118. Heraclitus, frag. 31. Cf. *Rep.* 400d, where Plato uses *tropē* with reference to
language as well as fire.

phors (*a*) and (*b*). Such metaphorization, as we shall see, is a unique and decisive contribution by Heraclitus to the history of thought.

Fragment 90 contains one simile, which compares the two statements that comprise the four metaphors. This simile extends the polar opposition from the physical or natural universe, statement (1), to the social or economic world, statement (2), or vice versa. The simile helps, but is not necessary, to explain the meaning of either statement.

In Heraclitus's fragment, simile serves a different function from metaphor. Metaphors (*a*) and (*b*)—or metaphors (*c*) and (*d*)—are interdependent, but together they compose the independent statement (1) — or statement (2). Each statement is half of the simile that is the whole fragment, but it is a half with a meaning whole in itself. The two terms of the simile that compose the whole fragment—statements (1) and (2)—are similar, yet independent. The terms of the metaphors, on the other hand, are in polar opposition to each other and are interdependent.

Fragment 67 uses simile and metaphor in a similar way. Of constancy and change Heraclitus wrote, "God is day and night, winter and summer, war and peace, satiety and want. But God undergoes transformations, just as . . . *x*, when it is mixed with a fragrance, is named according to the particular savor [that is introduced to it]."[119] The substance similar to God could be fire, olive oil, air, gold, or any pure substance able to receive many bodies.[120] Is the substance itself transformed by the reception? Fragment 67 makes ambiguous whether or not God is transformed into the predicate(s) of the first sentence. It also leaves unanswered whether that predicate can be "day" alone or "night" alone, or only the opposites "day and night" taken together. When God is transformed into the predicate, moreover, does he remain heterogeneous or does he become homogeneous with it? Is God immanent in, transcendent to, or himself the exchanges of, the predicate? The substance *x*, to which Heraclitus refers in Fragment 67, gives a clue not only to the answer to these questions but also to their significance. In the *Timaeus*, Socrates describes a substance—gold—that plays the same role as *x*.[121] Gold has a universal nature that, like the

119. Heraclitus, frag. 67, translation adapted from Philip Wheelwright, *Heraclitus* (Princeton, 1959; reprint ed., New York, 1964), p. 102. (The word that signifies the substance similar to God is not extant in the text; it is here represented by *x*.) Similar similes occur in frags. 73 and 124.

120. Wheelwright, *Heraclitus*, p. 155.

121. "Suppose a person to make all kinds of figures of gold and to be always remodeling each form into all the rest; somebody points to one of them and asks what it is. By far the safest answer is: That is gold, and not to call . . . the figures which are

sculptor's metal or the stamper's wax, can become something else and yet still remain itself. Gold minted into a coin, for example, is both homogeneous with itself (as gold) and heterogeneous with itself (as numismatic sculpture or as money).

Fragment 90 demands an interpretation of homo- and heterogeneity in which gold is considered as commodity, as coin, and finally as money. Statement (2) in Fragment 90 confuses students of Heraclitus who do not understand the relationship of gold to goods, or the opposition of metaphor (c) to metaphor (d). G. S. Kirk, for example, accuses Heraclitus of an "unavoidable looseness of speech" in statement (1) because Kirk does not understand statement (2). "Fire is said to be an exchange for 'all things;' but fire must itself be one constituent of 'all things,' if this means all the individual things in the world. . . . We cannot properly elucidate this difficulty; but probably it is simply due to an unavoidable looseness of speech."[122] Kirk's erroneous interpretation of the fragment is itself avoidable. Fragment 90, in fact, explains precisely how fire both is and is not one constituent of "all things" (that is, how it can be both homo- and heterogeneous with "all things"). Gold (the analogue to fire in the first statement) is both one constituent of "goods" (the analogue to "all things") and not one constituent of "goods." Insofar as gold is considered as a metal, it is a good (or commodity) like all other goods. Insofar as it is considered as coined money, it is a good unlike any other goods; perhaps, according to Heraclitus, it is not a good at all but rather a mere token or measure.[123] Gold is thus both a good and a nongood, as fire is both a thing and an

---

formed in gold 'these,' as though they had existence, since they are in the process of change while he is making the assertion. . . . And the same argument applies to the universal nature which receives all bodies—that must be always called the same, for inasmuch as she always receives all things, she never departs at all from her own nature and never . . . assumes a form like that of any of the things which enter into her. She is like wax, the natural recipient of all impressions" (Plato, *Ti.* 50a–b, 52).

122. Kirk, *Heraclitus,* p. 348.

123. Kirk, *Heraclitus,* (pp. 345 ff.) misunderstands why one side of the exchange seems homogeneous (namely, gold fire) and the other side heterogeneous (namely, *chrēmata*/all things). He also misunderstands why "Heraclitus did not fully integrate his opposite-doctrine with his doctrine of fire, though the two are connected by the doctrine of *metron*" (p. 348). To understand properly the doctrine of measure in Fragments 29 and 122, it is necessary to understand the apparent measure that is money and those fragments in which *metron* plays an implicit role (e.g., frag. 31, about *pyros tropai* and the measured divisions of the elements). Heraclitus closely associates measure (e.g. money) and that which it measures (e.g. commodity). Citing E. L. Minar ("The Logos of Heraclitus," *Classical Philology* 34 [1939]: 323), Vlastos writes that *logos* indicates not "computation" or "reckoning" but rather "value" in the double senses of "worth" (*pleiōn logos*) and "measure of worth" ("Equality and Justice," pp. 164, 166). (Cf. Gernet. "Choses visible," p. 411.) Harold Cherniss ("The Character of Pre-Socratic Philos-

exchange for all things. Gold/fire has at least three ontological statuses: commodity, coin, and money.[124] In the fragment, the word *chrysos* (and in some ways even *chrēmata*) suggests this triple meaning of gold/ fire.

Antamoibē, about which Fragment 90 seems to revolve, can signify the monetary and the barter forms of exchange. That the exchange of meanings that constitutes Fragment 90 is or involves monetary exchange can be indicated by comparing figures in which simple barter is involved. Archilochus, for example, sometimes exchanges meanings in the same way that goods are exchanged in barter. In one poem, he uses a surprising metaphor (or *antamoibē* of meaning) to describe an exchange (*antamoibē*) of qualities or possessions.

> There is nothing in the world unexpected, nothing to be sworn impossible nor yet marvellous, now that Zeus the Father of the Olympians hath made night of noon by hiding the light of the shining Sun so that sore fear came upon mankind. Henceforth is anything whatsoever to be believed or expected. Let not one of you marvel, nay, though he see the beasts of the field *exchange* pasture with the dolphins of the deep, and the roaring waves of the sea become dearer than the land to such as loved the hill.[125]

The transformation of noon into night (by solar eclipse) is like the exchange of pasture for sea. The land and sea animals exchange their abodes (possibly their properties) without an intervening third term or concept of all things. Archilochus barters without money.

In Heraclitus's Fragment 90, one thing is not simply exchanged for another thing; rather it is first exchanged for all things. The purpose of Archilochus's figurative exchange or metaphor would not have been furthered by having the animals re-exchange their abodes. But for Heraclitus, the double exchange within the statements of Fragment 90 is necessary. He considers exchange binocularly as one action in which two polar opposite transferences occur. In barter economy,

---

ophy," *Journal of the History of Ideas* 12 [1951]: 331; cited by Wheelwright, *Heraclitus*, p. 122) argues that fire in Heraclitus is neither a mere symbol of the universal process nor a substrate persisting as identical throughout its qualitative alterations. He speaks of it both as a token for exchange, like gold in trade, and as involved in change itself.

124. Konrad Axelos (*Héraclite et la philosophie* [Paris, 1968], p. 94) believes that it is significant that "l'or a la couleur... du feu." Oswald Spengler suggests interestingly that the abstract operations of gold as money are paralleled by its supposedly abstract color (*The Decline of the West* [New York, 1926], 1:247–49); see also Oswald Spengler, *Der Metaphysische Grundgedanke der Heraklitischen Philosophie* [Halle, 1904]. Such speculations are not necessary to understand the form of the fragment or the significance of "golden fire."

125. Archilochus, frag. 74. Italics mine.

one actor gives X to a second actor and this second actor gives Y to the first actor. Marine pastures can be bartered for land pastures. In a barter economy, no commodity (not even gold) attains the status of money. Heraclitus, however, considers gold not only as commodity but also as money. Statement (2) describes the exchange of gold for goods in polar opposition to the exchange of goods for gold. He splits the barter transaction into two opposite operations, namely, sale and purchase. This split presupposes an intermediating third term, money, which acts first as agent of the seller and then as agent of the buyer. The first actor sells and the second actor buys by means of money. In a money economy, one thing is not exchanged directly for another, but is first exchanged for money which seems to represent or be all things. The form of monetary exchange, then, is X-Money-Y except in the one case where Money and either X or Y are materially identical, that is, where both the coin and one of the commodities are made of gold.

In a monetary economy it sometimes appears to the actors that sale and purchase are separate operations. This appearance is deceptive, for there is no sale without purchase. (As we have seen, the Greeks believed there was no sale without payment.) This truth was becoming invisible to the Greeks who were already exposed to the new money form. X-Money and Money-Y seemed to be separate operations, and an ideological fetishization of the money form made money appear to be a mere token or measure. Heraclitus's fragment would explain the relation between the barter and money forms and hence limit the power of money (or Gyges' ring) to transform images into realities and realities into images.[126]

Heraclitus's interpretation of the money-symbol considers, from the point of view of the dialectic problems both of deposition (hypothecal and hypothetical) and of philosophical symbolization (whereby a thing both is and is not itself). In *Capital*, Karl Marx presents a theory of exchange similar to that which constitutes the content and form of Heraclitus's Fragment 90. Studying the formal exchange of commodities into use-value from nonuse-value and into nonuse-value from use-value, Marx suggests a Heraclitean theory of metaphor or exchange of meanings that distinguishes between gold as mere commodity and gold as the money form. In a short genetic analysis of the development of money from commodity, for example, Marx refers implicitly to the Heraclitean analysis.

> Commodities, first of all, enter into the process of exchange just as they are. The process then differentiates them into commodities and money,

126. See Chapter 1, "The Ideas."

and thus produces an external opposition corresponding to the internal opposition inherent in them, as being at once use-values and values. Commodities as use-values now stand opposed to money as exchange-value. On the other hand, both opposing sides are commodities, unities of use-value and value. But this unity of differences manifests itself at two opposite poles, and at each pole in an opposite way. Being poles they are as necessarily opposite as they are connected. On the one side of the equation we have an ordinary commodity, which is in reality a use-value. Its value is expressed only ideally in its price, by which it is equated to its opponent, the gold, as to the real embodiment of its value. On the other hand, the gold, in its metallic reality, ranks as the embodiment of value, as money. Gold, as gold, is exchange-value itself. As to its use-value, that has only an ideal existence, represented by the series of expressions of relative value in which it stands face to face with all other commodities, the sum of whose uses makes up the sum of the various uses of gold. These antagonistic forms of commodities are the real forms in which the process of their exchange moves and takes place.[127]

Throughout *Capital*, Marx regards money as the hero of a great historical drama. In the "act" about "the metamorphosis of commodities," for example, he describes the "scene of action, the market," in which "the exchange becomes an accomplished fact by two metamorphoses of opposite yet supplementary character—the conversion of the commodity into money, and the re-conversion of the money into a commodity."[128] As he suggests in a footnote, the act of exchange of which Marx here speaks elucidates that of Heraclitus's Fragment 90.[129] The two metamorphoses are considered (as by Heraclitus) in one vision, so that "the exchange of commodities is accompanied by the following changes in their form: Commodity—Money—Commodity."[130] Marx's "Money" is the combination of M_1 and M_2 in the equation that expresses barter exchange: $X-M_1-M_2-X$. It is the third term in many theories of metaphor.

127. Karl Marx, *Capital*, ed. Frederick Engels, trans. Samuel Moore and Edward Aveling (New York, 1967), 1: 104–5.
128. "Let us now accompany the owner of some commodity—say, our old friend the weaver of linen—to the scene of action, the market. His 20 yards of linen has a definite price, £2. He exchanges it for the £2, and then, like a man of the good old stamp that he is, he parts with the £2 for a family Bible of the same price. The linen, which in his eyes is a mere commodity, a depository of value, he alienates in exchange for gold, which is the linen's value-form, and this form he again parts with for another commodity, the Bible, which is destined to enter his house as an object of utility and of edification to its inmates" (Marx, *Capital*, p. 105).
129. *Ibid.*, p. 105n. Elsewhere, Marx compares the Heraclitean act of exchange to the act of translation in Goethe's *Faust*.
130. *Ibid.*, p. 105.

Both Marx and Heraclitus focus on money not as fetishized form but as the activity of transformation. In *Herr Bastiat-Schulze von Delitzsch*, however, the Hegelian Lassalle erroneously interprets golden money (in Fragment 90 and in reality) to be a mere symbol of abstract value.[131] As Marx argues, Lassalle makes the same error in *Die Philosophie Herakleitos des Dunkeln.*[132] Hegel had offered an interpretation of Heraclitus's fire as the fundamental element, but he had neglected Fragment 90.[133] Relying on the Hegelian interpretation of Heraclitean fire, Lassalle makes gold a mere idealist symbol of value. "Wenn Heraklit das Geld als Tauschmittel zum Gegensatz aller in den Tausch kommender reellen Producte machte und es an diesen erst sein wirkliches Dasein haben lässt, so ist also das Geld als solches nicht selbst ein mit einem selbständigen, stofflichen Werthe bekleidetes Product, nicht eine Waare neben andern Waaren . . . sondern es ist nur der ideelle Repräsentant der umlaufenden reellen Producte, das Werthzeichen derselben, das nur sie bedeutet."[134] Lassalle's interpretation of Heraclitean fire interprets gold only as abstract measure in its most alien form, and assumes the idealist position whereby money can be completely separated from its role as commodity. Lassalle ignores the polar opposition of money and commodity that in-

131. F. Lassalle, *Herr Bastiat-Schulze von Delitzsch, der ökonomische Julian, oder Kapital und Arbeit* (Berlin, 1864–67), p. 222.

132. Marx, *Capital*, pp. 7–8n., referring to F. Lassalle, *Die Philosophie Herakleitos des Dunkeln* (Berlin, 1858), pp. 222–23.

133. Hegel argues that Heraclitean fire is a "logical symbol" and suggests that the reason Heraclitus chose fire as the fundamental element is that fire (unlike earth, air, and water) is an ideal fluctuating element and is, perhaps, even fluctuation itself (G. W. F. Hegel, *Lectures on the History of Philosophy*, ed. and trans. E. S. Haldane [London, 1892] 1: 278–97). Lassalle applies this interpretation of fire to Fragment 90. His easy translation of *chrysos* as *Geld* assumes that money is the ideal, or abstract representative, of wares. In his history of philosophy, Hegel considered most of the available fragments of Heraclitus, the first known dialectician. No one fragment, he claimed, was omitted. Hegel did, however, omit explicit consideration of Fragment 90; perhaps it did not suit his interpretation of the other fragments.

134. Lassalle, *Herakleitos*, p. 224n. (cited in Marx, *Capital*, 1: 105n.). Lassalle also writes: "Heraklit beschreibt in diesem Vergleiche tiefer, als es auf den ersten Blick scheint, die wirkliche Function des Geldes" (p. 222). Lassalle offers his own interpretation of the *ideelle Einheit* of *Geld* and then continues to explain how gold represents things. "Das Geld ist somit *qua* Tauschagent nur der personificirte Werth, die herausgesetzte abstracte Einheit der wirklichen und als wirkliche eine unendliche Vielheit von bestimmten sinnlichen Dingen bildenden Producte. . . . Nach Heraklit war also alles Geld nur der Gegensatz und die herausgesetzte ideelle Einheit aller Dinge, aller umlaufenden Producte; diese ihrerseits wieder nur die dadurch in die Mannigfaltigkeit der sinnlichen Unterschiede aufgelöste Wirklichkeit jener ideellen Wertheinheit, des Geldes" (p. 223).

forms Fragment 90, of which he claims to be offering a close reading.[135]

Other students of Fragment 90 interpret gold only as material commodity. They argue that *chrysos* means "the commodity gold" and that *chrēmata* (which is usually translated as "wares," "commodities," or "goods") means "coins." Ingeniously, though incorrectly, they interpret the exchange of *chrysos* for *chrēmata* either as the purchase of coins or small change for gold or as the minting of coins. According to Karl Göbel, for example, "Einerseits sind alle Dinge Äquivalent des Feuers und anderseits Feuer Äquivalent für alle Dinge, wie Waren für Gold und Gold für Waren. Vielleicht sind hier unter *chrēmata* im Gegensatz zu den Goldmünzen oder Goldbarren die Scheidemünzen zu verstehen."[136] Göbel interprets metaphor (*d*) in Fragment 90 as referring to an exchange of small change ("Scheidemünzen") for gold. Such an exchange occurs both at the *agora* (where coins change hands) and at the mint (where a gold bar or ingot "purchases," or is transformed into, gold coins). Insofar as small coins are themselves commodities, Göbel's far-fetched translation of *chrēmata* as "small change" is unnecessary and misleading. Göbel focuses myopically on only one metaphor—(*d*)—of Fragment 90, but it is crucial to the articulation of Heraclitus's statement (2) about commerce that this metaphor have an interdependent polar opposite—(*c*). Ignoring the dialectical relationship between *chrysos* and *chrēmata*, Göbel misinterprets Fragment 90. Heraclitus does not consider minting alone, although he does refer in part to the exchange of the good that is gold for golden coins. In only a partial sense, however, can Fragment 90 be interpreted correctly in terms of the minting and purchase of coins, which do not fully express the money form.

In a sentence of the *Laws* about exchange in the marketplace, Plato mimics unmistakably the form of statement (2) in Fragment 90. "There shall be an exchange of coins (*nomisma*) for goods (*chrēmatōn*) and goods for coins, and no man shall give up his share to the other without receiving its equivalent; and if any does thus give it up, as it

---

135. Olof Gigon (*Untersuchungen zu Heraklit* [Leipzig, 1935]) argues, like Lassalle, that in Fragment 90 there is a wholly abstract notion of an invisible fire hidden in the appearance of other forms. He fails to consider the polar opposition between what is hidden and what is not hidden (frag. 54). The idealist interpretation fails to understand the material of gold/fire and tries to make Heraclitus into more of a "Platonist" than Plato himself would have allowed.

136. Karl Göbel, *Die vorsokratische Philosophie* (Bonn, 1910), pp. 49–50. Göbel also writes that "das Feuer ist auch die Kraft die diesen Umtausch durch sich selbst bewirkt."

were on credit, he shall make the best of his bargain, whether or not he recovers what is due to him, since in such transactions he can no longer sue."[137] By *chrēmata* Plato means goods and not coins.[138] Money transactions pose a special threat to Plato. He would carefully enforce the rules of the marketplace so that what is due a person (by justice or *dikē*) will not be lost.[139] The lawmaker seems to agree with Cephalus that purchase or sale must be according to the law (*kata ton nomon*); transactions must be scrutinized by law-wardens and *agora*-stewards. Such precautions in the marketplace (where Socrates and the moneylenders carry out their social intercourse and where Gyges was said to have had special powers)[140] will ensure that "no man shall give up his share to the other without receiving its equivalent." Although he tries to banish the problem of indiscriminately returning deposits (both hypothetical and hypothecal) from his philosophy, Plato seems to admit that the problem cannot be abolished from the marketplace. He tries, therefore, to control by law those Heraclitean exchanges which he dislikes and over which he fears that a man like Gyges might seize control.

The monetary form of exchange, which Plato feared, informs many fragments of Heraclitus.[141] Of these, one of the most telling is the simple fragment that reads, "The way up and the way down are one and the same."[142] Heraclitus of Ephesus refers not only to the trans-

---

137. *Leg.* 849e.

138. In this statement from the *Laws*, *chrēmatōn* could not mean *Scheidemünzen* (coins). Aristotle writes that "we call goods (*chrēmata*) all those things of which the value is measured in money" (*Eth. Nic.* 1119.b.26). Vernant (*Mythe et pensée*, p. 310) insists that the history of the meaning of *chrēmata* followed the development of money in the same way that Thomson insisted that Being or Idea followed it. "C'est en un autre terme [a term other than *ousia*] que se reflète l'effort d'abstraction qui se poursuit à travers l'expérience commerciale et la pratique monétaire. *Ta chrēmata* désigne à la fois les choses, la réalité en général et les biens, spécialement sous leur forme d'argent liquide."

139. *Leg.* 849e. See n. 39 above.

140. "He [a man such as Gyges] might with impunity take what he wished even from the market-place" (*Rep.* 360b).

141. On Fragments 12, 29, 31, 44, 54, 67, 73, 90, 122, 124, and 125, see above pages, and notes 20, 115, 118, 119, 123, and 135. On Fragment 93 (the epigraph to the Introduction), see below. On Fragment 22, see Ch. 5, n. 8. Heraclitus also writes: "The phases of fire are craving and satiety" (frag. 65); "It is hard to fight against impulsive desire, (for) whatever it wants it buys at the expense of soul" (frag. 85; cited Aristotle *Eth. Nic.* 2.3.10); and "An ass would prefer chaff to gold" (frag. 96; cited Aristotle *Eth. Nic.* 10.5.8). In Fragment 96, Heraclitus suggests (as does Aristotle) that gold as commodity is as useless to men as chaff is useful to donkeys, but that gold as money is the (human) "function" *par excellence* for men such as Midas.

142. Heraclitus, frag. 60.

formations of fire (*pyros tropai*) but also to its monetary exchanges (*chrysou antamoibai*). The way up and the way down refer to sale and purchase. Ephesus, a port on the Mediterranean, was a trading center between Sardis (the capital of Lydia, where gold was minted) and major trading nations (such as Phoenicia).[143] The way to which Heraclitus refers is (in part) a road like that between Sardis and its port, Ephesus.

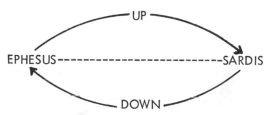

The road between Lydia and Ephesus was one, but the goods moved in both directions. Many commodities moved from Ephesus to Sardis. From Sardis to Ephesus, gold moved. There was no movement in one direction unless there was also movement in the other. One direction is the way of sale, the other is the way of purchase. In Greek, "up" and "down" have meanings that substantiate this interpretation of the fragment. *Katō* (down) refers to the road to the sea; *anō* (up) refers to the road from the sea. *Anō* is used, for example, by Herodotus to mean the inland road from the sea up to Heliopolis (Hdt. 2.8).[144]

Plato's *Republic* begins with the words, "I went down [*katebēn*] to the Piraeus [that is, along the road from Athens to its port city]." It

143. Heraclitus was acquainted with a monetary economy. Ephesus had close relations with Lydia (having been conquered by the Mermnadae), and the history and coins of Ephesus bear testimony to the impact of the numismatic economy. Certain critics, however, argue that Ephesus had a different kind of economy. For example, Vernant writes that Fragment 90 "ne nous parait pas se situer encore sur ce plan d'un rationalisme mercantile" (*Mythe et pensée*, p. 310n). Vernant, depending on an unsubstantiated argument of Clémence Ramnoux (*Héraclite, ou l'homme entre les choses et les mots* [Paris, 1959], pp. 404–5), believes that the Ephesian economy was one of "thesaurization;" thus, there exists for Heraclitus a fire in the invisible state and a fire in circulation, one corresponding to gold in coffers and the other to "liquid" gold. Such an interpretation fails to take into consideration the dialectical form of the fragment. Another critic, George Thomson (*Ancient Greek Society*, 2: 282), argues that Heraclitus's "concept of a self-regulating cycle of perpetual transformations of matter is the ideological reflex of an economy based on commodity production." Both Vernant and Thomson are probably mistaken about the historical facts and are certainly mistaken about the monetary (in)form(ation) of the fragment.

144. This interpretation of Fragment 60 is suggested by Clémence Ramnoux (*Héraclite*, pp. 404–5).

ends with a mythic upward way beyond earthly extremes of good and evil (*Rep.* 621c; cf. 614b–621b). The change from being good for fear of the gods of Hades (*Haidēs*) to being good for the sake of the Idea (*eidos*) of the Good is a movement "from Hades up to the gods" (*Rep.* 521c). The dialectic itself is supposed to rise above hypothesis and deposit (*kata-thēkē*). For Plato, the upward way (whether "up out of the cave" or "up the divided line") does not depend finally on its opposite, the downward way. Plato pretends that the etymology of *alētheia* (truth) is not "the unconcealed" but rather the unidirectional "way of the god," which does not imply any negation.[145] For Heraclitus, on the other hand, the upward way depends on the downward way. *Anō* is the polar opposite of *katō* as purchase is the polar opposite of sale.

The different interpretations in Plato and Heraclitus of the ways up and down affect their symbolic representation and metaphorization. *Katō* and *anō* refer directly to the lower and upper orders in a descending or ascending series of genera and species.[146] Metaphorization, which depends on such a series, is affected by whether or not there is an upper genus beyond all other genera, namely, the Idea. Heraclitus, who incorporated the money form into his thought as an active, changing rather than as a still, substantial concept, metaphorizes differently from Plato. Both Heraclitus and Plato, nevertheless, encounter and try to account for the internalization of economic form in their own thinking. Their thought—philosophy—confronts the economics of thought itself.

As Nietzsche argues in *The Genealogy of Morals*, the price-making of early man was not so different from our own.[147] Modern man returns to Greek philosophy with nostalgia, but he finds therein described only the origin or discovery of himself. The economics of thought, set down by Greek dialecticians at the origin of critical thinking, has not ceased to influence us.

145. Plato, *Cra.* 421b. On *alētheia* and the opposition of unseen or unknown things (*ta adēla*) to apparent things (*ta phanera*), see P. M. Schuhl, "Adéla."

146. Socrates suggests the analogy between classification and minting. "We ought to do our best to collect all such kinds as are torn and split apart, and stamp a single *charaktēr* on them" (*Philebus*, 25a).

147. Nietzsche, *Werke* 3: 811 ff.

THE LANGUAGE OF CHARACTER

An Introduction to a Poetics of Monetary Inscriptions

I would have some body put the Muses under a kind of contribution to furnish out whatever they have in them that bears any relation to Coins. – Addison, Dialogue upon the Usefulness of Ancient Medals

INSCRIPTION AND INSCRIBED

Heraclitus's study of signs (*sēmata*) deals with coins as well as words.[1] Numismatics, he knew, concerns both economics and esthetics.[2] The study of economic and verbal symbolization, and of the relationship between them, begins at the mint, where Greek poet-coinmakers considered the relationship between the writing on coins and that to which the writing refers.

1. See Heraclitus, frag. 93, in Hermann Diels, *Die Fragmente der Vorsokratiker,* 5th ed. (Berlin, 1934) with additions by Walter Kranz. (Epigraph to the Introduction, above.)
2. Marc Bloch, for example, deals with economic concerns ("The Problem of Gold in the Middle Ages," in *Land and Work in Medieval Europe* [Berkeley and Los Angeles, 1967]; originally published in *Annales d'Histoire Sociale* 5 [1933]: 7–16).
On esthetic concerns, see André Malraux (*Psychologie de l'art,* 3 vols. [Geneva, 1947–49], vol. 3: *La Monnaie de l'absolu,* p. 192), who aims to reintegrate Celtic coinage into the general history of art. "Leur nature [i.e., celle des monnaies celtiques dites gauloises], leurs dimensions, semblaient les exclure du domaine de l'art, où l'aggrandissement photographique les fait entrer." Malraux's essay is an analysis of the "régression invincible vers le signe" (p. 193) in the designs of Celtic coinage, of which the ideogram of the coin of Veliocassus is the best example. See also Cornelius Vermeule, *Numismatic Art in America* (Cambridge, Mass., 1971); C. H. V. Sutherland, *Art in Coinage* (New York, 1956); and Kurt Regling, *Die Antike Münze als Kunstwerk* (Berlin, 1924).

Coins were the first widely circulating publications or impressions in history.[3] The *charaktēr* (upper die used by the coinmaker or impressed mark on the coin) and the coin preceded by two millennia the printing press and the printed page (Plate 1). The writing on coins— "vocal monuments of antiquity"[4]—frequently referred to magistrates, political leaders, cities, mints, and denominations; dates and places of minting; and diemakers.[5] It could also refer to (*a*) social events or conventions; (*b*) some other impression in the coin (the type, for instance); (*c*) the material on which the writing appeared (a piece of metal); (*d*) the coin, into which the writing helped to transform the material (*c*); (*e*) the monetary system of which the coin (*d*) was a token; and so on.[6]

3. One of the first to recognize the importance of the analogy between the mint and the printing press was the economist and professional etymologist, A.R.J. Turgot. "Que les moindres progrès sont lents en tout genre! Depuis deux mille ans les médailles présentent à tous les yeux des caractères imprimés sur l'airain et, après tant de siècles, un particulier obscur soupçonne qu'on peut en imprimer sur le papier" (A. R. J. Turgot, "Tableau philosophique des progrès successifs de l'esprit humain" (1750) in *Ecrits économiques*, intro. B. Cazes [Paris, 1970], p. 57).

4. John Evelyn (*Numismata* [London, 1697]) wrote that coins are "the most lasting and (give me leave to call them) vocal Monuments of Antiquity" (*Coins and Vases of Arthur Stone Dewing, A Memorial Exhibition* [March–April 1971], The Fogg Art Museum, Harvard University, Cambridge, Mass.).

5. C. M. Kraay and Max Hirmer, *Greek Coins* (New York, 1966), pp. 15–16.

In most inscriptions, including those on the monuments of Babylon, the "inscriptions" of Wordsworth, journalistic ballads, and monetary inscriptions, notation of date and place is important. (See Geoffrey Hartman, "Wordsworth, Inscriptions, and Romantic Poetry," in *Beyond Formalism* [New Haven, 1970]), esp. pp. 208 ff.)

The names of artists were rarely important visual features on coins. David Bowers (*Coins and Collectors* [New York, 1964], p. 83) suggests that rulers did not wish such signatures to conflict with their own heraldic devices. However, Cimon sometimes signed both obverse and reverse of the coins he minted (Plate 2), Euaenetus worked for more than one state (Catana and Syracuse) and had no special allegiance to the rulers he served (Plate 3), and Publius Maenius Antiacus engraved a signature larger than the name of the Emperor (plate 4).

Signed coins are usually of very high artistic quality (as with Eucleidas's famous issue, Plate 5). Their makers seem aware of their "poetic" character. For example, on a coin issued at Clazomenae, *"Theodotus epoie"* (Theodotus made it) is inscribed to the left of the face of Apollo. In this instance *poiēsis* can refer to both die-making and to word-writing (Plate 6). (Cf. n. 20, below, on Bowes's heraldic device.)

6. For lists of monetary inscriptions, see A. Florance, *Geographic Lexicon of Greek Coin Inscriptions* (Chicago, 1966); Séverin Icard, *Identification des monnaies par la nouvelle méthode des lettres-jalons et des légendes fragmentées* (Paris, 1929) (English translation, *Dictionary of Greek Coin Inscriptions* [Chicago, 1968]); J.-M.-R. Lecoq-Kerneven, *Traité de la composition et de la lecture de toutes inscriptions monétaires... depuis l'époque Mérovingienne jusqu'à l'apparition des Armoiries* (Rennes, 1869); Stuart Mosher ("Coin Mottoes and Their Translation," *Numismatist*, April, May, July, September, and December, 1948); and M. N. Tod, "Epigraphical Notes on Greek Coinage," *Numismatic Chronicle* 5

The material or commodity (c) on which coin-writing appears is, unlike Gutenberg's paper, an especially valuable one. The pictorial or verbal impression in this material qualitatively changes it (esthetically) from a shapeless piece of metal into a sculptured ingot and, more significantly, qualitatively changes it (economically) from a mere commodity into a coin or token (d) of money (e). The sometimes beautiful impressions on ingots transform them into always useful tokens.[7] This transformation distinguishes minting from other kinds of sculpturing (even those that fashion equally valuable metals) and distinguishes monetary inscription from other kinds of inscription.

"The true inscription," writes Gotthold Lessing in *Über das epigramm*, "is not to be thought of apart from that whereon it stands or might stand."[8] According to Lessing's definition, we cannot properly consider an inscription (for example, the writing on a coin) without considering the material or thing (for example, an ingot) on which it stands. Yet some inscriptions (like Wordsworth's "Lines Left upon a Seat in a Yew-Tree") are written on one material but might also stand on some other material (a seat in a yew-tree).[9] To determine whether the writing on some coins might more suitably appear elsewhere is difficult. It is unclear, for example, in what ways coins (*nomismata*) constitute the proper material on which to write about social conventions (*nomoi*) (a).[10] However, there are numismatic writings that are

---

(1945): 108–16; 6 (1946): 47–62; 7 (1947): 1–27; 15 (1955): 125–30; 20 (1960): 1–24. Students of monetary inscriptions include Charles Patin, who tries to show that the ancients "despised all affectation, and dwelt more on the grandeur of the subject they described than on the cadence and the pomp of words, which they deemed unworthy of their attention" (*Thesaurus Numismatum* [Amsterdam, 1672]); and J. Eckhel (*Doctrina numorum veterum*, 8 vol. [Vienna, 1792–98]), who (as S. W. Stevenson suggests) argues that "brevity of inscriptions on medals is the character of a flourishing empire; whilst their loquacity, consequent upon flattery, vanity, and ambition, is, on the contrary, the sign of a state tottering to its fall." (See S. W. Stevenson, C. R. Smith, and F. W. Madden, *A Dictionary of Roman Coins*, s.v. "Inscription" [London, 1889; reprint ed., London, 1964]).

7. *Utile dulce* is a common coin motto (Mosher, "Coin Mottoes").

8. Gotthold Ephraim Lessing, *Zerstreute Anmerkungen über das Epigramm, und einige der vornehmsten Epigrammatisten* (Berlin, 1771); trans. H. H. Hudson, *The Epigram in the English Renaissance* (Princeton, 1947), pp. 9–10.

9. Cf. the paper-money inscription in *Faust* 2(6057 ff.).

10. Metal ingots, like postage stamps, are more suitable than some things for inscribing messages about social events (such as the Olympic games) and conventions or customs, but there is not always a necessary or proper connection between this medium and its messages. A similar difficulty arises in applying Lessing's definition, owing to his reliance on the particularity of the thing to which reference is made. "How specific, how occasional, must the object of the epigram be? If too general and abstract, does not the epigram become an apothegm or a maxim?" (Hudson, *Epigram*, p. 12).

clearly appropriate where they are inscribed. Inscriptions that refer to items (c), (d), and (e) can be considered to be monetary inscriptions *par excellence*. Whether an inscription refers to item (c), (d), or (e), it is evident that it should be thought of together with that into which it is impressed (that is, an ingot [c], which the inscription transforms into a coin or token [d] of the monetary system [e]).

The early poet-coinmakers, who impressed verbal symbols into monetary symbols, wrote about coins, and, as we shall see, they sometimes personified coins so that the coins could speak about themselves. It was ambiguous to these coinmakers whether a monetary inscription should refer to an ingot (c), a coin (d), or the monetary system (e). The ambiguity arises out of an ideological as well as esthetic confusion about the semiology of coins that marks the beginning of monetary theory.[11]

The *Sēma:* The Beginning of Monetary Theory

The first known inscribed coin (Plate 7) was minted in Ephesus around 600 B.C. On the reverse was punched (in reverse order): *"Phanēos eimi sēma"* (I am the *sēma* of Phanos). The inscription on the reverse calls the coin the *sēma* or token of the man Phanos, or it calls

11. The relationship between a numismatic inscription and the ingots inscribed is like that between a numeral or "number" (*Zahl*) and the group or "number" (*Anzahl*) of things represented or homogenized by it. A coin, like a number, is both a symbol and a thing: as a monetary unit it has symbolical properties, as has a numeral; as an ingot it has material properties, as have all things. The similarity suggests how minting may have affected Greek number theory and mathematical theory of ideas. (Cf. Chapter 1, "Hypothesis and Hypothecation," on *kermatidzein* and *diairesis*, and Chapter 1, n. 107 on the comparison between a unit [monad] and a drachma.)

The semiological similarity between number and coin may help to explain the etymology of "number" from the Latin *nummus* and the Greek *nomisma*, both of which mean "coined money" or "coin." See Oskar Wiedemann, who associates *numerus*, the direct etymon of "number," with cognates meaning "monetary interest" (*Das Litausche Präteritum* 5 [Strassburg, 1889–91]) and "money" (*Geld*) (*Beiträge zur Kunde der indogermanischen Sprachen*, ed. Adalbert Bezzenberger, 30 vols. [Gottingen, 1877–1906], 30: 216 ff.); A. Ernout and A. Meillet (*Dictionnaire étymologique de la langue latine* [Paris, 1967]), who relate *numerus* to *nummus*, which is a Sicilian dialect version of *nomisma*; and Sextus Pompeius Festus, who writes, "Nummus ex Graeco nomismate existimant dictum" (*De verborum significatione*, 176, 35). (Compare how the etymology of *numerus* puzzles Georg Curtius (*Principles of Greek Etymology*, trans. A. S. Wilkins and E. B. England, 2 vols. [London, 1875–76], 1: 389 ff.) and Emile Benveniste ("Trois étymologies latines," *Bulletin de la société linguistique de Paris* 32 [1931]: 85). On the transformation of the Greek *nemō* into the Latin *numerus*, see E. LaRoche, *Histoire de la racine nem- en grec ancien* (Paris, 1949), esp. pp. 260–64.

the figure of a stag impressed on the obverse the *sēma*, or heraldic badge of the goddess Artemis.[12] At the same time, the inscription helps to transform the ingot into a *sēma*, or coin. *Phanēos eimi sēma* is twice semiotic: it is a *sēma* on a *sēma*.

An inscription on a coin of Gortyna shows that the *sēma* to which the inscription of Ephesus refers may be the coin as well as the type: "This is the *paima* (striking) of the people of Gortyna" (Plate 8). *Paima* (a variant of *komma*) refers to the coin itself and not to the type (a lion). On the coins of Ephesus and Gortyna, the inscription refers to the coin itself, which is explained as a *sēma* or *paima*.

Ancient seals were often engraved with messages like those on the coins just mentioned. One gem, for example, is engraved "I am the *sēma* of Thersis. Open me not" (Plate 9). This inscription, which refers to a seal as *sēma*, is like that on the coin of Ephesus.[13] At the mint (*sēmantērion*) of Ephesus only a part of the political formulas of such seals and signet rings (*sēmeia*) was adopted, since the injunction against opening (as on a letter or vase) can hardly apply directly to a coin.[14] Unlike a sealed letter, a sealed ingot is unopenable, or infinitely circulating. Its valuable contents or powers to exchange are "closed," or made "invisible," to would-be seers. (That God, alone and universal, is "opener," is thus the theme of many monetary legends.[15] As we shall see, God, like money, is supposed to be a universal measure or equivalent.)

A signet ring is put to a new use when it mints coins. The growing consciousness of this new use was the beginning of that semiology, or science of signs, that is monetary theory.[16]

---

12. *Phanos* may be a variant of *"phaenō,* a possible epithet of Artemis, 'the bright one,' whose association with the deer is well known." It is more likely, however, that by *Phanos* "an ordinary human being is meant, ... a potentate or 'tyrant' either at Halicarnassus or at Ephesus, ... the stag being a common type at Ephesus" (George MacDonald, *Coin Types* [Glasgow, 1905; reprint ed., Chicago, 1969], p. 51). *Phanos* probably is a man and not (as others have thought) a city.

13. Cf. Seltman, *Greek Coins*, p. 28. Other analogues to the inscription on the coin of Ephesus include a bronze weight and coins of Thrace and Metapontum (Charles Newton, "On an Electrum Stater, Possibly of Ephesus," *Numismatic Chronicle* [1870], p. 238) and some Byzantine coins (MacDonald, *Coin Types*, p. 242).

14. J. Hangard, *Monetaire en daarmee verwante metaforen* (Groningen, 1963), p. 72. Cf. *sēmansis.*

15. *Aperiet Dominus thesaurum suum* (The Lord will open his treasures). *Aperiet cunctis* (He has opened to all). *Aperuit cunctia apostolor princeps* (The Prince of the apostles has opened to all). *Aperuit et clausit* (He opened it and he closed it).

16. *Sēmeion* is used by Greek writers to refer to the stamp (*charaktēr*) on a coin as a symbol of its size and weight. See Aristotle, *Pol.* 1257a.

Conundrum: The Canting Badge

Into the surfaces of many of the earliest coins were impressed images intended to suggest the sounds of words not actually imprinted. These pictures, which seem to recall an oral or hieroglyphic culture, are usually called *types parlants*, canting badges, or *redende Zeichen*. [17] Although they make writing itself unnecessary, they often depend (like conundrums) upon language and its homonyms. The sound of the name of the image sculpted into the surface of the coin is like that of the name of the issuing city. This sound yokes together two *signifiés*: the type and the city. It is often ambiguous what kind of linguistic relation exists between them. In the case of the coins of Selinus (Plate 10) and Rhodes (Plate 11), the types are plants that grow abundantly in the areas of their issuing cities. From these plants, as folk etymology might teach us, the cities were named. (Moreover, the types represent the surrounding environment of the city, and hence perhaps the city itself, without the need of intermediating language.) A coin (*nomisma*), however, is as conventional (nomic) as language and its puns. Many canting badges took advantage of purely linguistic or conventional homonymic relations between type and city. They are punning badges that purposely do not rely on images of things native to the region of the issuing city. A coin of Melos (Plate 12), for example, employs such a pun: *mēlon* means apple, but apples did not grow in the area of Melos. Similarly, the coins of Euboea (Plate 13), which means "rich in cattle," and those of Side (Plate 14), which means "pomegranate," are conventional canting badges. The unwritten puns of such coins play the same role with regard to the two *signifiés* they yoke together (type and city) that the coins (into which they are impressed) play with regard to the commodities they exchange on the basis of a conventional measure.

Most early canting badges were not impressed with inscriptions that helped the reader interpret the type. [18] In a canting badge of Phocaea (Plate 15), however, the letter ϕ is such an inscription. It is the first letter of the name of the issuing city, Phocaea (*Phōkaia*), and also the first letter of the type, a seal, (*phokē*), that appeared on earlier canting badges of Phocaea without any inscription. On this coin, then, the letter ϕ serves the same purpose of linking type and city as did the unwritten puns on the canting badges previously considered (Plates 12–14). The relationship between the widespread use of writing and the development of sophisticated numismatic semiology,

17. See Wilhelm Fietze, "Redende Abzeichen auf Antiken Münzen," *Journal International d'Archéologie numismatique* 15 (1913): 11 ff.

18. See MacDonald, *Coin Types*, pp. 51–52.

which this coin might suggest, is not part of the present inquiry. The short inscription of this coin, however, suggests a historical transition from the ordinary canting badge with no inscription to the long punning inscriptions that often explain much later coin types.

One coin with such a canting badge and long explanatory inscription is the fiorino d'oro (florin) of Florence (Plate 16). "There was no motto on the [original] fiorino, but only a lily or flower blossom (*fiore*) to indicate the city of Florence (*Firenze*)."[19] The silver piece issued after the fiorino d'oro, however, did have an explanatory running Leonine hexameter: "*Det tibi florere, Christus, Florentiam vere.*" The Florentines developed a whole series of short epigraphs that imitate the canting badge. Such poems were widely circulated as the first printed verse poems in the West.[20]

The Canting Ducat

Venetian ducats minted after 1284 bear an inscription that surrounds a mandorla of stars. Inside the stars is the figure of Christ, to whom the inscription seems to be addressed.

Impression: SIT.T.XRE.DAT.Q.TV.REGIS.ISTE.DUCAT
Reading: *Sit tibi Christe datus, quem tu regis, iste ducatus*
Translation: Let this duchy, which thou rulest, be dedicated to thee, O Christ

(Plate 17)

An unscientific etymology based on a pun has it that the name of the coin is derived from the last word of the legend.[21] "The word *ducat* was first applied to the silver grossi of Venice before any appearance in monetary [inscriptions]."[22] The poet of the first inscribed ducat (1284) was aware of the linguistic affiliation of *ducatus* (the political state) with *ducat*, and of the way in which the type (a doge [*dux*] pictured on the coin) made the ducat a canting badge. *Ducatus* is the

19. It is unclear whether *fiore* and *Florence* are related by folk or scientific etymology. See MacDonald, *Coin Types*, pp. 254 ff.

20. Canting badges also play an important role in the Renaissance. In England, for example, "Sir Martin Bowes, master of the mint under Henry VII and Edward VI, sometimes placed a bow as a symbol on coins for which he was responsible" (MacDonald, *Coin Types*, p. 257). The canting badges of Granada portrayed a pomegranate (as did those of Side).

21. MacDonald, *Coin Types*, p. 254. Similar false etymologies exist for the noble and the angel.

22. Herbert E. Ives, *The Venetian Gold Ducat and its Imitations*, ed. and annotated Philip Grierson (New York, 1954), p. 6.

culmination of the sounds of *datus* (the last word of the first phrase) and *regis* (the last word of the second phrase). As *ducatus* follows *iste* (the word that modifies it), so *datus* follows *Christe* (to whom the *ducatus* is given). The coin maker seems to put the words of his inscription into the mouth of the doge (*dux*), who kneels before Saint Mark. The doge offers to Christ either his duchy or his ducat or both. Christ had warned against offering Him the coins of secular political rulers.[23] To many pseudosecularized men, however, money appeared as abstract and limitless as the holy grail and as infinitely desirable as the grace of God. (Aristotle comments that sometimes money and grace may be infinitely desired in similar ways.)[24] Perhaps the supposedly merciful merchants of Venice did not so much wish to give ducats to God as they wished Him to give (ducats of) grace to them. The posture of the doge, perhaps, is like that of the devil when he offered Christ all the riches of the material world with the words *"tibi dabo."*[25] *Ducat* is the gift that the *dux* would give to Christ; grace is that which he would receive from Him. *"Pro gratia gratis"* and *"Dat accipit reddit"* are favorite Christian mottoes for coins.[26]

The Noble

One of the great numismatists, John Ruskin, writes that the English noble is "the most important in all English history, having been struck to commemorate the first great naval victory over the French [at Sluys] on Midsummer day, June 24th, 1340."[27] Ruskin finds the motto on the noble ambiguous.

Impression: I H C AUTEM TRANSIENS PER MEDIUM ILLORUM IBAT
Translation: He, however, passed through the middle of them
                                                                      (Plate 18)

He interprets this motto (from Luke 4) by clever references to Sir Edward Creasy's *History of England,* in which a naval victory at Sluys is chronicled.

---

23. See Chapter 2, "Literature about Coins."
24. Aristotle, *Politics,* 1256b.
25. "All this dominion *will I give to you* and the glory that goes with it" (Luke 4.6).
26. Mosher, "Coin Mottoes."
27. *The Works of John Ruskin,* ed. E. T. Cook and A. Wedderburn, 39 vols. (London, 1903–12), 30: 272–77. Ruskin is fond of showing the supposed relationship between monetary inscriptions and the political events that inspired them. See John Ruskin, "Catalogue of Coins in St. George's Museum" (*Works,* 30: 268 ff.), where he interprets inscriptions as symptoms of political and economic reality, but does not consider that the coin maker was aware of this role.

Wroth proposes a similar passage from Thomas de Burton's chronicle of the battle to explain the popular legend.

> Quod videns Edwardus rex, ordine disposto per medium ipsorum transibat, et de illis victoriam . . . adeptus est. Quapropter ipse rex Edwardus impressionem monetae suae aureae fecerat commutari. Unde in suo nobili . . . ex una ejus parte navem cum rege armato in eo contento, regio nomine circumscripto, et ex altera ejus parte crucem imprimi constituens, hanc circumscriptionem adhibuit "Jesus autem transiens per medium illorum ibat."[28]

The king passed through his enemies just as Jesus passed through his enemies. If this were the only interpretation of the legend, the inscription would not bear the relation to that on which it is impressed that makes it a true monetary inscription. The inscription, however, was supposed to have a power in its own right apart from its impression on Edward's coins. It was commonly impressed into many magic objects of the fourteenth century and especially into rings.[29] A fourteenth-century version of the ring of Gyges, for example, was impressed with the same words as the noble: "An elegant method [to become invisible] is to wear the Ring of Gyges on your finger; you can then become visible or invisible at will simply by turning the stone inward or outward. . . . Round the stone must be engraved the words, 'Jesus passant par le milieu d'eux s'en allait.' You must put the ring on your finger, and if you look at yourself in a mirror and cannot see the ring it is a sure sign that it has been successfully manufactured."[30] At the battle of Sluys, the king passed through his enemies. He was as invisible as Plato's Gyges, who had a ring that made him invisible and who was said to have been the first minter of coins.

Longer Monetary Inscriptions

Speculation such as that about nobles is not necessary to understand most monetary inscriptions, which state explicitly their relation to that on which they are impressed. Sometimes the topic is the monetary system: *"Sans changer"* (Without changing) or *"Dedit pig-*

---

28. W. Wroth, "The First Gold Noble," *Numismatic Chronicle* 2 (1882): 299.

29. The quote from Luke is known "as the inscription of a gold ring of the fourteenth century, found at Montpensier in Auvergne; . . . [as] occurring in treatises of alchemy; . . . [as] the text carved upon the wooden front of a druggist's shop . . . attached to a house of the Templars in Toledo; . . . [as being] mentioned in the well-known passage of Maundeville [*Travels*, ch. 10]" (ibid).

30. Grillot de Givry, *Witchcraft, Magic, and Alchemy*, trans. J. Courtenay Locke (London, 1931), p. 185.

nus" (He has given a pledge).[31] The subject can be the manufacture of money, as when coins explain pictorially or verbally their own minting.[32] Sometimes the theme is wealth: *"Die menschen der weldt trachtn also nack gelt"* (The men of the world aim thus for money), or *"Crescite et multiplicamini"* (Increase and multiply).[33] Often the topic may be the relationship between the coin as commodity and the coin as medium of exchange: *"Non aes sed aere"* (Not money, but the things it will buy), or *"Det klipperne yder vor bergmand vnderyder vyadhytten da gider af mynter vinyder"* (What the mountains hide the miner brings up; from that we get money for our use).[34]

Among the longer monetary inscriptions are the legends in verse (usually distich) published on Muslim coins. The topics of these inscriptions often include coin and money.

> To the Shah Jahangin belongs the whirligig (circle or passing) of time;
> In Agra by his name gold shines brightly:
> So long as the pomp (ceremony or ritual) of the Five Guards (the five daily
>   prayers) lasts in the world.
> May the stamp of his Five Muhrs (stamps) be current.[35]

The only other mark on this riddling coin is the number 5. The reader must guess what unit is being numbered.

Minting itself is an important topic in many Persian monetary inscriptions.

> I make madness till on my head a tumult (noise) falls.
> Coin I strike on metal (gold), till its master (owner) be found.[36]

This legend, beautiful and riddling, suggests the full potential of poems on coins.

Similar monetary inscriptions include the following:

> Since on my soul I struck the stamp of Ali's love,
> The world obeyed my rule by grace of God above.[37]

---

31. Mosher, "Coin Mottoes."
32. A coin of Paestum, for example, illustrates pictorially the process of coin manufacture. (Cf. MacDonald, *Coin Types,* p. 4.)
33. Mosher, "Coin Mottoes."
34. Ibid.
35. Coin of Jahangir (Hindustan) (Oliver Codrington, *A Manual of Musalman Numismatics* [London, 1904], p. 107). Cf. C. J. Rodgers, "Couplets on Coins of Jahangir," *Journal of the Asiatic Society of Bengal* (1888) and "Couplets on Coins of Kings after Jahangir," *Journal of the Asiatic Society of Bengal* (1888).
36. Coin of Muhummad Jan. Codrington, *Musalman Numismatics,* p. 106.
37. Coin of Safi II, Sulaiman (Persia). Ibid., p. 96.

Ashraf laid hold on majesty;
Let his coin's legend read "Requited by unright."[38]

Silver and gold through all the world have now become the moon and sun,
Thanks to the true Imam's imprint, the Age's Lord (the rightful one).[39]

The order proceeded from the Incomparable Creator to Ahmad the king:
"Strike coins in silver and gold from the ascension of Pisces up to the
moon."[40]

The revolution (of the heavens) brings gold and silver from the sun and
moon, that it may make on its face the impression of the coinage of Taimur
Shah.[41]

The explicit topic of these lengthy inscriptions is the coined money of
which they are part and into which they are impressed. These widely
published and circulated verses are about and on reverse and obverse.

LETTER AND LETTERED

One problem facing Muslim and other inscribers of coins is the
small number of words to which they are limited by technique, space,
and state regulations.[42] Attempts to overcome spatial limitations led

38. Coin of Ashraf (Persia). Ibid., p. 98.
39. Coin of Karim Khan, Abu Al-Fath, Sadik, Ali Murad, and Aka Muhammad
(Persia). Ibid., p. 101.
40. Coin of Ahmad Shah (Duranni). Ibid., p. 102.
41. Coin of Taimur (Persia). Ibid.
42. "Consider the limitations and difficulties that beset the [American] designer.
Artistic rendering and a super-abundance of lettering do not go hand in hand towards
the best results. Our artists at the start are handicapped by having to place on the coin
'United States of America,' 'E Pluribus Unum,' 'Liberty,' 'In God We Trust,' the date,
and the denomination" ("The New Dime," in Selections from the Numismatist, p. 155.
Cited by Vermeule, Numismatic Art in America, pp. 13–14).
With the development of printed paper monies, of course, long and elaborate inscriptions were made possible. The difference between these impressed objects (economically valuable gold and economically worthless paper) made one especially serious
concern of paper-money inscriptions the explanation and prohibition of counterfeiting.
Persian paper money contemporaneous with that described by Marco Polo in China
(see Ch. 1, n. 10) and bearing lengthy inscriptions is described by Colonel Sir Henry
Yule (The Book of Ser Marco Polo, ed. and trans. Yule [London, 1929], p. 428n). Among
the first modern paper monies is the famous issue of Georgia (1769), with an acrostic
puzzle: "At the base of the note the comical counterfeiting warning is upside down, the
words read from right to left like Hebrew, the words are in both English and Latin, and
the word order is scrambled. Reconstructed, the warning reads "TO COUNTERFEIT IS

to the employment of symbolic dots and dashes, impressions into the perimeters or edges of coins, canting badges, and calligraphy.[43] Calligraphy, which would make beautiful designs out of letters of the alphabet and the words they compose, appears particularly suited to coin-writing because coins and letters are similar to each other and lend themselves to similar kinds of interpretation. Both coins and letters may be understood as symbols and also as material things: coins, for example, as commodities interpreted apart from any "symbolic" mediation of economic exchange, and letters as designs without phonetic meaning.[44]

Theorists of calligraphy, such as Emilio Marinetti, believe that the fetishization of letters into designs is the "liberation of the letter" that the spatialist poets defended.[45] Their analogy from coin to letter is misleading because commodity and design are fundamentally different. Yet such an analogy, and the corresponding theory of letter as design (image) and also as symbol, influenced numismatic calligraphers who impress well-designed literal symbols (letters) into the symbols of the economic exchange system (coins). In numismatic calligraphy, lettering may seem to imitate on a coin, which is a commodity, the objectification or fetishization of the coin as mere symbol.

Religion also helps to explain widespread calligraphy on coins. Calligraphy enables Muslim minters, many of whom are prohibited from making pictures, to produce beautiful and lengthy inscriptions.[46] For example, in Persia, the obverse of a dinar of the seventh

---

DEATH WITHOUT BENEFIT OF CLERGY VIDE ACT" (Eric P. Newman, *The Early Paper Money of America* [Racine, Wisconsin, 1967], p. 93).

43. "The 'Tombac' nickel of 1943 had an arrangement of Morse Code dots and dashes around the perimeter, instead of the usual beading or denticles. Decoded, the dots and dashes read: WE WIN WHEN WE WORK WILLINGLY" (Bowers, *Coins and Collectors*, p. 198). Warnings to counterfeiters often were printed in the perimeter or edge of coins. One well-known coin, for example, reads: RODAT AVARA MANUS NE ME FALSIFICANS (The greedy hand cannot betray by clipping me).

44. Massin (*Letter and Image*, trans. Caroline Hill and Vivienne Menkes [New York, 1970], p. 19) writes that "the essential job of the letter is to be as unobtrusive as possible." Letters, he suggests, are hardly sensible (material). "Perceptible, but invisible, silent, and yet a mental projection of speech, a letter has only the weight of ink" (p. 19). Similarly it might be argued that a coin as money is a weightless or nonmaterial symbol. Massin also writes that "one has only to pause in the slightly illogical process of reading, dissect the construction of the sentence and untie the links of a word, to get at the letters" (ibid.). By such dissection, the letter may be fetishized as mere design. Similarly, one has only to pause in the process of economic exchange, sale, and purchase of commodities to get at the commodity aspect of money.

45. Ibid.

46. "The Muhammadan coinage, with some few exceptions, avoids, in accordance with religious tenets, the representation of living objects or indeed of any objects at all

century fitted circles of writing (adapted from the Koran) to a square. "There is no god but Allah alone. He has no partner. Muhammad is the Apostle of Allah whom He sent with guidance and the religion of truth that He may make it victorious over every other religion."[47] Square calligraphy (Plate 19), circular calligraphy (Plate 20), monogrammatization (Plate 21), and simple script (Plate 22) played the principle roles in Muslim coinage.

Calligraphy on European coins is rare. Nevertheless, such coins do appear from time to time, during the reigns of Charlemagne (Plate 23) and, as Ruskin notes, William the Conqueror.[48] In 1643, moreover, the artist Nicholas Briot minted a famous calligraphic coin (Plate 24). "The reverse of these noble coins," writes C. H. V. Sutherland, "is movement pure and simple: by a conception unique in English monetary history a banner floats, fold upon fold, across the field of the coin, proclaiming the king's adherence to the Protestant religion, the laws of England and the liberty of Parliament. It is doubtful if English designers have ever achieved anything more fluid or more original."[49] Briot's coin, however, is not entirely calligraphic, since the banner is more important to the design than the letters that fill it.

Calligraphic design and similar techniques would eliminate that conflict between design and lettering on which John Ruskin based his theory of numismatics. In *Modern Painters,* he emphasizes the importance of images for Greek minters and de-emphasizes that of letters.

---

and both sides of the coins are devoted to inscriptions" (R. A. G. Carson, *Coins of the World* [New York, 1962], p. 475). Cf. Codrington, "Ornamentation," in *Musalman Numismatics,* pp. 17 ff.; and Oleg Grabar, *The Formation of Islamic Art* (New Haven, 1973), p. 95 ff.

47. Gold dinar of Umaiyad Caliphate (696-97 A.D.), trans. Carson, *Coins of the World,* p. 478. Other purely religious inscriptions are recorded by Codrington (*Musalman Numismatics*), for example: "Allah is One, Allah is the Eternal; He begets not, neither is he begotten."

48. Ruskin, *Works,* vol. 30, plate 37.

Philip Grierson ("Note on the Stamping of Coins," in *History of Technology,* ed. Charles Singer, E. J. Holmyard, and A. R. Hall, 5 vols. [Oxford, 1954–58] 2: 490) points to technical aspects of the minting process that necessarily affected the reproduction of letters. He suggests that "in Carolingian times... both device and letters could be formed by a limited range of punches capable of producing straight lines, large and small crescents and curves, annulets, pellets, triangles, and so forth." He also remarks that "the lettering on the coins of eleventh- and twelfth-century France was often produced by the use of little more than a small selection of wedge-shaped punches, which yielded patterns that bore only the vaguest resemblance to the letters they were intended to represent."

49. Sutherland, *Art in Coinage,* p. 182.

He seeks to explain why "in the finest Greek coins the letters of the inscriptions are purposely coarse and rude, while the *relievi* are wrought with inestimable care" (7: 356). Ruskin's first observation (about the Greek sculptor's unwillingness to engage in difficult and time-consuming work) is hardly a convincing explanation of the supposed crudeness of letters on Greek coins.[50] His second explanation of the supposed crudeness of the letters is more convincing.

> 'Letters are always ugly things. . . .' Titian often wanted a certain quantity of ugliness to oppose his beauty with, as a certain quantity of black to oppose his colour. He could regulate the size and quantity of inscription as he liked; and, therefore, made it as neat—that is, as effectively ugly—as possible. But the Greek [sculptor of coins] could not regulate either size or quantity of inscription. Legible it must be, to common eyes, and contain an assigned group of words. He had more ugliness than he wanted, or could endure. There was nothing for it but to make the letters themselves rugged and picturesque; to give them, that is, a certain quality of organic variety. (7: 356)

Ruskin suggests that the Greek coin maker can make something unnatural or inorganic (letters) appear natural or organic. A mere symbol of a sound, he says, can look like an organ. In "Athena Ergane" (in *The Queen of the Air*), Ruskin explains the verbal unimportance and organic importance of the letters in the inscription of "The Hercules of Camarina" (Plate 25).

> Look, for instance, at the inscription in front of this Hercules of the name of the town—Camarina. You can't read it, even though you may know Greek, without some pains; for the sculptor knew well enough that it mattered very little whether you read it or not, for the Camarina Hercules could tell his own story; but what did above all things matter was, that no K or A or M should come in a wrong place with respect to the outline of the head, and divert the eye from it, or spoil any of its lines. So the whole inscription is thrown into a sweeping curve of gradually diminishing size, continuing from the lion's paws, round the neck, up to the forehead, and answering a decorative purpose as completely as the curls of the mane opposite. (19: 415)

Of course, letters (however crudely made) play a fundamental role in the design of many coins. In an "owl" of Athens (Plate 26), the eyes

50. "In an English coin, the letters are the best done, and the whole is unredeemably vulgar. In a picture of Titian's, an inserted inscription will be complete in the lettering, as all the rest is; because it costs Titian very little more trouble to draw rightly than wrongly, and in him, therefore, impatience with the letters would be vulgar, as in the Greek sculptor of the coin, patience would have been. For the engraving of a letter accurately is difficult work, and his time must have been unworthily thrown away" (Ruskin, *Works*, 7:356).

(which see at night, when things are invisible to other animals) are massed on the coin like two letters: *OO*. Plain letters become beautiful eyes.

In his discussion of "The Hercules of Camarina," Ruskin argues that the legibility of numismatic inscriptions is unimportant to the art of minting. Elsewhere, however, he asserts that the esthetics of a great coin (including its literary aspect) must be as pure as its metal. Metallic purity is costly "since there is a loss by wear" but "if a nation can afford to pay for the loyal noise and fancies in fire [salutes and fireworks], it may also, and much more rationally, for loyal truth and beauty in its circulating signs of wealth" (28: 430–31). In *Fors Clavigera* Ruskin offers a detailed proposal, for coins for the Companions of Saint George, that includes consideration of the inscription "*Sit Splendor*" from Psalm 90 (28: 430–31). Part of the "truth and beauty" of this inscription lies in its relation to other impressions in the coin and to Ruskin's crucial definition of the work of the Companions and their "Economy of Life" (28: 541). The seriousness with which Ruskin considers his own inscription belies his argument that inscriptions are necessarily unimportant and "irredeemably vulgar" (7: 356). "*Sit splendor*" plays no small part in his thinking, and he intended his coin to have literary and philosophical beauty. The relation that Ruskin notices, between the truth and beauty of an inscription and the purity of the material upon which it is inscribed (28: 430–31), aids in understanding both his proposed coinage and the "Economy of Life" of which it is the visible and legible symbol.

SCULPTURE AND SCULPTED

A monetary inscription can be defined by its relationship to that upon which it is inscribed and together with which it forms an integral, whole coin. This coin is a work of sculpture, whose economic value is defined by the supposed commodity value of the material sculpted and whose beauty derives in part from its formal relationship to the physical properties of the material sculpted. The form or architecture of coins is important to the specific study of monetary inscriptions only insofar as the inscription itself suggests consideration of the material problems of design, value, or meaning. The unique shape of some coins, however, does make their architecture significant. For example, incuse coins (Plates 27–29) are different in appearance from any other Greek money: "Each piece displayed in relief the state's blazon and some letters of its name, all within a

round cable border, and each piece had on its reverse side the identical picture but sunk in intaglio."[51]

It has been suggested that there was a philosophic basis for the
form of incuse coins. Manufactured by stamping obverse and reverse
with one punch (die) at one time, incuse coins are associated with
Pythagoras of Samos, the city where hollowcasting was invented. A
student of metalwork, Pythagoras was the son of Mnesarchos, the
stone engraver. During the reign of the tyrant Polycrates, Pythagoras
left his home for Croton in Sicily, where he "made incuse coinage,
introduced a philosophy, and founded Pythagorean brotherhoods,"
which minted the only incuse coins.[52] Historians argue that the
Pythagoreans represented the "new class of rich industrialists and
merchants."[53] The purpose of the incuse form cannot be deduced
from this observation alone, but rather must be inferred from
Pythagorean philosophy itself. George Thomson writes that " 'the
Pythagoreans believed that the upper and lower parts of the universe
stood in the same relation to the centre, only reversed.' Evidently,
therefore, . . . they were intended to symbolize the Pythagorean unity
of opposites."[54] This interpretation of Pythagorean coinage is difficult
to substantiate. Ideological significance, however, can properly be
attributed to different kinds of minting processes. Pythagorean
philosophers are only the first of many political thinkers to become
involved in minting. Hume, Locke, Copernicus, Newton, and
Franklin all interpret the representational system of wealth.[55]
Pythagoras, too, was a philosopher-minter interested in the relation
of form—the shape of a coin—to that which is formed—the metallic
commodity—and the relation of the money form to the philosophic
One.[56]

The architecture of incuse coins unites or doubles obverse and re-

51. Charles Seltman, *Book of Greek Coins* (London, 1952), pp. 10–11; cf. George
Thomson, *Studies in Ancient Greek Society*, 2 vols. (London, 1949–55), 2: 252.

52. Seltman, *Book of Greek Coins*, p. 11. Incuse coins were probably first minted in
Croton (plate 27) about the same as the arrival of Pythagoras. The end of the
minting of incuse coins in the middle of the fifth century corresponds to the liquidation
of the Pythagorean brotherhood.

53. Thomson, *Ancient Greek Society*, 2: 263–64.

54. Ibid., p. 252; cf. Seltman, *Greek Coins*.

55. See, for example, Franklin's famous *fugio* coins.

56. The analogy between philosophical being and the money form helps to explain
further a general relationship between coinage and the Pythagoreans' philosophy. The
Pythagoreans established special conventions or laws, such as the ordinance against
wearing signet rings. (See G. S. Kirk and J. E. Raven, *The Presocratic Philosophers*
[Cambridge, 1971], p. 227.)

verse.[57] Verbal inscriptions, like the incuse technique, can also unite (or at least consciously relate) obverse and reverse. In one early and very long Persian monetary poem, for example, "one verse of the couplet is on the obverse and the other on the reverse of the coin: the poem begins at the top of the obverse and continues at the bottom of the reverse."[58]

Some Byzantine coins (like Pythagorean coins) are architecturally designed so that one side complements the other. A Byzantine coin of the eleventh century, for example, has a convex side and a concave side, and is one of the first coins impressed with an original verse poem (Plate 30).[59] On the reverse are the words PARTHENE SOI POLUAYNE, which Jean Sabatier translates: *"En ton honneur, Vièrge très-glorieuse."* The inscription probably refers to the picture of the Virgin holding the infant Christ in her arms. On the obverse are the words: OS ELPIKE PANTA KATORTHOI, which Sabatier translates: *"Qui espère en toi réussit en tout."* These words are written around the figure of the emperor, a cross in his right hand and a goblet surmounted by a smaller cross in his left hand. George MacDonald, however, translates the two inscriptions together, reading the reverse first and the obverse second: "Whoso hath set his hopes on thee, most glorious Virgin, he succeedeth in all things."[60] The inscriptions on obverse and reverse being intelligible both together (as in the case of the Persian coin) and separately, the two sides of this coin are united architecturally and also verbally. Architectural design is thus integrated with inscription.

COINS ABOUT LITERATURE AND LITERATURE ABOUT COINS

The consideration of the relations of coins and numismatic semiology to literature includes two studies I have not yet mentioned: that of coins depicting or quoting works of literature and that of works of literature interpreting coins.

57. Oftentimes coin makers present double images not by relating obverse and reverse but rather by conflating two opposing images on a single verse. See, for example, the silver drachm of Istrus (fourth century B.C.), showing two heads, one upside down and the other right side up (*Ancient Coins*, ed. G.M.A. Hanfmann and M. S. Balmuth, The Fogg Art Museum, Harvard University [Cambridge, Mass., 1956], Plate 19).

58. Codrington, *Musalman Numismatics*, p. 95. (Cf. similar coins discussed by Codrington.)

59. On the architecture of this coin (of John II), see Jean Sabatier, "De la Monnaie byzantine," in *Description générale des monnaies byzantines*, 2 vols. (Paris, 1862), 2: 26.

60. Sabatier, "Monnaie byzantine," 2: 172, cf. 2: 28; and MacDonald, *Coin Types*, pp. 242–43.

Coins about Literature

In Addison's *Dialogue upon the Usefulness of Ancient Medals,* Philander argues that "there is a great affinity between Coins and Poetry, and that your Medallist and Critic are much nearer related than the world generally imagines."[61] The kind of relation between verse and reverse that Philander suggests is based on a mistaken belief, that "a man may see a metaphor or an allegory in picture as well as read them in a description" (p. 448), and that the arts are merely "Comments on each other" (p. 449). "When ... I confront a Medal with a Verse," says Philander, "I only shew you the same design executed by different hands, and appeal from one matter to another of the same age and taste" (p. 448). Philander counts coins as he accounts for literature: "I have by me a sort of poetical cash, which I fancy I could count over to you in Latin and Greek verse" (p. 450). This relation between coins and poems is nevertheless useful to the historian. "A reverse often clears up the passage of an old poet, as the poet often serves to unriddle a reverse" (p. 446). And indeed, many students of coins do little more than unravel reverses by referring to verses (see Plate 31 and Aeschylus, *Agamemnon,* v.110 ff.).[62] Other characters in Addison's dialogue, however, mock the "learned avarice" (p. 436) and "Medallic eloquence" (p. 438) of Philander, who charges his "Coins with more uses than they can bear." Their arguments are directed only against the accuracy of his historical *explications des textes.* They should have been aimed also against the assumed identity of the designs of medal and verse.

In the *Laokoon,* Lessing argues that the assumption of a formal identity between medal and poetry is methodologically misguided.[63] He mocks philandering numismatic zeal that will "sooner find the Prosodia in a Comb as Poetry in a Medal" (Addison, *Ancient Medals,* p. 447). Arguing that Addison and his epigone Spence do not take

61. Joseph Addison, *Dialogue upon the Usefulness of Ancient Medals,* No. 1, in *Works* (London, 1921), 1:446.

62. See *Coins and Vases of Arthur Stone Dewing, A Memorial Exhibition* (March–April 1971), The Fogg Art Museum, Harvard University, Cambridge, Mass., p. 5. The numismatist argues that "the reverse of the coin (plate 31) shows two eagles tearing a pregnant hare, a type probably referring to a passage in the *Agamemnon* of Aeschylus."

63. G. E. Lessing, *Laokoon,* trans. Ellen Frothingham (New York, 1969), appendix, n. 17. Lessing also attacks the accuracy of some of Addison's interpretations, such as that of an ancient coin (in Addison's *Travels*) that Joseph Spence (in *Polymetis* 7) believes to explain a passage of Juvenal. Though he admits that "illustrations of this kind are not to be despised though neither always necessary nor always conclusive" (p. 52), Lessing suggests that such interpretations are perforce incomplete.

into account the differences between coin-making and poem-making, he regrets the easy substitution of a passage of a literary work for a coin type, and vice versa.[64] Lessing himself tries to consider coins as integral works of sculpture. In the *Laokoon*, however, he seems to ignore the fact that coins are also literature. This ignorance is strange since, as we have seen, his theory of the epigram necessarily includes the kind of literature called the monetary inscription.

Coinmakers not only depict works of literature but also quote them. For example, *Expectate veni* (Plate 32) recalls a phrase of Virgil, whose context (in the *Aeneid*) helps to explain its suitability as a Roman monetary legend. Aeneas is telling Dido about the plunder of Troy by "gold-hungry Greeks." Just before he describes the final Greek victory, Aeneas reports the words he spoke to the vision of the dead Hector: "*Quibus Hector ab oris exspectate venis?*" (From what shores, Hector, comest thou, the long looked-for?)[65] Hector (the dead hero of the *Iliad*) responds by encouraging Aeneas (the living hero of the *Aeneid*) to prepare for the founding of Rome. Hector gives Aeneas the following advice: "All claims are paid to king and country; if Troy's towers could be saved by strength of hand, by mine, too, had they been saved. Troy commits to thee her holy things and household gods [Penates]; take them to share thy fortunes: seek for them the city—the mighty city which, when thou hast wandered over the deep, thou shalt at last establish" (*Aeneid* 2:291 ff.). Hector *exspectatus* frees Aeneas of debt to his country and transfers to him the Trojan household gods.[66] Thus he helps Aeneas to purchase the establishment of Rome with the disestablishment of Troy and to transform Troy into the mighty city that supervised the minting of this token of exchange.

---

64. Addison's *Travels* and *Dialogue* inspired Spence's *Polymetis*, in which the latter tried to show direct relations between works of several art forms, among them coins and poems. On Addison, Spence, and Lessing, see Austin Wright (*Joseph Spence* [Chicago, 1950], esp. pp. 90 ff.). On the relation between the visual and verbal arts, see Lessing, *Laokoon*, p. 50. On numismatics in English literature, see Mark Jay Levin, *Literature and Numismatics in England, 1650–1750* (Ph.D. diss., University of Pennsylvania, 1974).

65. Virgil, *Aeneid*, 2: 282–83 in *Virgil*, trans. H. Rushton Fairclough (London, 1935). Cf. MacDonald, *Coin Types*, p. 243; Eckhel, *Doctrina numerum veterum*, 8: 45; and William Stukeley, *The Medallic History of Marcus Aurelius Valerius, Emperor in Britain* (London, 1759), 1: 66–67, 2: plates 23 (no. 6) and 26 (no. 5).

66. These symbols of the transference of power are mentioned again when Aeneas confronts Helen at Vesta's shrine, when Panthus carries certain holy things and vanquished gods (Virgil, *Aen*, 2: 320, 567 ff.), and when Aeneas asks his father to carry the sacred things (*cape sacra manu patriosque Penatis*) (Virgil, *Aen*, 2: 717).

Literature about coins

Writers often aid the student of coins by interpreting monetary inscriptions within a larger political and linguistic framework. The role of the paper money inscription in *Faust*, Part 2, is perhaps the most interesting example,[67] but numismatics also derives inspiration from Jesus' interpretation of a Roman denarius. In the Gospels (which articulate the redemption of the human economy of credit and debt through the divine economy of belief and grace), Jesus' interpretation of Caesar's coin helps to define the Christian relationship of man to God. The telling of the story illustrates Jesus' prudent economy of truth (withholding the bare truth)[68] as well as his political economy.

> 'Tell us, then, what you think. Is it lawful to pay taxes to Caesar, or not?' But Jesus, aware of their malice, said, 'Why put me to the test, you hypocrites? Show me the money for the tax.' And they brought him a coin. And Jesus said to them, 'Whose likeness and inscription is this?' They said, 'Caesar's.' Then he said to them, 'Render therefore to Caesar the things that are Caesar's, and to God the things that are God's.' (Matt. 22:17–21. Cf. Luke 20:21–25 and Mark 12:14–17.)

Jesus escapes his enemies' attack by offending neither the nationalist parties (with an overt approval of paying taxes) nor the seat of the empire (with an overt disapproval of paying taxes). He is a prudent steward or economist of the truth.

It is significant that Jesus asks for a coin. Ordinary commodities could have served equally well as examples of that with which taxes might be paid. The special kind of commodity that is a coin, however, offers Jesus a manifold interpretation. The likenesses and inscriptions on Roman coins often displayed religious signs. Many denarii, probably including the one that the Pharisees and Herodians bring to Jesus, bore inscriptions claiming that Caesar was divine (just as some of Jesus' followers believed that Jesus was the Son of God).[69] If Caesar is a God, what are "the things that are Caesar's"? If Caesar is

---

67. Johann Wolfgang von Goethe, *Faust* 2 (Hamburg, 1964): 6057–62. In context, the fictional inscription in Part 2 suggests that verbal and economic media are semiologically identical and that an explicit explanation of (paper-) money is also an implicit explanation of language.

68. On the "economy" of truth, see Chapter 3, below.

69. James Ross Snowden (*The Coins of the Bible and Its Money Terms* [Philadelphia, 1864]) suggests that the New Testament refers to a silver denarius of Tiberius Caesar (14–37 A.D.). On the obverse of this coin was a portrait of Caesar, with the inscription TI. CAESAR.DIVI.AUG.F.AUGUSTUS (Tiberius Caesar Augustus, son of the divine Augustus). On the reverse was inscribed PONTIF.MAXIM. (chief priest).

the human or secular head of state, what then are his things—the thing from which the denarius was made (probably a silver ingot) or only the likeness and inscription impressed on it? The likeness and inscription on the coin are "of Caesar;" they are among his things. Like any commodity in the political economy, however, the ingot that these impressions transform into a coin belongs to its current owner. Or, like anything in the natural world (including, perhaps, Caesar himself), the coin belongs to God. Thus Jesus defines taxation in terms of the relationship between the inscription and the material on which it is stamped; he raises implicitly a question about the divine and political authority of money.[70] (Curiously, the impression of divine images on coins may have precipitated the destruction of the divine aura and cult worship of the gods. As we shall see, coins may have secularized the gods in much the same way that cinematography may have destroyed the aura of "original things.")

Herman Melville's interpretation of economic symbols suggests a similar theory of numismatic semiology. In *Moby Dick, Pierre,* and *The Confidence Man,* Melville implies that there is a necessary relation between an inscription and that upon which it is written, and also that money (of which the coin is a symbol) and language (of which the letters of the inscription are symbols) are similar media of social exchange. The pattern of "The Doubloon" in *Moby Dick,* for example, is the pattern of the book.[71] Interpretations of the doubloon nailed to the mast of the ship begin by zeroing in on an object at once esthetic and economic. "On its round border it bore the letters, REPUBLICA DEL ECUADOR: QUITO. So this bright coin came from a country planted in the middle of the world, and beneath the great equator, and named after it; and it had been cast midway up the Andes, and in the unwaning clime that knows no autumn."[72] The doubloon is a coin shown to be not merely an economic token with exchange value but also an esthetic symbol to be infinitely interpreted.

During the course of "The Doubloon" (the ninety-ninth chapter of *Moby Dick*), many members of the crew reveal themselves through their thoughts about it, none more significantly than Ahab.

---

70. The tension between earthly and divine economies is often posed with reference to Jesus' interpretation of the coin. See Thomas Aquinas, *Tractatus de regimine principum,* in *Opera omnia,* ed. St. E. Fretté and P. Maré, 34 vols. (Paris, 1871–80), 27: 367 ff. Aquinas ends his interpretation with the words *"quasi ipsum nummisma sit causa ut in pluribus tributa solvendi."*

71. Charles Feidelson, *Symbolism in American Literature* (Chicago, 1953), p. 32.

72. Herman Melville, *Moby Dick,* eds. Luther S. Mansfield and Howard P. Vincent (New York, 1962), p. 428. Cf. ch. 90, "Heads or Tails."

> One morning, turning to pass the doubloon, [Ahab] seemed to be newly attracted by the strange figures and inscriptions stamped on [the doubloon], as though now for the first time beginning to interpret for himself in some monomaniac way whatever significance might lurk in them. And some certain significance lurks in all things, else all things are little worth, and the round world itself but an empty cipher, except to sell by the cartload, as they do hills about Boston, to fill up some morass in the Milky Way.[73]

What is true of interpreting the doubloon is true of interpreting *Moby Dick* itself. Ishmael must explain his book "else all these chapters might be naught."[74] The book as naught and the round world as empty cipher: these are one and the same possibility entertained as the literary hypothesis of Symbolism. Melville's theory of symbolism and his diatribe against the superficiality of economic exchange and representation in the markets of Nantucket is a warning to those who would interpret any coin outside the whole system of linguistic, economic, and pictorial exchanges in which it operates. "The Doubloon" (probably modeled, ironically, on Addison's *Dialogue upon the Usefulness of Ancient Medals*) illustrates a relationship that Melville saw between the verbal and economic worlds.[75]

Emerson, who also considered himself knowledgeable about verbal and economic symbolization, wrote that "nature itself is a vast trope, and all particular natures are tropes."[76] All language, in this sense, is figurative. The American Symbolists loved this configuration but did not always see in it precisely the same economic exchange system that they themselves pretended to abhor. For them God is the "algebraic x," like the money form itself.[77] For Melville, the doubloon (or indeed any such symbol) is hardly such a "polysensum" or "plenum" of meaning; its ontological status remains undefined and uncreditable: we never know whether it is an empty or a full cipher.[78]

Melville opposes the coin's role as exchange value to its role as "navel" nailed onto the mast in the center of the ship. Is this opposi-

73. Ibid, p. 427.
74. Feidelson, *Symbolism*, p. 31.
75. "Explanatory Notes," in Melville, *Moby Dick*, p. 804, deals with the similarity to Addison's work. On the doubloon in *Moby Dick*, see William Ellery Sedgewick, *The Tragedy of Mind* (Cambridge, Mass., 1944), pp. 111 ff.; Russel and Clare Goldfarb, "The Doubloon in *Moby Dick*," *Midwest Quarterly* 2 (Spring, 1961): 251 ff.; and John D. Seelye, "The Golden Navel: The Cabalism of Ahab's Doubloon," *Nineteenth Century Fiction* 14 (March 1960): 350ff. On economic symbolism in Melville's writings, see Feidelson, *Symbolism*, and W. W. Holdheim, *Theory and Practice of the Novel* (Geneva, 1968).
76. Feidelson, *Symbolism*, p. 145.
77. Ibid., p. 159.
78. Ibid., p. 179.

tion real, or is one kind of exchange (economic), like the other (esthetic), endlessly tropic and infinitely hermeneutic? Melville's numismatic semiology is a biting theory of language and economics in which the ontological status of the world itself is threatened with annihilation.

ESTHETICS AND ECONOMICS

The tension between a coin as an esthetic object and as an economic object often gives rise to ideological confusion. Aristotle, for example, detects a difference between a coin as an inscription or sculpture and as a monetary token. On the one hand he suggests that minting and ring-sealing produce imitative or natural copies of the original die (*On Memory and Recollection*, 450–51). Similarly, mental impressions (*pathēmata*) or affections are likenesses (*homoiōmata*) of the soul and not mere symbols like spoken or written words (*On Interpretation* 16a). Works of art are also likenesses (*homoiōmata*) or reproductions of originals and not symbolic representations of them.[79] On the other hand, Aristotle suggests that the copied impression (*charaktēr*) on a coin is a conventional symbol (*sēmeion*) of weight or issuing authority (*Politics* 1257a). Such symbols, like spoken and written words and unlike affections and works of art, bear no natural relationship to the things signified. Thus, coins are both natural (as stamped art) and unnatural (as monetary tokens).[80] This tension between the superstructural (or esthetic) and the substructural (or economic) roles of the mint implies a corresponding tension between nature and convention (*nomos*), a tension that the mechanical reproduction of coin (*nomisma*) helped to emphasize in ancient Greek thought.

In "Art in the Age of Mechanical Reproduction," Walter Benjamin tries to relate superstructure (artistic reproduction) to substructure (economic production) by relating photography or cinematography to statistics.[81] In the modern age, he argues, photography (an art) and statistics (an economic science) both seem to equalize things. Benjamin allies this sense of the universal equality of things only with the modern age. However, at no time was this sense greater than when

79. S. H. Butcher, ed., *Aristotle's Theory of Poetry and Fine Arts* (New York, 1951), p. 124. Like Plato, Aristotle often employs words such as *typos* (cf. English "type") to signify the perception (*aisthēsis*) by which memory is impressed.

80. In the *Politics* (1258b) Aristotle argues that monetary interest (*tokos*), which is a homogeneous likeness of its principal, is unnatural. Cf. Chapter 3, below.

81. Walter Benjamin, "Art in the Age of Mechanical Reproduction," trans. Harry Zohn, ed. and intro. Hannah Arendt, in *Illuminations* (New York, 1968), pp. 219–20.

coins (or mechanically reproduced works of art) or money itself (of which coins are the tokens) were being developed. Money is the universal equivalent *par excellence*. Benjamin mentions coinage only once in his essay,[82] although it serves better than photography as a case study of the relation between or confusion of reproduction and production. The esthetics of coinage, after all, does not demand metaphorical reference to an apparently unrelated economic science like statistics. Coins are themselves both artful reproductions and active participants in the sum total of the relations of production. They are things ontologically equal to each other as products of the same die, and money, which they symbolize, equalizes *in potentia* all (other) things.

In his essay, Benjamin challenges the Aristotelian theory of imitation by arguing that photography annihilated the ontological status of the original and its imitation.[83] "The technique of reproduction detaches the reproduced object from the domain of tradition. By making many reproductions it substitutes a plurality of copies for a unique existence. And in permitting the reproduction to meet the beholder in his particular situation, it reactivates the object reproduced. These two processes lead to a tremendous shattering of tradition" (p. 223). Even more than photography in the modern world did the mint in the ancient world shatter tradition. Coins destroyed the aura of individual objects and encouraged a sense of the universal equality of things. The mechanical reproduction of the mint, Benjamin might argue, liberated men from dependence on divine cults and on the cult value of art. Stamping out impressions of the gods and other "originals," coinage had less cult value and more exhibition value than previous forms of art. With the advent of the mechanical reproduction of coins (often bearing, ironically, impressions of the gods), "the criterion of authenticity [of the original] ceased to be applicable to artistic production, [and] the total function of art [was] reversed. Instead of being based on ritual, [art began] to be based on another practice—politics" (p. 226). Benjamin generally asserts that mechanical reproduction must be a catalyst for democracy, since its products

82. Benjamin suggests that the Greeks knew only two methods of mechanical reproduction: casting and stamping ("Mechanical Reproduction," p. 220). Most coins are made by stamping; a few large coins of the Roman period and some counterfeits of the modern period were cast. Since both casting and stamping were techniques older than the first coins, coinage was not a true invention, but rather the culmination of certain forms of knowledge of counting and sculpting.

83. "From a photographic negative . . . one can make any number of prints; to ask for the 'authentic' print makes no sense" (Benjamin, "Mechanical Reproduction," p. 226).

require some sort of universal testing when they cease to be the center of a cult. Coins, of course, must and can be weighed by everyone.[84] Coinage, a new kind of sculpture, shattered the Greek view of statues as objects of cult veneration confronting the beholder with their uniqueness and aura. It heralded the modern age of mechanical reproduction.

In our time, weighing and criticizing coins no longer seem necessary or pleasurable, despite large fluctuations in the gold markets. The artlessness of modern coins (the result in part of modern modes of mechanical reproduction) has worked to dim our appreciation of older coins.[85] Photography and photographic enlargement (another modern mode of mechanical reproduction) have helped renew the study of coins, however, and have made it easier and perhaps more interesting for us who live in the modern age of mechanical reproduction.[86] The study of coins as examples of visual and literary art in an

84. A money weigher, of course, must give his testing full attention. The test of a coin is its weight as well as its beauty. Ibid., pp. 226, 242–43.

85. Ancient coins often lack the technical finesse sometimes associated with "high art." Hegel notes that "in the art of stamping coins the ancients created veritable masterworks of beauty, although from the purely technical point of view they obtained results inferior to those which we obtain nowadays" (G. W. F. Hegel, *The Philosophy of Fine Art*, trans. F. P. B. Osmaston, 4 vols. [London, 1920], 3: 198). The mindless, apothegmatic advertising slogans on today's coins may correspond to the new mode of numismatic reproduction. The modern artist allows a reducing machine (which the ancients did not have) "to transform his large clay model into miniature size" (Sutherland, *Art in Coinage*, p. 200). Some die-casters use a reducing glass in making their models, but the design suffers. "A reduction is about as true to model," writes Sir George Hill, "as a cheap colour-process illustration is to the original picture" (Sutherland, *Art in Coinage*). Modern coins, moreover, lack the contours in portraiture for which ancient coins are famous. "The contours are fogged, however infinitesimally: the impression is slightly soft: the definition—by contrast with coins struck from directly made dies—is quite certainly impaired. Thus the peculiar distinction of the coin-design, namely, its fineness of clear line—a distinction for which the master-artists of all ages were famous, is lost" (Sutherland, *Art in Coinage*, p. 203). Parts of the original model are made invisible by reduction, so that the modern artist is doubly separated from the "original." Mechanical reproduction had separated the artist from his original in ancient Greece. Nowadays the artist no longer makes even a die directly.

86. The artful photographic enlargement of coins has been a tool of the numismatist since Ruskin (who notes its influence in *Works*, 19: 410). A photograph of a coin is the mechanical reproduction of a mechanical reproduction, changing the popular appearance of the coin and destroying its "aura." Malraux believes, however, that photography "qui réproduit un original" (*La Monnaie*, p. 192), merely rescued coinage from being forgotten by the art historian. He did not consider how photography may have transformed numismatics and how photography, like minting, seems to reproduce an original.

age of mechanical reproduction suggests the consideration both of economic production and representation and of esthetic reproduction or imitation. Coins should be studied as *sēmata* at once artful and economic. In this sense, numismatics not only counts coins but also accounts for the significance of and the relationship between economic and esthetic signs.

THE GOLDEN FLEECE AND THE VOICE OF THE SHUTTLE

Economy in Literary Theory

"Economy" has been an important term in literary theory since Aristotle, but it is usually ignored by literary critics and omitted from the dictionaries and histories of poetics. "Economy" refers etymologically to the conventions (*nomoi*) of and distribution (*nemesis*) within the household (*oikos*).[1] Domestic economy concerns production and distribution in the household, and relations between master and slave, husband and wife, and father and son. Political economy concerns production and distribution in the polis, and relations between political groups, such as tyrants and subjects, and citizens and slaves.

An earlier form of this chapter appeared in *The Georgia Review*, Summer 1976.

1. The complex relationships among *nomos, nemesis,* and *oikonomia* (by which political theorists elucidate arguments about the law) are considered by E. LaRoche (*Histoire de la racine nem- en grec ancien* [Paris, 1949], pp. 144 ff.), M. I. Finley (*The Ancient Economy* [Berkeley and Los Angeles, 1973], pp. 17–34), D. R. Bender ("A Refinement of the Concept of Household," *American Anthropologist* 69 [1967]: 493–504), O. Brunner ("Das 'ganze' Haus und die alteuropäische Ökonomik," *Neue Wege der Sozialgeschichte* [Göttingen, 1956], pp. 33–61), and K. Singer ("Oikonomia: An Inquiry into Beginnings of Economic Thought and Language," *Kyklos* 11 [1958]: 29–54).

Nemesis refers to *"distribution of what is due,* but in usage always *retribution"* (H. G. Liddell and Robert Scott, *A Greek-English Lexicon* [Oxford, 1940; reprint ed., 1966], s.v. *"nemesis."* On retributive justice (cf. *dikē*), see Chapter 1, "Heraclitus and the Money Form." On *oikos* (house) and *oikia* (household)—Aristotle and Xenophon suggest the distinction between them can be transcended—see Aristotle (*Politics* 1278b) and Leo Strauss (*Xenophon's Socratic Discourse: An Interpretation of the Oeconomicus* [Cornell, 1970], esp. pp. 92 ff.).

Literary economy concerns similar problems of production, distribution, and relations.

The use of the word "economy" in literary theory seems to have begun with Aristotle's *Poetics*.

> A tragedy, then, to be perfect according to the rules of art, should be of this construction [i.e., ending in misfortune, etc.]. Hence they are in error who censure Euripides just because he follows this principle in his plays, many of which end unhappily. It is, as we have said, the right ending. The best proof is that on the stage and in dramatic competitions, such plays, if well worked out, are the most tragic in effect; and Euripides, faulty though he may be in economy [*oikonomia*], is felt to be the most tragic of the poets.[2]

Some scholars argue that *oikonomia* is a synonym of *taxis* (order) and should be translated as "construction," "general management," or "disposition."[3] Aristotle himself, however, criticizes the use of unnecessary synonyms in prose and dislikes Alcidamus's sloppy metaphoric misuse of the word *oikonomia* in reference to rhetoric.[4] In the *Poetics*, Aristotle carefully employs the possibly pre-Aristotelian technical term *oikonomia* in a way that comprehends esthetic and political philosophy.[5] He distinguishes between households (*oikoi*) suitable for depiction in comedy and those suitable for depiction in

---

2. Aristotle, *Poetics*, 1453a22 ff. Quotations from the *Poetics* are from *Aristotle's Theory of Poetry and Fine Art*, ed. S. H. Butcher (New York, 1951). Quotations from other works of Aristotle are from *Aristotle*, 23 vols., The Loeb Classical Library (Cambridge, Mass., and London, 1926–70).

3. On "order," see A. Gudeman, *Aristotles Poetik* (Berlin and Leipzig, 1934), pp. 248–49. Cf. *katorthōthōsin* (*Poetics* 1453a28). For advocates of "construction" and "general management," see Gerald F. Else, *Aristotle's Poetics: The Argument* (Cambridge, Mass., 1957), p. 404–5; and Butcher, *Aristotle's Theory*, p. 47, respectively.

4. Aristotle, *Rhetoric* 1405a. Aristotle writes that "those who employ poetic language [in prose] by their lack of taste make their style ridiculous and frigid, and such idle chatter produces obscurity; for when words are piled upon one who already knows, it destroys perspicuity. For example, Alcidamus has spoken of 'the dispenser (*oikonomos*) of the pleasures of the hearers'" (*Rhetoric* 1406a). Aristotle does not object to a similar use of *oikonomia* in poetry, but he does argue that it is "too epithetic for prose" and that it is "metaphorical, hence ridiculous and obscure." Perhaps Aristotle also has a political reason for attacking Alcidamus's use of *oikonomia*. Alcidamus is a champion of nature (*physis*) against convention (*nomos*); he asserts that "god has set all men free, that nature has made no man a slave," and that *nomoi* alone make men slaves (W. K. C. Guthrie, *A History of Greek Philosophy*, 4 vols. [Cambridge, 1969], 3: 313). The aristocratic Aristotle, taking another viewpoint, asserts that there is such a thing as a slavish nature. He attacks not only the rhetoric but also the politics of Alcidamus's metaphor that "philosophy is a bulwark against the laws (*nomoi*)" (*Rhetoric* 1406b) and his phrase "the laws (*nomoi*), the ruler of states" (*Rhetoric* 1406a).

5. Cf. Else, *Aristotle's Poetics*, pp. 404 ff.

tragedy, such as Oedipus's household. When Aristotle suggests that Euripides has faulty economy, he means, in part, that Euripides' tragedies do not always depict families suitable to the genre.

The family depicted in tragedy must also be suited to the supposed family of the audience, from which the tragic hero elicits pity. In the *Rhetoric* (1386a) and the *Ethics* (1155a), Aristotle argues that men experience not pity but fear when they see members of their own household in great danger. In seeing their own families threatened, men are able to fear only for themselves, only for those who are homogeneous with them in danger; and in this case fear drives out pity. Great fear, like indignation (*nemesis*), is to be avoided by the tragedian (*Rhetoric* 1387a). He must manage a household on stage in such a way as to ensure that it is somewhat familiar to that of his audience (hence eliciting fear) but not too familiar (since that would make pity impossible). The poet-economist, then, must be a master of familiarities and unfamiliarities, of similarities and differences. He must be a master of metaphorization between human families and between families of words: "Metaphors should be drawn from objects which are proper to the object, but not too apparently familiar (*apo oikeiōn kai mē phanerōn*); just as, for instance, in philosophy it needs sagacity to see the similarity (*to homoion*) in things that are apart" (*Rhetoric* 1412a). Metaphors should be drawn from objects that are generally homogeneous with each other, that is, of similar families (*genē*) or households (*oikoi*), but not too obviously homogeneous. Only in this way can metaphorization reverse (our perceptions of) familial relations between households and between households of words.

The esthetic theory of *mimēsis* and of the *homoion* is informed by theories of economic and biological production (*poiēsis*). In the *Politics*, for example, Aristotle makes a crucial distinction between nature and convention, or between good and bad production, on which his esthetics depend. He distinguishes between a supposedly natural economics (whose end is just distribution or *dikē*) and a supposedly unnatural chrematistics (whose end is profit or *kerdos*).[6] This distinction informs Aristotle's political and esthetic writings. The tyrant, for example, is defined as a chrematistical profit-making ruler interested only in selfish ends. On the other hand, the statesman is defined as

6. Aristotle did not have a separate science of "economics" (as Alfred Marshall called it in 1890, in *Principles of Economics*), nor was he an *économiste*. However, the power of money is one subject of his *Economics*, which chronicles the rise to and fall from power of many wealthy men. Aristotle recommends studies of such men; one example is the interpretative tale about Thales (*Politics* 1259a). (The author of the Aristotelian *Economics II* suggests that such stories can be adapted to tragedy [1346a].)

an economist who dispenses or disposes but does not make a profit. Aristotle defines both domestic and political economy by focusing on these two kinds of production:

> And we can also see the answer to the question whether the art of wealth-getting (chrēmatistikē) belongs to the householder (oikonomikou) and the statesman, or whether on the contrary supplies ought to be provided already, since just as statesmanship does not create (poiei) human beings but having received them from nature makes use of them, so also it is the business of nature to bestow food by bestowing land or sea or something else, while the task of the householder is, starting with these supplies given, to dispose of them in the proper way. For it does not belong to the art of weaving to make fleeces, but to use them, and also to know what sort of fleece is good and suitable or bad and unsuitable. (Politics 1258a)

The poet (poiētēs) is a maker. Aristotelian poetics considers whether a poem is the product of an economical treatment of objects provided by nature or of a chrematistical attempt to make or provide such objects themselves. It would determine whether a poem is "the voice of the shuttle"[7] or the golden fleece. Aristotle suggests that the chrematist desires to earn an unnaturally infinite profit: "Wealth-getting (chrematistikē) has no limit in respect of its end, and its end is riches and the acquisition of goods in the commercial sense. But the household branch (oikonomikē) of wealth-getting has a limit, inasmuch as the acquisition of money [as opposed to goods] is not the function of household management" (Politics 1257b). Chrematistics, unlike economics, supports the unnatural illusion that "wealth consists of a quantity of money" (Politics 1257b) that can purchase and so seems to be homogeneous with anything in the market. To men such as Midas gold becomes everything, just as to some poets metaphor appears to be all.

In Aristotelian literary theory there is a purposeful ambiguity whether poetry is an economic or a chrematistical production. Indeed, Aristotle argues that a work of art is a homogeneous likeness (homoion) of an original, natural thing as it appears to the senses and not a symbolic representation of it.[8] Symbolic representations such as words do not represent naturally (physei); words are merely conventional symbols (symbola) of mental impressions (pathēmata) and are heterogeneous with those impressions (On Interpretation 16a). The mental impressions themselves, however, are homogeneous likenesses (homoiōmata) of natural objects, "which are the same for the whole of

7. Fragment from the Tereus of Sophocles, recorded by Aristotle (Poetics 1454b36).
8. Cf. Butcher, Aristotle's Theory, p. 124.

mankind," so that these impressions stand in the same relation to natural objects as works of art stand in relation to originals. The metaphor that informs this theory of heterogeneous symbolization and homogeneous imitation is derived in part from the image of the mechanical impression of wax by a seal-ring or of a globule of metal by a stamp. In Aristotle's thought, sealing and minting, or the transformation of a natural object (for example, a metal as commodity) into a supposedly unnatural medium (for example, the same metal as money), is often a metaphor for the impression of the mind by a memory (*On Memory and Recollection* 450–51).[9] On the one hand, an impression on a coin is like art: it is the homogeneous imitation or *pathēma* of the stamp, as art is homogeneous with the thing it signifies. On the other hand, an impression on a coin is like a word: it is the symbolical and heterogeneous *sēmeion* of the natural weight of the coin where it is impressed (*Politics* 1257a), as a word is a heterogeneous symbol of the thing it signifies. These conflicting aspects of numismatic impressions suggest how the development of minting may have confused an earlier understanding of the relation between sign (for example, verbal art and word) and thing signified, and between natural things (*pathēmata*) and conventional things (for example, *symbola*); they also suggest how money itself (of which coins are the tokens) helped to confuse the relation between the (economic and chrematistic) problem of the just price and the (philosophic and rhetorical) problem of the *mot juste*.[10] Minting and money made possible a revolution in art and esthetic theory of which Aristotle is an articulate spokesman and critic.

Money interest, the theory of which is a key to Aristotelian economics, helped to precipitate from archaic Greek thought a new theory of imitation or of like things (*homoiōmata*). In the Greek language after the development of money, words such as *tokos* came to refer not only to the biological generation of likenesses but also to monetary generation or interest.[11] Aristotle objects to this easy metaphor from natural,

9. On this and similar metaphors, see J. Hangard, *Monetaire en daarmee verwante metaforen* (Groningen, 1963).

10. A similar confusion informs Ezra Pound's economics. See Richard G. Landini, *A Guide to the Economic Thought in Ezra Pound's Cantos* (Ph.D. diss., University of Florida, 1959); and Wayne McIntyre, *Aesthetics and Economics in Ezra Pound* (M.A. thesis, University of Toronto, 1968), esp. pp. 67 ff.

11. Monetary interest and offspring are both signified by *tokos* (offspring of animals), *sitos* (offspring of plants), and *ekgonos* (offspring). Cf. Latin *faenus*, from *fecundus*. Many peoples accepted the analogy between animate and inanimate generation (see F. M. Heichelheim, *An Ancient Economic History* [Leyden, 1964], 1: 104–13, 212–22). On the history of the idea of usury, see Benjamin Nelson, *The Idea of Usury: From Tribal Brotherhood to Universal Otherhood* (Chicago, 1969).

animate to nomic, inanimate things and writes that it is "natural [*kata physin*] to all . . . to draw provision [economically] from the fruits of the soil and from animals" but that usury or monetary generation draws not from nature (*physis*) but from money (*nomisma*):

> Usury is most reasonably hated, because its gain comes from money itself and not from that for the sake of which money was invented. For money was brought into existence for the purpose of exchange, but interest increases the amount of the money itself (and this is the actual origin of the Greek word *tokos:* offspring resembles parent [*homoia ta tiktomena*] and interest is money born of money); consequently this form of the business of getting wealth is of all forms the most contrary to nature. (*Politics* 1258b)

In this consideration of production and reproduction, Aristotle argues that interest does not stand in the same relation to a monetary deposit as a child (for example, a lamb) stands in relation to a parent (for example, a ram or ewe). Natural generation is economic, and monetary generation is chrematistic. In the *Politics*, Aristotle distinguishes between natural economics and unnatural chrematistics not only in terms of their ends (*dikē* and *kerdos*) but also in terms of their circuits of exchange. As Marx suggests, "Aristotle sets forth two circuits of circulation, C[ommodity]$_1$–M[oney]–C$_2$, which he calls 'economics,' and M$_1$–C–M$_2$, which he calls 'chrematistics.'" [12] In economics, the "offspring" of trade is qualitatively different from its "parent": C$_1$ and C$_2$ are heterogeneous. In chrematistics, the "offspring" of trade is qualitatively identical to its "parent" even if it is quantitatively unequal to it: M$_1$ and M$_2$ are homogeneous. The chrematistic "offspring" resembles its "parent" as interest may be said to resemble principal. As Aristotle argues in the *Generation of Animals,* it is the nature of some animals and some plants to produce their likenesses (*homoiōmata*),[13] but it is not the nature of metallic money to do so.

Aristotle's distinction between natural and unnatural production informs his theory of the poetic production of likenesses of human beings. The nature of human beings, however, is identical neither to that of animals or plants (which do not live in a polis) nor to that of metal (which a polis may transform into money). What kind of generation is natural to human beings? This is one of the questions which

---

12. Karl Marx, *A Contribution to the Critique of Political Economy,* ed. Maurice Dobb, trans. S. W. Ryazanskaya (New York, 1970), p. 137n.

13. Exceptionally, in the *Generation of Animals* (71a ff.), Aristotle argues that reproduction resulting in nonidentical offspring is typical of "creatures which come into being not as the result of copulation of living animals, but of putrescent soil and out of residues."

informs Aristotle's favorite play, *Oedipus Tyrannus*, the economy of which may help to explain his theory of *poiēsis*.

In the works of many writers of classical Greece, *tokos* has a double significance as "offspring" and as "interest." For example, in the *Republic* Socrates is a midwife to philosophy; he is a dispenser of the offspring (*tokos*) of the truth that has been deposited with him and that he pays out to his interlocutors as interest (*tokos kai ekgonos*) homogeneous with its principal.[14] In the same dialogue, Gyges the tyrant is depicted as being as keen in the pursuit of monetary profit as Socrates in the pursuit of truth. Both philosopher and tyrant, Oedipus of Thebes also dominated the Greek imagination, and Sophocles tells his tale as if Oedipus were himself an unnatural *tokos*.[15] In *Seven against Thebes* and *Antigone*, in which members of Oedipus's family are presented, the word *tokos* and the explicit image of money play important roles.[16] The economy of *Oedipus Tyrannus*, however, directly confronts the problem of unnatural production. Generation, at once biological and monetary, is the informing principle. Norman O. Brown suggests that "the institution of interest presupposes not only cumulative time but also the displacement of the parental complex from the totemic group to the totemic possession money," so that "money in the civilized community comes to have a

14. *Republic* 507a, cf. 551e. Sophocles' Arcesilaus rebukes a usurer, saying that he is like a bird that heeds the wind only when its offspring (*tokos*) is near (frag. 477). Aristophanes suggests that a banker is a hatcher of owls, the coin-type of Athens (*Birds* 1106 ff.). A similar pun informs much of *Thesmophoriazusae* (esp. 830 ff.) and *Clouds* (esp. 240 ff. on Socrates, and 1970–71 on Thales).

15. Oedipus, like Gyges, comes to power by killing a king and marrying the queen. In *Oedipus Tyrannus*, however, the king is his father and the queen is his mother. The violation of *nomoi* is even greater in Sophocles' drama than in Herodotus's *Histories*. *Oedipus Tyrannus* portrays Oedipus's detection of his political and domestic being, just as Plato's *Republic* delineates the detection of the injustice of the hypothetical Gyges. In *Oedipus Tyrannus* Oedipus ends by blinding himself, but his crime, like the injustice of Gyges in the *Republic*, remains visible to all. Cf. Bernard M. W. Knox, *Oedipus at Thebes* (New Haven, 1957), esp. pp. 160, 213.

16. In Aeschylus's play, the chorus calls Eteocles *oidipou tokos* (*Seven* 372) and Eteocles speaks of himself as *tokos* (*Seven* 407). On monetary imagery in Sophocles (esp. *Antigone*), see A. A. Lang (*Language and Thought in Sophocles* [London, 1968], esp. pp. 50–51, 151), Robert Goheen (*The Imagery of Sophocles' "Antigone:" A Study of Poetic Language and Structure* [Princeton, 1951], Herbert A. Musurillo (*The Light and the Darkness: Studies in the Dramatic Poetry of Sophocles* [Leiden, 1967]), Jan C. Kamerbeek (*The Plays of Sophocles: Commentaries* [Leiden, 1967], pt. 4, esp. p. 26), and Seth Benardete ("A Reading of Sophocles' *Antigone*," *Interpretation*, vols. 3/4 [Spring 1975], 5/1 [Summer 1975], 5/2 [Winter 1975]).

psychic value it never had in the archaic community."[17] In *Oedipus Tyrannus* a kind of sexual generation as unnatural as usury acts to transform Thebes into a tyranny.[18]

Oedipus Tyrannus presents a human offspring (*tokos*) who unwittingly violates the laws (*nomoi*) of household (*oikos*) and state (*polis*). As the result of this violation he comes to rule the household as its father and the state as its tyrant. The play opens with a fatherly Oedipus addressing the people of Thebes with the word *tekna* ("children").[19] He believes that he is heterogeneous with the people, but he addresses them metaphorically as if he were homogeneous, as if he were their father. At the end of the play Oedipus addresses not the people of Thebes but rather his own children-siblings with the same words, as if he were only their father.[20]

The people of Thebes need Oedipus's help because their city is plagued with famine and childbirths without issue (*tokoisi agonois* 26–27). Like children, they suppose that Oedipus correctly answered the riddle of the sphinx by recognizing the familiar (man) in the unfamiliar (riddle) and so saved Thebes from the horrible ransom (36) it had to pay. His answer is believed to be the touchstone (*basanos* 493, 510) by which Oedipus was tried and found to be no counterfeit. The plot of the touchstone that is *Oedipus Tyrannus*, however, will reveal that he who is supposed to have recognized the being of man in the riddle and to have paid the ransom is an unnatural counterfeit, and that the great detective is also the great criminal who does not know his own

17. N. O. Brown, *Life Against Death* (New York, 1959), p. 279.

18. George Thomson (*Marxism and Poetry* [New York, 1946], p. 47; *Aeschylus and Athens: A Study in the Social Origins of Drama* [London, 1946], p. 282; and *Studies in Ancient Greek Society*, 2 vols. [London, 1949–55], 2: 194) and Roland Barthes (*On Racine* [New York, 1964], p. 41) assert that *peripeteia*, the "transformation of the action [in drama] into its opposite" in tragedies such as *Oedipus Tyrannus* (*Poetics* 1452a), is like the historical transformation of the Greek aristocracy after the invention of money. Blind wealth, which can "raise the worst among the highest" (Euripides, frag. 91) and vice versa, is a *topos* that informs even the Aristotelian *Economics*. Many revolutions in wealth, however, have not produced great tragedy; and as both Aristotle and Marx (*Economic and Philosophic Manuscripts* [New York, 1964], pp. 165 ff.) argue, money is merely a medium of exchange and is not itself productive or transformative. Louis Gernet's suggestion that Greek cultural history must be understood in the context of money as a "homogeneous material" (*Anthropologie de la Grèce antique* [Paris, 1968], p. 410) better defines the numismatics of Greek tragedy.

19. Sophocles, *Oedipus Tyrannus*, line 1. Translations are usually from *Oedipus the King*, trans. Thomas Gould (Englewood Cliffs, 1970), unless indicated as my own. Greek quotations are usually from Sophocles, *Ajax—Oedipe Roi—Electre*, ed. Alphonse Dain and trans. Paul Mazon (Paris, 1968).

20. Cf. Seth Benardete, "Sophocles' *Oedipus Tyrannus*," in *Sophocles*, ed. Thomas Woodward (Englewood Cliffs, 1966), esp. p. 107.

being and who must pay a ransom of himself. *Oedipus Tyrannus* reveals the domestic and political unnaturalness of Oedipus, just as Aristotle's *Politics* discovers the unnaturalness of monetary interest. This revelation is what can save Thebes.

The revelation of Oedipus's being begins with Creon's announcement that the oracle (to which Oedipus himself had sent Creon) suggested that the city could be ransomed again (101) by punishing the murderer of the previous king, Laius. Demonstrating a mercenary suspicion typical of tyrants, Oedipus suggests that the killers were probably hired assassins, since only money (*argyrion* 124) could convince men to act so unnaturally as to kill a king. He wishes to find a clue (*symbolon* 221), and offers a profitable reward (*kerdos* and *charis* 232) to the person who provides one. From this point, the movement of the play is from the polis and the problem of who killed Laius to the family and the problem of who generated Oedipus, or who Oedipus is. Oedipus's almost familial self-interest in finding the political killer is manifest. "As it happens, it's I who have the power that he [Laius] had once, and have his bed, and a wife [Jocasta] who shares our seed, and common bond had we had common children (had not his hope of offspring [*genos*] had bad luck [*edystychēsen*]—but as it happened, luck [*tychē*] lunged at his head): because of this, as if for my own father, I'd fight for him" (258 ff.). Oedipus suggests that the events of his life and generation were and are ruled by *tychē* (luck). Aristotle argues that dramatic plots should proceed by *technē* (art) as opposed to *tychē*. [21] In *Oedipus Tyrannus* the concept of *tychē* confronts that of its near homonym, *technē*, and in the course of the play Oedipus learns that his own status as *tokos*, another near homonym, is the *technē* that informs the plot of his life.

After hearing of their obligation to detect the criminal, the chorus appeals to "golden Pytho" (152–53) or "golden Hope" (159), "Artemis, whose famous throne is the whole circle of the marketplace" (161), and "Athena, golden goddess, daughter of Zeus" (187). The Lycēan Lord, perhaps Apollo (Oedipus's enemy), is called golden (204–5), and the head of Bacchus is said to be bound in gold (209). Hades, another deity of commerce, seeks vengeance on Oedipus because Oedipus's answering the sphinx ended Hades' enrichment (*ploutidzein* 30) from the bodies of dead Thebans. Such golden and commercial gods are supposed to affect the destiny of Thebes, but the chorus seems not to know their exact technique.

In the interview with Tiresias, Oedipus expresses his distrust of

---

21. *Eth. Nic.* 1140a, *Poetics* 1454a. Cf. Butcher, *Aristotle's Theory*, pp. 180 ff.

Tiresias's famous *techne* (357) and his trust in his own ability to answer riddles. Tiresias the seer accuses the tyrant of a kind of incest (*homilia* 367, cf. 1185). Oedipus concludes that Tiresias has sold his story for wealth: "Oh, wealth (*ploute*) and tyranny (*tyranni*) and art surpassing art (*techne technes hyperpherousa*) in the life that has much admiring envy in it!" (380–81). Oedipus allies wealth and tyranny to *techne technes hyperpherousa*, but he does not yet know whose or which artful technique informs all others. He intends merely to accuse the blind Tiresias of being a charlatan and a beggar (*agyrtes* 388), with eyes always open for profit (*kerdos* 388) and always closed to his art (*techne* 389) of which he believes that he, Oedipus, is the true master. Tiresias warns Oedipus about the criminal he seeks:

> A seeming stranger, he shall be shown to be
> a Theban born. . . .
> To his beloved children, he'll be shown
> a father who is also brother; to the one
> who bore him, son and husband; to his father
> his seed-fellow (*homosporos*) and killer.

(452–60)

Reminding the tyrant that "he who was rich (*plousios*) will beg" (455), Tiresias leaves the stage. Oedipus, who had guessed that the answer to the riddle of the sphinx was "Man" (in general), does not yet guess or know that the answer to the riddle of the insightful Tiresias is "Oedipus" (in particular).

In the following episode, Oedipus accuses Creon of having conspired with Tiresias. He taunts Creon for not fighting with the aid of wealth (*chremata* 542), which, Oedipus suggests, is necessary to win and to maintain a tyranny. Creon insists that he does not want a tyranny (586) and that he regards tyranny as essentially without profit (*kerdos* 595).

Oedipus then tells Jocasta that Creon has been plotting against his life with a malignant *techne* (643). Again opposing *techne* (which he now appears to fear) to *tyche*, he describes to Jocasta the events of his life as though they were ruled by chance (*tyche* 773). Oedipus speaks of a chance event (*tyche* 776) in the home of King Polybius and Queen Merope of Corinth, whom he believes to be his parents. One day, he says, someone in the court called him *plastos* (780) (meaning "counterfeit" as well as "bastard").[22] Oedipus went to the oracle and received

---

22. This is the only occurrence of *plastos* in the extant works of Sophocles. *Plastinx* is the word for the balance used by a moneychanger. In the *Republic*, Socrates suggests that a youthful creature "is best moulded and takes the impression that one wishes to

the warning that he would kill his father and marry his mother. He tried to heed the warning by leaving Corinth. At a crossroads he met a supposedly unfamiliar man (Laius, as it turns out) whose arrogance he repaid (810) with death.

Oedipus was and is afraid of killing his father, supposedly Polybius. He is relieved, therefore, when a messenger arrives from Corinth and announces that Polybius is dead. Oedipus believes that he now has only to fear marrying his mother (*tekousa* 985), supposedly Merope. The messenger from Corinth, however, says that he found the baby Oedipus by chance, that he did not purchase him from another (1025), and that he gave the baby to Polybius as a gift. He even calls Oedipus *teknon* (1030), as if he were the tyrant's father, and explains the chance (*tychē* 1036) by which he was named Oedipus. Oedipus quickly detects that the reward-seeking messenger did not actually find him by chance (1039), but rather received him from another. At an earlier crossroads on his way from Thebes to Corinth, the infant Oedipus was given by a Theban freeman (1123) to the Corinthian hireling (1029). Again Oedipus calls himself the son of chance (*tychē* 1080, cf. 1025), but the doubting chorus now wonders who are the parents of the tyrant who called them *tekna* (1): "Who was your mother, son (*teknon* 1098)?" To the chorus, Oedipus is no longer only a tyrant or political father, but also a son.

In the interview with the Theban freeman almost all is revealed. The freeman does not wish to speak freely (*charis* 1152, cf. 232), but when threatened by Oedipus, he tells of the prediction that a child would kill his parents (*tekontes* 1176) and of his parents' decision to destroy it. "Poor mother (*tekousa* 1174)," cries Oedipus. Still ignorant that he is familiar, or homogeneous, with the mother, Oedipus can pity her. Finally, however, the time of the play reveals his generation: "Time, all-seeing, surprised you living an unwilled life, and sits from of old in judgment on the marriage, not a marriage, where the begetter is the begot as well (*tekounta kai teknoumenon*)" (1213–15). The price of all-seeing time (1213) is the rate of interest. Oedipus is the son (*teknon* 1216) of Laius, revealed as a *tokos*, both begetter and begot. His mother-wife's suicide is described as if to reinforce that revelation: "She called to Laius, dead so many years, remembering the ancient seed which caused his death, leaving the mother (*tiktousan*) to the son to breed again an ill-born (*dysteknon*) progeny. She mourned the bed

---

stamp (*plattetai*) on it" (377b). Oedipus was adopted by the Corinthian monarchs. If he were the bastard son of either Polybius or Merope, however, he could conclude either that murdering Laius was not patricide or that sleeping with Jocasta was not incest. Thus, in the later scenes of the play Oedipus hopes that he is a bastard.

where she, alas, bred double—husband by husband, children by her child (tekn'ek teknōn tekoi)" (1245–50). What Oedipus once interpreted as bad luck (dys-tychia 262) is now revealed to be bad birth (dys-teknia 1248, cf. 423 and 425). Dysteknia produced the patricidal and incestuous tokos in Oedipus Tyrannus.

The technē technēs hyperpherousa, or technique of techniques, that informs Oedipus's tyranny is socially perverse, if not unnatural, human production. Like the product of monetary generation, Oedipus is homogeneous (or, as he calls himself, ekgonos) with his progenitors: "I am without god and the son of unholy parents, but I am also of the same kind (homogenos) as those from whom I was born" (1360–61). Indeed, he is as much like (or the homoion of) Laius as interest is qualitatively equal to its principal. The most general formula for chrematistical usury, M_1-C-M_2, represents an unnatural transaction in which there may be some quantitative but no qualitative difference between M_1 and M_2. Oedipus is often warned about this homogeneity (414–15); words such as homosporos, homilia, and homos dominate the language of Oedipus Tyrannus. But what distinguishes Oedipus from other men is not that he is like, but rather that he is qualitatively equal to, his progenitor. Seth Benardete writes that Oedipus "is equally husband and son of Jocasta, father and brother of Antigone, and killer of Laius who gave him life. By killing his father and marrying his mother he has destroyed the triad of father, mother and son. He is not a third one over and beyond his origins, but is at one with them."[23] The tyrant-detective discovers his genus by discovering his crimes of homogeneity: patricide and incest. Geoffrey Hartman writes that "Oedipus is redundant: he is his father, and as his father he is nothing, for he returns to the womb that bore him."[24] Oedipus is his own progenitor. Tiresias says, "This day you will be born and die at the same time" (438). By becoming his father, Oedipus the tokos makes his own birth impossible and so commits political (and, in Colonus, domestic) suicide.

At the end of the play, Oedipus thinks not of the political "children" he now knows that he has lost, but of his familial children-siblings. He addresses them with the word that opened the play, tekna (1375, 1480, 1484, 1501), and tells the tale of a violation both his and theirs: "Your father killed his father, plowed the one who gave him birth (tekousa), and from the place where he was sown from there he got you, from that place he too was born" (1496–99). He who is at

23. Benardete, "Sophocles' Oedipus Tyrannus," pp. 115-6.

24. Geoffrey Hartman, "The Voice of the Shuttle: Language from the Point of View of Literature," in Beyond Formalism (New Haven, 1970), p. 348.

one will be atoned at Colonus. In Sophocles' tale of the counterfeit Oedipus's family, Antigone is the incestuous patricide's daughter-sister and his only possible offspring or outcome. Like her father-brother, she will stand finally against generation (*anti-gonē*).

In his discussion of *oikonomia*, Aristotle demonstrates that the family of Oedipus is suitable for depiction in tragedy. He determines the relation between the family life depicted on stage and the family life of the spectator. If the spectator considers Oedipus to be a little like or homogeneous to himself, he can pity Oedipus. If, however, the spectator identifies wholly with Oedipus (as do some Freudians), fear may drive out pity. Oedipus, who answered the riddle of the sphinx, was unable until the end of *Oedipus Tyrannus* to recognize his homogeneous familiars and heterogeneous unfamiliars. We know probably no better than he who answered the sphinx whether Oedipus is like us. Modern man is puzzled and charmed by *Oedipus Tyrannus*. He can pity the tyrant or perverse monarch of old despite and because of the appearance that his is another political economy.

The disposition of Sophocles' play focuses on the most vexing social problem of generation in human families, incest, which exists naturally in the state of nature and abhorrently in conventional societies. *Oedipus Tyrannus* may be interpreted as a study of tyranny in which is discovered not its monetary genesis, as in Plato's *Republic*, but rather its perverse sexual genesis. Monetary and sexual theory are informed by the same tension between nature and convention that Aristotle writes about in his condemnation of interest and in his partially anti-Platonic defense of poetry. Poetry is a counterfeit human production as vexing as incest. In Aristotelian theory, poetry is a dispensation or offspring (*tokos*) of the truth, but an ambiguity exists whether it is a natural, economic production or an unnatural, chrematistic production. Aristotle acknowledges the problem of the original thing of which art may be said to be a likeness (*homoion*) and the problem of what happens to an artistic production when it becomes or is, like Oedipus, identical to its supposedly homogeneous progenitor. Such problems, crucial in the articulation of Platonic esthetic theory, exist only at the marginal extremes of Aristotle's economics and theory of *mimēsis*. His poetic economy depends nevertheless on theories of natural reproduction, and, inevitably, on studying productions such as *Oedipus Tyrannus*. How much Aristotle depends on a theory of natural dispensation that moderns can adapt or adopt is a problem still to be considered.

Despite Aristotle's integration of esthetic and economic theory, the term "economy" soon came to mean, as if by a bad metaphor, merely the internal disposition (*dispositio*) of a literary work. Polybius, Dionysus of Halicarnassus, Philodemus, Quintilian, Racine, Milton, Lessing, Schiller, Dryden, Henriot, and perhaps even Rousseau are among those who use the term in this narrow depoliticized sense of internal organization.[25] Indeed, the history (in literary theory) of economy is, like that of *mimēsis*, often little more than the description of why and how fundamental philosophical and political categories were stripped of their explicit philosophical and political implications. In this history there are some exceptional theorists who attempt to integrate disposition with dispensation; among these are the Aristotelian scholiasts, who often consider the poet as an economist (*oikonomos*) dispensing (*tamieuomenos*) parts of a drama,[26] and Longinus.

Longinus's *Treatise on the Sublime* presents a theory of literary economy that considers more than disposition. Longinus argues that sublimity (*hypsos*) is the polar opposite of economy and that the effect of

25. Polybius (1.4.3; cf. 1.13.9), Dionysus of Halicarnassus (*Epistula ad Pompeium* 4.2; cf. *Ars Rhetorica* 25), and Philodemus of Gadara (*Peri parrēsias*, ed. Alexander Olivieri [Leipzig, 1914], p. 47) use *oikonomia* to refer to the order and rules of literature (LaRoche, *Histoire*, pp. 144, 159). Marcus Fabius Quintilianus ("De dispositiona utilitate," in *Institutio Oratoria*, bk. 7) translates *oikonomia* into Latin as *dispositio*, and tries to separate problems of disposition from problems of acquisition, production, and dispensation. Although some Latin commentators retain the Greek word in their works (for example, Aelius Donatus's *ad Ter. Eun.* 719; and Marius Servius's *ad Aen.* 1.226), they too do not consider disposition in relation to dispensation.

Racine considers *l'économie* of his *Britannicus* (*dédicace* to *Britannicus*) and notes that he "changed somewhat *l'économie* and *la fable* [the story] of Euripides" (*préface* to *Iphigénie*). Milton writes of "the economy or disposition of the fable" (introduction to *Samson Agonistes*). G. E. Lessing writes about "the customary *ökonomie* of French tragedies" (*Sammtliche Schriften*, ed. K. Lachman, 13 vols. [1838–40], 6: 111, letter, February 1760) and about the *ökonomie* of works of literature in general (letter, June 24, 1759).

In such criticism "economy" usually applies to drama, but it is applicable to any genre. Dryden writes about the economy of an epic (*Of Dramatic Poesy and Other Critical Essays* [New York, 1964], 2: 225) and argues that in "the economy of a poem Vergil much excells Theocritus" (ibid., 2: 91). Emile Henriot discusses the *économie* of Balzac's novels (*Portrait de femmes d'Héloïse à Katherine Mansfield* [Paris, 1951], p. 338). Charles Rollin writes about the *économie* of discourse in Demosthenes' speeches (*Traité des études* [Avignon, 1808], bk. 4, ch. 4). Jean-Jacques Rousseau (*Essai sur l'origine des langues* [Paris, 1970], p. 536) considers the internal dispositions of "langages" such as music and painting: "Multiplier les sons entendus à la fois, ou développer les couleurs l'une après l'autre, c'est changer leur économie, c'est mettre l'oeil à la place de l'oreille, et l'oreille à la place de l'oeil."

26. See, for example, sch. *Eumenides* 47 and sch. *Electra* 1098. Passages in which the scholiasts use the term *oikonomia* are collected in Adolfus Trendelenburg's *Grammaticorum Graecorum de Arte Tragica Iudiciorum Reliquiae* (Bonn, 1867), esp. pp. 94–105.

sublime language is transport, while the effect of economy is persuasion:

> Our persuasions we can usually control, but the influences of the sublime bring power and irresistible might to bear, and reign supreme over every hearer. Similarly, we see skill in invention and economy emerging as the hardwon result not of one thing or two, but of the whole texture of the composition, whereas Sublimity flashing forth at the right moment scatters everything before it like a thunderbolt, and at once displays the power of the orator in all its plenitude (*athroan*).[27]

The sublime dispenses plenitude and precipitates chrematistic production. "Our soul is naturally uplifted by the truly great [sublime]; we receive it as a joyous offering; we are filled with delight and pride as if we had ourselves created what we heard" (7). In order to elicit this possibly false feeling in his reader, the writer or orator is encouraged to employ techniques such as natural high-mindedness, selection and organization of material, and amplification. Amplification includes the economic arrangement or disposition (*epoikonomia*) of facts or of passions (11). These techniques, however, cannot by themselves produce sublimity: "The orator must remember that [amplification by economy] apart from sublimity does not form a complete whole. . . . If you take away the sublime, you will remove . . . the soul from the body" (11). Sublimity is to the soul as economy is to the body. Economy can form a complete or independent whole only when pity is to be excited or an opponent is to be disparaged. Economy, then, appears to signify mere disposition, but it is a polar opposite of, and is necessarily dependent on, sublimity.

Longinus prefers the dispensing sublime poet (for instance, Archilochus) to his polar opposite, the disposing economic poet (Eratosthenes is an example): "Eratosthenes in the 'Erigone' (a little poem which is altogether free from flaw) [is not] a greater poet than Archilochus with the rich and un-economic [*anoikonomēta*] abundance which follows in his [Archilochus's] train and with that outburst of the divine spirit within him which it is difficult to bring under the rules of law [*hypo nomon taxai*]" (33.5). Archilochus is a sublime and uneconomic dispenser. His "revolutionary" spirit is difficult, perhaps impossible, to bring under the control of *nomoi*. (A similar difficulty,

---

27. Longinus, *On the Sublime*, sect. 1. *Oikonomia* in *On the Sublime* has been translated as "arrangement" (*Longinus on the Sublime*, ed. and trans. W. Rhys Roberts [Cambridge, 1899]), as "disposition" (*Longinus' "On the Sublime*," ed. D. A. Russell [Oxford, 1964]), and as "economy" (*Dionysius Longinus on the Sublime*, trans. William Smith [London, 1752]). The translation of sect. 1 is adapted from Roberts. The following translations are from G. M. A. Grube, *On Great Writing (On the Sublime): Longinus* (New York, 1957).

perhaps, underlies Aristotle's dismissal of Alcidamus's interpretation of *oikonomia* in rhetoric, for Aristotle strongly disapproves of Alcidamus's revolutionary theory of *nomoi*.)[28] Longinus's polar opposition of economy to sublimity implies a corresponding opposition of work (resistance) to beauty. The audience, like the writer, may be inventive and skillful, and may work hard at understanding the events that it sees or reads. The audience, however, cannot control its reaction to the sublime (14). As in the philosophy of Kant, moreover, the beautiful is that which can, and indeed must, be comprehended without work. The sublime is that which we feel we ourselves have created or produced effortlessly. It is the *Verschwendung* (dispensation) that Goethe depicts in *Faust* and that, finally, Goethe shows to be uncreditable.[29] Without work there is no production; without resistance there is no justifiable feeling of liberation from resistance. The supposedly liberated *Sublime* remains at best a partial study of one aspect of esthetics.

Aristotle suggests that the writer or philosopher is an *oikonomos* who dispenses likenesses (*homoiōmata*) of impressions (*pathēmata*) that he receives from nature. Plato's Socrates suggests that the philosopher is a kind of artful midwife who dispenses to his interlocutors a teaching that he hopes to be the offspring (*tokos*) of the Good, or the interest (*tokos*) on the principal that is the Good, or homogeneous to (*ekgonos*) the Good. The Platonic and Aristotelian theory, that there is something given to or deposited with man (for example, the Good) that it is his duty to dispense to others, generally influenced the art of writing as well as the study of writing and *mimēsis*. In "How to Write History" (50–51), for example, Lucian argues that the historian does not make but rather receives the events of history as the dispensation of God, and that he is required to dispense these events to his readers without misrepresentation. Lucian asserts that the historian is like a sculptor who does not make but rather receives his material (gold, for example) from nature and who works this material into a sculpture: "The sculptor's art [lies] in handling [*oikonomesthenai*] his material properly. . . . The task of the historian is similar [to that of the sculptor]: to give fine arrangements to events and illuminate them as

28. See above, n. 4.
29. In Goethe's *Faust*, the opposition of disposition to dispensation (Longinus's "economy" and "sublime") creates a tension between real (creditable) and unreal (uncreditable) activity. Figures such as Homunculus (a "soul" without a "body") and Knabe-Wagenlenker (who calls himself *Verschwendung*, or dispensation) and his double Euphorion end in a sublime and uneconomic manner. Cf. Goethe's dispensing *Pandora*.

vividly as possible." Lucian also states that the historian is like a
mirror that reflects or dispenses the shape of things and events just as
it receives them. Things must be allowed to "speak for themselves,"
"without false colouring, distortion, and misrepresentation."[30] As in
Aristotle, the crucial argument is that the economist-poet is not the
same kind of maker as is the chrematist-poet of idle tales.

Another example of the influence of the Aristotelian theory of dispensation is the religious and philosophical doctrine that the wise
man is an *oikonomos* (steward) who dispenses the divine teaching.
Unlike Lucian's historian but like Plato's philosopher, he alters the
mirror economically, that is, according to the spiritual level of his
audience. In the parable of the sower, for instance, Jesus suggests
that the steward should match his ability to give with his students'
ability to receive the truth. In order to dispense truth, it may even be
necessary to tell a kind of untruth. This doctrine of the economy of
truth, which justifies a kind of lying, is easily misused. It may become
a rationalization for lying in order to help not the hearer but rather the
liar. Edmund Burke writes that "falsehood and delusion are allowed
in no case whatever," but that "there is an economy of truth . . . a sort
of temperance, by which a man speaks the truth in order to speak it
the longer."[31] Saint Paul argues that he is a steward (*oikonomos*), but
often seems to consider in his theory of economy only the good of the
steward himself. "In your teaching," he writes, "show gravity and
sound speech that cannot be censured, so that an opponent may be
put to shame, having nothing evil to say of us. Bid slaves to be
submissive to their master. . . ."[32] Paul implies that in order not to be
censured, one can tell a lie or even seem to become the friend of
slavery.

The doctrine of economy may also be misused when the medium
(for example, speech or writing) by which the truth should be dispensed is misunderstood. The Reverend F. W. Robertson, for exam-

30. Cf. Diodorus Siculus, *Historical Library*, 5.1.

31. Edmund Burke, *Letters on the Proposals for Peace with the Regicide Directory of
France*, no. 1, in *Works* (London, 1842), 8: 208.

32. Titus 2.7. Cf. Titus 1.7. Paul would reinterpret the economy of the Old Testament
(Genesis 43.16, 43.19, 44.1; 2 Kings 18.3) on a supposedly higher spiritual level. He
would give to the gentiles the "grace" that is "the unsearchable wealth of Christ"
(Ephesians 3.8): "As each has received a gift, employ it for one another, as good
economists of God's varied grace" (1 Peter 4.10). In the Christian economy, grace is the
plenitudinous source of abundance. It is not the work of man, nor can man alone cause
it to be dispensed (2 Corinthians 2, 3); man is only the steward of the mysteries of God
(1 Corinthians 4.1). In the New Testament the word "economy" also refers to God's
plan for salvation (Ephesians 3.9, 1.10). Cf. Adhémar d'Ales, "Le Mot *oikonomia* dans la
langue théologique de Saint Irénée," *Revue des études grecques*, 32: 1–9.

ple, speaks of the "economic management of the truth" but erroneously believes that words "are the coins of the intellect."[33] Because men are sometimes morally bad or intellectually mistaken, the doctrine of the economy of truth demands that only saintly and wise men be entitled to employ "the withholding of the full and explicit truth." Jesus is supposed to have been such a man. When asked about taxation, he answered that "man should render unto Caesar what is Caesar's and unto God what is God's." This answer is said to illustrate how "economy" benefits both speaker and hearer.

The attempt to define the difference between falsehood and pious economy gives rise to theories of metaphor and fiction. Cardinal Newman, for example, compares economy with the *disciplina arcani*. Economy is "setting [the truth] out to advantage," as when "representing religion, for the purpose of conciliating the heathen, in the form most attractive to their prejudices," and the *disciplina arcani* is a "withholding [of] the truth" in the form of allegory, by which the same text may express the same truth at different levels to different people.[34] Economy is necessary to "lead children forward by degrees" (p. 72) and may employ similes and metaphors. Newman maintains, for example, that "the information given to a blind man, that scarlet was like the sound of a trumpet, is an instance of an unexceptionable economy, since it was as true as it could be under the circumstances of the case, conveying a substantially correct impression as far as it went" (pp. 72–73). All men are children blind to truth, and, as Newman argues, every poet accommodates to (and sometimes even flatters) the feelings and prejudices of the hearer.

Like metaphors, whole histories and fictions can be economical. The events of the New Testament are economical versions of the truth, just as the events of the Old Testament are economical "simulations" of the New Testament. The first chapter of the book of Job and "the Mosaic Dispensation [were] Econom[ies] simulating (so to say) unchangeableness, when from the first [they were] destined to be abolished" (p. 77). This simulation is as economic as the simulation of sight by sound. Newman, indeed, seems to interpret all good teaching as "Economia of greater truths untold:" "All those so-called Economies or dispensations, which display His character in action, are but condescensions to the infirmity and peculiarity of our minds, shadowy representations of realities which are incomprehensible to creatures such as ourselves..." (p. 75). The motives of ordinary men

33. Reverend F. W. Robertson, *Sermons*, 1st ser., no. 1; 4th ser., no. 6.
34. Cardinal Newman, *The Arians of the Fourth Century* (London, 1919), ch. 2, sect. 3, p. 65.

(for example, fear of saying the truth or desire to profit from saying an untruth) can make economy a mere rationalization for telling self-serving untruths. Thus an evil or ignorant poet-liar may do others more harm than good. Newman argues that "it is plain that [some men, for example] Justin, Gregory or Athanasius, were justifiable or not in their Economy, according as they did or not practically mislead their [hearers]" (p. 73) and that it was by economy that "to the Jews [Paul, wishing to save his life] became as a Jew" (p. 65), since he did not "practically mislead" his judges. He advises, however, that the ordinary man may "lie, or rather utter a lie, as the sophists say" (p. 74), only "as physician, for the good of his patients" (pp. 73–74).

The economy of truth, of course, informs secular as well as religious literature. In "Economies de paroles," Voltaire defines economy merely as "speaking according to the time and place" and cites the passage in the New Testament in which Paul speaks "by economy" before the Pharisees in order to save his life as "a pious artifice."[35] Influenced by Saint Jerome, who praised the "art of speaking that which seems true (le vraisemblable) rather than that which is true (le vrai)," Voltaire catalogues many non-Christian writers who wrote economically. Plato, Theophrastus, Xenophon, Aristotle, and others are said to have said "non quod sentiunt, sed quod necesse est dicunt." Voltaire suggests that not only specific biblical metaphors and fictions but also literature in general may be economic, and, significantly, that proper rules for the economy of the truth can be determined not from theology but rather from domestic and political economy.[36]

Esoteric economic writing hides its deepest message from those to whom a writer does not wish to reveal it. The ones to whom the message is revealed are either those extraordinary good or wise men who can understand without work or those ordinary men who are willing and able to work. As Maimonides argues, the work of interpretation is part of literary production. Without the effort required to interpret his difficult Guide of the Perplexed, it cannot guide.[37] Some modern critics have argued, however, that literature and philosophy should be easy and that the writer should husband the reader's ener-

35. Voltaire, "Economie de paroles," in Dictionnaire philosophique, in Oeuvres, ed. M. Beuchot, 72 vols. (Paris, 1829–40), 39: 451 ff. My translation.

36. Voltaire, "Economie domestique," in Dictionnaire philosophique.

37. See Leo Strauss, "Introductory Essay," in Maimonides, The Guide of the Perplexed, trans. Shlomo Pines (Chicago, 1969); and Leo Strauss, Persecution and the Art of Writing (Glencoe, Ill., 1952).

gies. Herbert Spencer's "economy of creative effort" emphasizes "the importance of economizing the reader's or the hearer's attention. To so present ideas that they may be apprehended with the least possible mental effort, is the desideratum."[38] Spencer suggests that "the more simple, . . . the greater will be the effect produced" and that brevity, assuming it does not work against ease, is admirable because it conserves the reader's energies.

According to Spencer, a writer should be sparing with words because "language is a hindrance to thought." "This general principle of economy" implies that "the sensitiveness of the faculties of the reader must be continuously husbanded" according to a theory in which words and sentences are supposed to be separate from the ideas they express. "The more time and attention it takes to receive and understand each sentence, the less time and attention can be given to the contained idea; and the less vividly will that idea be conceived."[39] Spencer even suggests that metaphor is superior to simile because it uses fewer words to express the same idea: "The superiority of the Metaphor to the Simile is . . . the great economy it achieves. . . . When the comparison is an involved one, the greater force of the metaphor, consequent on its greater brevity, becomes much more conspicuous."[40] Spencer would rule out all abstract or fiduciary words because he supposes that the effort required to conjoin a concrete word with its object is less than the effort needed to conjoin an abstract word with its object. In the English language, he believes, "the economy of the recipient's mental energy, into which are thus resolvable the several causes of the strength of Saxon English, may equally be traced into the superiority of specific over generic words." Spencer's supposition that words and ideas can be separated would make ideas (if they exist at all) inaccessible, and his preference for concrete words would make abstract and universal thinking almost impossible. The feeling of freedom from work that Spencer's economy might give to the reader would erase from his life that resistance without which beauty (or thought) is impossible. Spencer would flatter the reader or citizen in a way inimical to the philosophy of art and political theory but supportive of the conservative politics he espouses.

The relation between the literary and political aspects of Spencer's thought is similar to that of a writer like Ben Jonson, who discusses "the economy and disposition" of poems and asserts that the poet is a

38. Herbert Spencer, *The Philosophy of Style* (New York, 1882), pp. 2–3.
39. Ibid., p. 45.
40. Ibid., pp. 30–31.

"husbandman" who "should not protect [his] sloth with the patron-
age of difficulty." Jonson argues that "translation [or metaphor] must
serve only necessity . . . or commodity." The political implications of
"commodity" are manifest in Jonson's assertion that language is un-
commodious when "a privy councillor at the table take[s] his
metaphor from a dicing house." Metaphorization should not mix social classes (Aristotelian political *oikoi*) that are unfamiliar to each
other. Jonson thus suggests that language should support the regime
in the same way as the mint. "A man coins not a new word without
some peril," he writes. "Custom is the most certain mistress of language, as the public stamp makes the current money. . . . We must
not be too frequent with the mint, every day coining [new words] . . .
since the chief virtue of a style is perspicuity, and nothing so vicious
in it as to need an interpreter." Jonson knows that interpretation
sometimes acts as a catalyst to new logical and political organization,
and so relegates Mercury or Hermes (whom he calls *deorum hominum-
que interpres*) to a conservative "presiden[cy] of languages," the "letters" of which "are the bank of words."[41]

The conservative political implications of the argument that literature ought to be easy or commodious for the reader should not be
ascribed to the arguments that literature should liberate the reader or
that literary organization should not be wasteful. Longinus's wish to
give to the reader a feeling of liberation may appear to be like the ease
of which Spencer writes, but for Longinus economy is a difficult
disposition that makes possible the apparently easy dispensation that
is sublimity. The scholiasts' suggestion, that it is "uneconomical" to
waste (*diatribein*) the presence on stage of characters or actions[42] may
seem to aim at the abbreviation of which Spencer writes. However,
the scholiasts would abbreviate not the reader's energies, but rather
the play itself, and this abbreviation often makes the play more difficult for the reader or spectator to comprehend. The scholiasts'
theory of the economy of plays has been applied to words by some
modern critics, who argue that writing is "supremely economical"
when "every word is doing a fantastic amount of work."[43] Yet in all
these cases, economy does not necessitate abbreviating the work of
the reader.

41. Ben Jonson, *Timber or Discoveries,* ed. R. S. Walker (Syracuse, 1953), pp. 41–60.
42. Sch. *Electra* 1384, sch. *O.C.* 887 and sch. *Eumenides* 47. Cf. sch. *Hippolytus* 803 and
sch. *Hippolytus* 521 on the economy of the absence of truth; sch. *Hippolytus* 569 on the
economy of sound; and sch. *Electra* 312, sch. *Hippolytus* 659, and sch. *Ajax* 342 on the
economy of character.
43. G. P. Hibbard, "Words, Action and Artistic Economy," *Shakespearian Survey,* 23:
37, 49–58.

Many critics do admit that Spencer's "economy of the recipient's mental energy" may be a good guide for writing prose but argue that it should not be transferred to poetry. Victor Shklovsky, for example, attacks Spencer directly in his argument that the literary theorist should "speak about the laws of expenditure and economy in poetic language not on the basis of an analogy with prose, but on the basis of poetic language."[44] He attacks theories of literature that would make poetry easy, automatic, or "algebraic" for the reader. Shklovsky draws an analogy between prosaic literature (in which the first letters of words sometimes seem to replace the words) and speech (in which the sounds of words sometimes replace thoughts or objects). The insidious disappearances of words in the first case and of thoughts or objects in the second case are described in terms of algebraic familiarization. "We perceive the object as if it were packaged: we know that it exists from the space which it occupies, but we see only its surface." As Shklovsky suggests, words misunderstood as abstract fiduciary symbols have the same effect on the objects they are supposed to represent that money has on the commodities it is supposed to measure. "The object, perceived thus in the manner of prose perception, fades and does not leave even a first impression; ultimately even the essence of what it was is forgotten."[45] The mind is transformed by modern thrifty language into a homogenized and homogenizing agent. Shklovsky argues that "the process of perception is an esthetic end in itself and must be prolonged" and that poetry is or should be an agent of defamiliarization in an apparently universally familiar world.

As we have seen, the debate about literary economy can be transposed from the level of words and metaphors (about which Spencer and Shklovsky write) to the political level. Adorno makes such a trans- or re-position when he objects to the apparent homogeneity and one-dimensionality of modern society, and argues that "defiance of society includes defiance of its language."[46] This defiance, which depends on difficult defamiliarization, may inform musical as well as verbal "languages." Adorno argues, for example, that modern com-

---

44. Victor Shklovsky, "Art as Technique," in *Russian Formalist Criticism: Four Essays,* trans. and intro. Lee T. Lemon and Marion J. Reis (Lincoln, 1965), p. 10. Shklovsky compares Spencer to Robert Avenarius and Alexander Veselovsky. Cf. Stéphane Mallarmé (*Oeuvres complètes*, ed. Henri Mondor [Paris, 1945], pp. 368, 656), who employs a similar metaphor to distinguish between prose and poetry.
45. Shklovsky, "Art as Technique," p. 11.
46. Theodor W. Adorno, *Prisms*, trans. S. Weber and S. Weber (London, 1967), p. 225. See Martin Jay, *The Dialectical Imagination: A History of the Frankfurt School and the Institute of Social Research, 1923–1950* (Boston, 1973), p. 176.

mercial music is too familiar. (It is, so to speak, as confident of and blind to itself as was Oedipus in Corinth.) Only the difficulty and "willed ugliness" of its antagonist, modern music, can free its listeners from the "state of pathological hebetude and insensibility" that commercial music encourages. In Adorno's esthetics, as Fredric Jameson notes, "only the painful remains as a spur to perception."[47] Pain is the unfamiliarity in sound that will force us to transform the unconscious contents of daily perceptual life. In Adorno's criticism, "we begin to glimpse what is the profound vocation of the work of art in a commodity society: not to be a commodity, not to be consumed, to be unpleasurable in the commodity sense."[48] Perhaps the pain of one who listens to modern music, like the pain of Oedipus in Thebes, can reveal to him what is familiar and unfamiliar.

Pain is a spur or gadfly that, like metaphor, helps us to recognize or to remember our own being in the apparently unfamiliar. A modern economy of literature, however, cannot rest with defamiliarizing the apparently familiar, whether it be commercial music or the word "economy." "Commodity society" can hardly be destroyed or even understood by the merely negative goads of pain.

Like Aristotle, modern theorists must undertake not only to defamiliarize the being of man but also to comprehend in a single vision the social and esthetic problems that arise in the philosophy of art. Aristotle's theory of economy, which responds to and rises above negative goading, was fractured by subsequent thinkers into theories of disposition and dispensation. Modern literary theorists are beginning to recover from this uncritical and apolitical bifurcation. Unlike Aristotle, however, modern theorists cannot depend on the distinction between nature and convention that made possible the theoretical rigor of the Aristotelian distinction between chrematistics and economy, or between the exchange value of a commodity and the use value of a good. Indeed, modern thinkers can hardly comprehend the idea of a nature that distributes goods to be redistributed by stewards. The tension between Aristotelian economics, in which nature is given to man, and modern economics, in which nature is changed through exploitation, informs much of modern philosophy and literature.[49] In

47. Fredric Jameson, *Marxism and Form* (Princeton, 1971), p. 24; cf. p. 5.
48. Ibid, pp. 395–96.
49. Works of Shakespeare, for example, are informed by a conflict between a supposedly unnatural (chrematistic) merchantry and a supposedly natural (economic) mercy. The conflict extends to language. ("An if my word be sterling yet..." [*Richard II* 4.1.264]; "What he speaks is all in debt; he owes/For every word" [*Timon of Athens* 1.2.204–5].) In *The Merchant of Venice* (1.3.79–93), Shylock defends usury by using language to conflate the monetary generation of "use" from a principal (which the

the modern era, men argue (as did Locke) that nature must be exploited actively or (as Marx) that there is no nature, but only human history and work, of which language is a part. We can no longer take for granted the ontological status of the biological and spiritual things of which Aristotle contends art and memory offer homogeneous likenesses.

The theory of Aristotle gives way, but it also points the way toward a modern and equally political economy of literature. This modern theory must avoid the post-Aristotelian fracture of economy into disposition and dispensation and must overcome the Aristotelian distinction between chrematistics and economy, between the golden fleece and the voice of the shuttle.

---

gentile merchants of Venice believe to be unnatural) with the sexual generation of lambs from rams and "ewes" (which they believe to be natural). (Cf. *tokos.*) Sigurd Burckhardt (*Shakespearean Meanings* [Princeton, 1968], pp. 214–15) notes that "Shylock is imaginative not only about money and flesh but also speech." Cf. Edward Hubler (*The Sense of Shakespeare's Sonnets* [Princeton, 1952], pp. 69 ff., 95 ff.), who discusses "the economy of the closed heart," the concept of stewardship whereby a "man has an obligation to nature [because] he is the steward and not the owner of his qualities," and "the association [in the sonnets] of husbanding and begetting."

Modern political economy of literature
must overcome Aristotelian economics

THE LIE OF THE FOX

Rousseau's Theory of Verbal, Monetary, and Political Representation

Tout bien considéré, je crois que je ferai mieux de jetter mon anneau magique [de Gygès] avant qu'il m'ait fait faire quelque sotise. –Rousseau

Aristotle warned that Aesopian fables were dangerous to the political order.[1] Despite his warning, however, the fables are usually read as apolitical stories with nice moral endings. During the eighteenth century, for example, John Locke urged that young students memorize Aesop. Locke thought that the fables were devoid of "useless trumpery" and "principles of vice and folly," and that they were perfect pedagogic devices "apt to delight and entertain a child."[2] In

An earlier form of this chapter was first published in *Sub-Stance*, no. 10 (1974).

1. Aristotle tells how Aesop once gave a clever interpretation of "The Fox and the Hedgehog," in which a fox refuses the kind offer of a hedgehog to remove his fleas. The fox prefers to keep his fleas because they are already sated with his blood. Any new fleas, who would certainly replace the old ones, would take even more blood from him. Wishing to defend the tyrant (or incumbent flea) of Samos, Aesop concludes thus: "You men of Samos, let me entreat you to do as the Fox did; for this man, having got money enough, can have no further occasion to rob you; but if you put him to death, some needy person will fill his place, whose wants must be supplied out of your property" (Aristotle, *Rhetoric* 2.20.6). The fables of Aesop were written "during the suppression of free speech in the Age of the Tyrants" (Marian Eames, "John Ogilby and his *Aesop*," *Bulletin of the New York Public Library* 65 [1961]: 78).

2. John Locke, *Some Thoughts concerning Education*, ed. F. W. Garforth (London, 1961), p. 189 (written in 1693). On Locke's own translation of Aesop, see p. 17. Other important versions and political interpretations of Aesop during this period include those of Roger Lestrange, Samuel Croxall, and Samuel Richardson.

113

France, Voltaire insisted that La Fontaine's translations were "naïv-
etés élégantes." Referring to "Le Corbeau et le renard," he argued
that children should memorize fables because these stories are simple
and moral. "La Fontaine," he wrote, "est pour tous les esprits et pour
tous les âges."[3] Against this happy view, Jean-Jacques Rousseau argued throughout his writings. Re-introducing the Aristotelian problem of rhetoric and politics (as the study of society) into the study of
the fable and literature in general, he lifted to a higher level the debate
about the merits of fables. Rousseau's interpretation of "Le Corbeau
et le renard" plays an integral role in his theory of verbal, monetary,
and political representation.

In *Emile* Rousseau quotes all of La Fontaine's fable:

Maitre Corbeau sur un arbre perché
    Tenoit dans son bec un fromage.
Maitre Renard par l'odeur alléché,
    Lui tint à peu près ce langage.
    Eh! bon jour, monsieur le Corbeau!
Que vous étes charmant! que vous me semblez beau!
    Sans mentir, si vôtre ramage
    Répondoit à vôtre plumage,
Vous seriez le Phénix des hôtes de ces bois.
A ces mots le corbeau ne se sent pas de joye.
    Et pour montrer sa belle voix
Il ouvre un large bec, laisse tomber sa proye.
Le Renard s'en saisit et dit: mon bon monsieur,
    Aprenez que tout flateur
    Vit aux dépends de celui qui l'écoute
Cette leçon vaut bien un fromage, sans doute.
    Le corbeau, honteux et confus,
Jura, mais un peu tard, qu'on ne l'y prendroit plus.

(Maître Crow, perched on a tree,
was holding a cheese in his beak.
Maître Fox, attracted by the smell,
held a conference with him in almost this language.
"Well! hello, Monsieur le Crow!
How charming you are! How beautiful you seem to me!
Without lying, if your warbling
Should correspond to your plumage,
You would be the phoenix of the hosts of these woods."
At these words the crow could not contain his joy.
And to show his beautiful voice
He opened a large beak, let his prey fall.

3. Voltaire, *Oeuvres*, ed. M. Beuchot, 72 vols. (Paris, 1829–40), 39: 216–18.

The fox seized it, and said, "My good Monsieur,
Learn that every flatterer
Lives at the expense of him who listens.
This lesson is worth a cheese, without doubt."
The crow, ashamed and confused,
Swore, but a little late, that he wouldn't be taken again.)[4]

Rousseau begins his analysis of "Le Corbeau et le renard" with apparently childish *naïveté*. *Maître*—the first word of the poem—is the first item in an interpretative catalogue of signs: "*Maitre!* Que signifie ce mot en lui-même? Que signifie-t-il au devant d'un nom propre? Quel sens a-t-il dans cette occasion?" (*Oeuvres*, 4: 353). No catalogue of signs can teach a child what mastership is, just as it cannot teach who is the master in this fable and who is the servant. If the child does not know this before he reads the word *maître*, the masterful fable will act to enslave him.

Words (such as *maître*) that seem to signify things are a fundamental problem for Rousseau as he considers memorization and education. A child should be taught signs only after he knows the things they signify: ideas, objects, and passions. "Que sert d'inscrire dans leur tête un catalogue de signes qui ne réprésentent rien pour eux? En apprenant les choses, n'apprendront-ils pas les signes?" (*Oeuvres*, 4: 350). Whenever possible, the tutor should teach by experience rather than by mere verbal memorization. A child, for example, must be injured before he can understand justice. In *La Nouvelle Héloïse* (2: 578–80), Julie suggests that the tutor should wrong the tutee (as the tutee has wronged his sibling) in order to teach him the experience of being injured. Through such play-acting the child can come to know injury and finally justice. Rousseau argues that to encourage "la mémoire des mots" is to cultivate "la mémoire au profit [du] jugement." The work of memorizing mere words is not worth the tears it costs (*coûte*) the student. Verbal memorization is harmful: "Ce [n'est] rien que d'instruire un enfant à se payer de mots, et à croire savoir ce qu'il ne peut comprendre." Julie's children do not memorize the fables of poets or even the catechism. "Fables sont faites pour les hommes," argues Rousseau, not (as Voltaire urged) for everyone.

In *Emile* Rousseau again states that a price must be paid for memorizing mere words: "C'est du premier mot dont l'enfant se paye, c'est de prémiére chose qu'il apprend sur la parole d'autrui sans en voir l'utilité lui-même que son jugement est perdu . . ." (*Oeuvres*, 4: 350). The properly tutored child should not begin to memorize or

4. Jean-Jacques Rousseau, *Emile*, in *Oeuvres complètes*, 4 vols. (Paris, 1959–), 4:353–55. As we shall see, Rousseau alters some words of La Fontaine's poem.

study words, such as *maître,* until he has erred (for instance, by mistaking flattery for praise). "Le tems des fautes est celui des fables" (4: 540). Verbal memorization is dangerous to an inexperienced child because he cannot understand the relationship between sign and thing signified.[5]

Rousseau flatters us, readers and potential tutors, by pretending that we do understand things. He speaks of a "science des mots" that have no significance for the student but that may have significance for the tutor. Rousseau carefully holds in abeyance the problems of how to teach things to children (possibly by sight or speech) and of how words do signify; he proceeds to the next word whose meaning may be questioned by the tutee.

Corbeau is the second in a series of words that Rousseau seems to empty of meaning. "Si l'enfant n'a point vû de corbeaux, que gagnez-vous à lui en parler?" To speak to a child about something he has not seen is—even if one speaks the so-called truth—a kind of flattery, relying as heavily on mere signs as does the fox.

At this point Rousseau slips into a discussion of signs that signify nothing in natural life. There is a retreat of the reality of the things signified. Even if the child has seen a crow, it is unlikely that he has ever seen a crow carrying cheese in its beak. It is certainly impossible to see a crow understanding the human language of a fox. The image is unnatural. Rousseau, of course, argues that we should always make our images according to nature and that children should be taught only "la vérité nue."[6]

The word *phénix* represents an extreme in this series of increasingly unnatural signs. It is even more unlikely that the child has ever seen a phoenix (to which the fox, waxing poetic, compares the crow) than that he has ever seen a crow holding a piece of cheese in its beak and listening to a talking fox (which La Fontaine, waxing poetic, describes). As Rousseau comments: "Qu'est-ce qu'un Phénix? Nous voici tout à coup jettés dans la menteuse antiquité." The child is not so sophisticated as to understand the nature of such lies, and a tutor can hardly put himself easily into the place of a child on the threshold of learning language. "Nul de nous," writes Rousseau, "est assés philosophe pour savoir se mettre à la place d'un enfant." For the child the strange statement of the fox—"Vous seriez le Phénix des hôtes de ces bois"—is surrounded by all the mystery of the noun *phénix* and the conditional and subjunctive copula *seriez,* which articulates the

---

5. See J. Derrida, *De la grammatologie* (Paris, 1967), p. 291.
6. For this argument in *Emile* and *La Nouvelle Héloïse,* see Rousseau, *Oeuvres,* 4: 352, 2: 581.

metaphor.[7] "Vous seriez le Phénix" was the favorite line of Voltaire, who wrote of it approvingly: "Il est bien naturel de nommer *phénix* un corbeau qu'on veut flatter."[8] But in this same line Rousseau discovers the enemy of the tutor and the unnatural corrupter of children: the fox-flatterer who makes senseless words seem sensible and who pretends that children are as wise as philosophers. He interprets metaphor itself as a kind of flattery or unnatural verbal trickery. Metaphor can be as harmful, in the pen of a poet, as the fox's flattery. *Phénix*, like *seriez*, is an abstract, algebraic cipher. There is no reason to question the correspondence between the song of a phoenix and its plumage, since *phénix* has no natural significance.

From the discussion of signs without natural significance (based on a theory of natural imitation), Rousseau proceeds to a discussion of the possibly unnatural process that is the fox's metaphor itself. The recitation of the speaking fox is a metaphorical poem-within-a-poem that Rousseau strips naked. Rousseau's contemporary, César C. du Marsais, defined metaphor as a figure "par laquelle on transporte, pour ainsi dire, la signification propre d'un nom (j'aimerais mieux dire d'un mot) à une autre signification que ne lui convient qu'en vertu d'une comparaison qui est dans l'esprit."[9] The spirit, however, errs, especially when it is flattered. Rousseau fears the Heraclitean state in which anything can be exchanged for one thing and then reexchanged for any other thing. In this state it will appear to a child that he needs to understand not things but rather only words, which compare or can be exchanged for things.

The lie of the fox depends not only on *seriez* but also on *répondoit*.

Sans mentir, si vôtre ramage
Répondoit à vôtre plumage.

As if trying to stress the importance of speaking correspondences, Rousseau changes La Fontaine's *se rapporte* to *répondoit*. No longer focusing on the metaphorical relationship between words and things, he turns his attention to the related problem of metaphorical correspondence or metaphor itself. *"Répondoit!"* the child asks, "Que signifie ce mot?" The tutor, if he is wise, knows that the supposed correspondence of *ramage* (or a bird's song) to *plumage* is a *mensonge*. These two cannot be compared except by unnatural metaphor or by harmonious rhyme, as illusionary as the *ramage* itself. To compare *ramage* (which one hears) and *plumage* (which one sees) is the same as

---

7. Rousseau changes La Fontaine's *être* to the conditional *seriez*.
8. Voltaire, *Oeuvres*, 39: 220.
9. Derrida, *De la grammatologie*, p. 389.

to compare music and painting. Rousseau argues in the *Essai sur l'origine des langues* and elsewhere that there is a dangerous and "fausse analogie entre les couleurs et les sons."[10] Painting and music are of two different *économies:* the first is diachronic, the second synchronic. Rousseau is as critical of the comparison between music and painting as he was of the word *phénix.*

For adults, perhaps, the lie of the fox is easy to spot; the lie of the poet (who made the fox) is less evident. We are all craven ravens. It is childish to identify only with the fox. The flattered crow confuses painting and music; he loses his cheese in an attempt to show (*montrer*) the supposedly beautiful voice (*sa belle voix*) that the fox suggested he had. One cannot show a voice but only a painting; it is as impossible to show a voice as to compare *plumage* with *ramage.* The flattered crow imitates in life the impossibilities suggested to him in the fox's language.

As the crow opens his mouth to sing, he drops the cheese. No sound, not even a caw, issues. "Il ouvre un large bec, laisse tomber sa proye." The cheese (*proie*) is exchanged, but it is unclear whether fox or crow is the antecedent of *sa.* While falling, of course, the cheese is the property of neither animal: the fall signals the property transfer that the reader cannot see but that he believes he hears. Rousseau admires the harmony of the verse: "Ce vers est admirable; l'harmonie seule en fait image. Je vois un grand vilain bec ouvert; j'entends tomber le fromage à travers les branches" (*Oeuvres* 4:355). Rousseau admires the clever, onomatopoetic rhyme of *oix* and *oie*, whereby sounds of nature are imitated by the probably conventional sounds of human language.

In the *Essai sur l'origine des langues,* however, Rousseau argues significantly that harmony is the potential enemy of melody or natural imitation. He rejects harmony "as a mistaken illusion of consonance

---

10. Jean-Jacques Rousseau, *Essai sur l'origine des langues* (Paris, 1817; reprint ed., Paris, 1970), p. 535. The tutor must consider whether it is better to teach students to watch or to listen. In *Emile* Rousseau writes that "l'impression de la parole est toujours foible et l'on parle au coeur par les yeux bien mieux que par les oreilles" (*Oeuvres,* 4: 645; cf. *Essai,* p. 503). Vision, however, is not always possible. "J'entends dire qu'il convient d'occuper les enfans à des études où il ne faille que des yeux; cela pourroit être s'il y avoit quelque étude où il ne falut que des yeux; mais je n'en connois point de telle" (*Oeuvres,* 4: 348). Moreover, what one can see is not always true. John Locke wished his translation of Aesop to be replete with pictures (Locke, *Education,* p. 190). A picture, however, may be merely the visual sign of an idea of something-that-is-not. One who relies too much on vision may unwittingly become the ignorant victim of sound. "L'impression successive du discours... vous donne bien une autre émotion que la présence de l'objet même, où d'un coup d'oeil vous avez tout vu.... Concluons que les signes visibles rendent l'imitation plus exacte, mais que l'intérêt s'excite mieux par les sons" (*Essai,* p. 503).

within the necessarily dissonant structure of the moment." Melody does not partake of this mystification: "It does not offer a resolution of the dissonance, but rather its projection on a temporal diachronic axis."[11] Melodious music, in fact, is naturally imitative because its melody imitates directly the inflexions of the human voice (p. 533), and because, as indirect sign of the human voice, music is the catalyst that creates in listeners an emotion like that created by other things.[12] Harmony takes its energy of expression from melody, but it is a supplement to the human voice.[13] "En voulant faire mieux que la nature [as does the crow, duped by the fox] vous faites plus mal" (p. 533). Unnatural harmonious music, when stripped of melody, is the perfect tool for the fox. Harmonious praise is the power to which the crow falls prey. Fontenelle writes that "la louange est la voix la plus harmonieuse."[14]

La Fontaine puts the moral of our fable into the mouth of the speaking animal: "Apprenez que tout flateur / Vit aux dépends de celui qui l'écoute." As Rousseau phrases it in the Discours sur l'origine et les fondements de l'inégalité parmi les hommes," men "ne purent... s'aggrandir qu'aux dépends des autres" (Oeuvres 3: 175).[15] The flatterer depends on the flattered and lives at his expense. It is costly (coûteux) to listen to (écouter) a flatterer. Rousseau is skeptical, however, that a child can ever understand the economic relationship between the value of what the flatterer gives (words) and what the flattered gives (cheese). He comments, "Il y aura bien peu d'enfans qui sachent comparer une leçon à un fromage et qui ne préférassent le fromage à la leçon" (Emile, in Oeuvres 4:355). Rousseau doubts that a child can understand the terrifying common denominator that makes possible the economic exchange of flattering words (which the fox gives) for objects (which the fox receives).

Rousseau studies the fable—and implicitly all literature—from the point of view of its propensity to obscure the operation of linguistic

11. Paul de Man, "The Rhetoric of Blindness," Blindness and Insight (New York, 1971), p. 130.

12. "L'art du musicien consiste à substituer à l'image insensible de l'objet celle des mouvemens que sa présence excite dans le coeur du contemplateur.... Il ne représentera pas directement ces choses, mais il excitera dans l'ame les mêmes sentimens qu'on éprouve en les voyant" (Essai, pp. 537–38). Flattery, like music, excites in the listener sentiments similar to those the listener would experience in the presence of an object. However, flattery depends on the absence of the object everywhere except in the esprit.

13. "Il faut... dans toute imitation, qu'une espèce de discours supplée à la voix de la nature" (Essai, p. 534).

14. Prosper Soullié, Critique comparative des fables de La Fontaine (Reims, 1881), p. 14.

15. "On achette l'aggrément aux dépends de la clarté," writes Rousseau in Emile (Oeuvres, 4: 352).

and economic representation and exchange. In *Emile* he contends that the fox in La Fontaine's "Le Corbeau et le renard" is a subversive who exchanges flattering words for cheese.[16] Speaking animals confound the proper distinction between words and things by exchanging one for the other. Rousseau argues that the fable corrupts the student's innocent (and pedagogically useful) distinction between verbal and economic representation and teaches him to respect a representation more than the thing represented. The corrupting power of language alters the very nature of things by exchanging them for words. Therefore, Rousseau does not wish to teach young students this meaning of the fable. He would rather teach us (readers, who are potential tutors) the meaning of the fable and of literature in general for those who live in the modern age. If there is a retreat of the signified in Rousseau's interpretation of the fable, it is to the end of bringing us to the adult world in which not animals, but human beings, seem to speak of things.

Verbal flattery is the art of supplementing (or even creating) nature with words so that the listener, not acquainted with nature or willing to forget it, believes more in words than in things. The fox supplements nature, as does a usurer. "De tous les usuriers," writes Ségur, "les flatteurs sont les pires."[17] Language is the economic go-between, apparently mediating desires and their satisfaction. (The fox desires to eat the cheese because he—like us—is hungry and needs food, and he desires to trick the crow because his foxy nature asserts itself.) A fox-admiring reader who does not comprehend the mastery of the fable will try to imitate it. He will try to use the fable just as the fox uses the poem within the fable. Fables thus train children to become usurers and financiers.[18] Modern society is filled with grown children who, educated by fables, misunderstand the economic and verbal media. It is to the language, economics, and politics of this society that Rousseau devotes his attention.

The economist and professional etymologist Turgot was the first thinker to present a systematic comparison of words and money as social symbols of exchange.[19] For Rousseau, who goes well beyond

16. *Fromage* (a food, which enters into the mouth) and *langage* (words, which exit from the mouth) are "tenable." (See "tenoit un fromage" and "tint ce langage.") They rhyme with and are exchanged for each other.

17. Soullié, *Critique comparative,* p. 14.

18. In *Emile* (*Oeuvres,* 4: 542), Rousseau refers briefly to a student of "Les Deux Mulets" who will become a financier.

19. A. R. J. Turgot, "Tableau philosophique des progrès successifs de l'esprit humain" (1750) and "Valeurs et monnaies," in *Ecrits économiques,* intro. B. Cazes (Paris, 1970).

Turgot's analogies between *monnaie* and *langue*, the description of discourse is like that of money.[20] Other thinkers argued that language and money could accomplish the same end; Rousseau considered that they accomplished it in the same way. As Derrida writes, "all the thought of Rousseau is a critique of representation, whether in the linguistic or the political sense."[21] Rousseau's comparison of language and money includes the argument that coins, like words, are mere signs. "L'argent," he writes, "n'est pas la richesse, il n'en est que le signe" (*Considérations sur le gouvernement de Pologne,* in *Oeuvres,* 3: 1008).[22] Rousseau argues that asking a child to memorize what he does not understand is like giving him pieces of money the value of which he does not understand.[23] It is as difficult to explain money to a child as to explain the operation of words such as *seriez* and *phénix.*[24] Moreover, the child can be subverted by monetary exchange as by verbal memorization.

In *Emile,* Rousseau writes that "la societé . . . du commerce [consiste] en échanges de choses; celle des banques en échanges de signes et d'argent" (*Oeuvres,* 4: 461). Banks and other financial institutions exchange not things (by barter) but only signs (by monetary transactions and transfers). Society, however, is founded necessarily upon "mesures communes." Conventional equality (measure) between things "a fait inventer la monnoye" (as opposed to the law) "car la monnoye n'est qu'un terme de comparaison pour la valeur des choses de différentes espéces" (4: 461). Money, then, is the great trope—a comparative term for the value of things of different species. In the fable, metaphor compares *ramage* and *plumage;* so money (the measure of value) compares *leçon* and *fromage.* "La monnoye," Rousseau says, "est le vrai lien de la societé" (ibid.). In the modern age men as well as things are equalized, but only because they share the same comparative relation of equality to the *maître.* The modern age, writes Rousseau in *Discours,* is one of extreme equality. "C'est ici le dernier terme de l'inégalité, et le point extrême qui ferme le Cercle et touche

20. Derrida, *De la grammatologie,* p. 423. Cf. J. Starobinski (*Jean-Jacques Rousseau: la transparence et l'obstacle* (Paris, 1971), pp. 365 ff.
21. Derrida, *De la grammatologie,* p. 417. My translation.
22. Cf. *Essai,* p. 536: "un son quelconque n'est rien . . . naturellement."
23. Rousseau, *Emile* (*Oeuvres,* 4: 338).
24. "Si vous prétendiez expliquer aux enfans comments les signes font négliger les choses, comment de la monnoye sont nées toutes les chiméres de l'opinion, comment les pays riches d'argent doivent être pauvres de tout, vous traitteriez ces enfans non seulement en philosophes mais en hommes sages, et vous prétendriez leur faire entendre ce que peu de philosophes mêmes ont bien conceu" (Rousseau, *Emile,* in *Oeuvres,* 4: 462).

au point d'où nous sommes partis: C'est ici que tous les particuliers redeviennent égaux parce qu'ils ne sont rien, et que les Sujets n'ayant plus d'autre Loi que la volonté du Maître, ni le Maître d'autre regle que ses passions, les notions du bien, et les principes de la justice s'évanouissent de rechef" (3: 191). Money, the development of which plays a crucial role in the origin and development of inequality, is like modern commercial language; both are perversely equalizing common denominators in a one-dimensional society, depending on a false sense of "universal equality."

Monetary and verbal representation are principal targets for Rousseau. Modern men, like children, are able to understand nothing about things and their representation. They are crows educated by foxlike tutors. As things can be alienated by money, so too can these men be alienated by political symbols of exchange—so-called political representatives. In a chapter of *Du Contrat social* entitled "Des Deputeés ou réprésentans," Rousseau—like Plato—complains that many citizens are more interested in their private *bourses* than in public service (*Oeuvres*, 3: 428). Money (as language) distorts the proper relation between things and signs, and corresponds to private greed in the bad city. From the good city both political representatives and financial institutions are, like poetry and word merchantry in Plato, absent. "Ce mot de *finance*," writes Rousseau, "est un mot d'esclave; il est inconnu dans la Cité" (3: 429). There is no money in the good city because money, which can seem to be an exchange for all things, corrupts. Rousseau's dictum, in both *Du Contrat social* and the *Essai sur l'origine des langues*, is "Donnez de l'argent, et bientôt vous aurez des fers" (3: 429; cf. *Essai*, p. 542).

As finance—economic representation—enslaves, so too does the institution of political representatives. The legislative power of the people cannot be represented.[25] Political sovereignty cannot be represented.[26] The good ancients, Rousseau argues, did not even have a word for political representation. "L'idée des Réprésentans est moderne" (*Oeuvres*, 3: 430). Not the representative but the thing or person supposedly represented is important, for precisely the reason

25. "La Loi n'étant que la déclaration de la volonté générale, il est clair que dans la puissance Législative le Peuple ne peut être réprésenté" (Rousseau, *Du Contrat social*, in *Oeuvres*, 3: 430). The inability of both things and popular sovereignty to be represented does not make them ontological equals. Nature (in *Les Rêveries du promeneur solitaire*), however, is similar to the political General Will. One loses oneself asocially in Nature as one loses oneself socially in the General Will.

26. "La Souveraineté ne peut être réprésentée, par la même raison qu'elle ne peut être aliénée.... Les députés du peuple ne sont donc ni ne peuvent être ses réprésentans" (Rousseau, *Du Contrat social*, in *Oeuvres*, 3: 429).

that representation is impossible. John Locke is wrong to confuse political representation with sovereignty, as he is wrong to urge students to memorize fables. Rousseau argues that the English are a nation of shopkeepers, free only at the moment they exert their sovereignty and elect their Members of Parliament. At other times they are slaves of commissioners.

There is a language of slaves as well as a politics and an economics. In the *Essai sur l'origine des langues*, Rousseau presents an apocalyptic vision of the "signal" language of slaves, in which only signs circulate: "Les sociétés ont pris leur dernière forme: on n'y change plus rien qu'avec . . . des écus; et comme on n'a plus rien à dire au peuple, sinon, donnez de l'argent, on le dit avec des placards au coin des rues" (p. 542). A language that has thus come full circle is "one-dimensional." It is the language least favorable to liberty.

The language of modern men is a spoken language imitating written language. Rousseau considers the difference between hieroglyphic writing, by which things are represented, and modern abstract alphabetic writing, by which only sounds are represented. Alphabetical signs, in fact, encourage the reader to forget things; the representation must pass through sounds rather than directly to things. For Rousseau, the historical development of the alphabet corresponds to that of a monetary economy and to that of a police state. "L'alphabet," he writes, "[convient] aux peuples policés" (*Essai*, p. 508). Rousseau explains the origin of commercial language and, perhaps, what we call "commercials:" "Cette manière d'écrire, qui est la nôtre, a dû être imaginée par des peuples commerçans, qui, voyageant en plusieurs pays et ayant à parler plusieurs langues, furent forcés d'inventer des caractères qui pussent être communs à toutes" (p. 508). These characters are common measures of sounds, or alphabetical symbols, that permit translation through signs of sounds of words. Such characters are like money, which is a common measure not of all languages (as the alphabet) but of all commodities. Monetary characters permit the translation of these commodities; similarly, alphabetical characters (and puns) permit the sonal representation of two languages in one medium. The fox, having well digested the power of the *double entendre*, turns out to be an excellent poet. He makes language, alien and alienating, serve his own ends, as did the Greek sophists. Like Gyges, he is the banker-tyrant of the modern world.[27]

Voltaire assumed, perhaps too readily, that the fable was an unim-

27. On Rousseau and Gyges' ring, see *Les Rêveries du promeneur solitaire* ("Sixiéme Promenade"), in *Oeuvres*, 1: 1057–58.

portant form of literature. He argued that it was merely a minor genre,[28] and that La Fontaine, though excellent in his own way, could not be considered as excellent a writer as Corneille, because drama is a greater literary form than the fable. For Rousseau, however, the fable is potentially as important as any other genre. In fact, his interpretation of "Le Corbeau et le renard" implies a consideration of its relation to one of the revolutionary genres of the eighteenth century: the novel.

The novel, not the fable, is the literary genre most associated with the modern age. One of the first novels, Richardson's *Pamela*, lays claim to a moral purpose not unlike that of his *Aesop*.[29] Richardson is interested in the generic and moral criticism of literature about economic life; Rousseau, however, is more interested in the deepest internalization of economic representation into a narrative. He suggests a theory of narration in the novel.[30]

Rousseau's theory of the novel—like his theory of all literature—begins with his distrust of language. He claims in *Emile* that he hates all books: "Ils n'apprennent qu'à parler de ce qu'on ne sait pas" (*Oeuvres*, 4: 454). More than other books, however, Rousseau admires *Robinson Crusoe*. In *Emile* he gives an interpretation of Defoe's novel that opposes it to the Aesopian fable (which was Locke's favorite reading for children). Rousseau wishes to convince so-called adults to teach children first "ce que sont les choses en elles-mêmes" (4: 458) by transporting them in the imagination to Crusoe's island. Rousseau depends on islands, such as those in *Rêveries* or in *La Nouvelle Héloïse*.[31] They serve him as necessary tropes or ciphers, standing at the center of his theory of language and economics, and informing his theory of literature.

Robinson Crusoe lives on an island with no language and no money.[32] Imagining himself on such an island without exchange, the tutee can come to know things as they are; the fiction makes it possi-

28. Voltaire, *Oeuvres*, 48: 270.

29. Samuel Richardson, *Pamela*, Letter 29. On the relationship of Richardson's *Aesop* to *Pamela*, see Catherine Hornbeak, "Richardson's *Aesop*," *Smith College Review of Letters* (1938).

30. See Jacques Ehrmann, "The Minimum Narrative," *Substance* 2 (Winter, 1971–72): 3–14. Cf. Friedrich Nietzsche (*Die Geburt der Tragödie*, in *Werke in drei Bänden* [Munich, 1966], sect. 14, p. 80), who suggests that the novel "als die unendlich gesteigerte äsopische Fabel zu bezeichnen ist."

31. J. Starobinski ("Economie," in *Rousseau*) suggests that the same distrust of money leads to a supposedly good society (Clarens) in *La Nouvelle Héloïse* and a supposedly bad action (theft) in the biographical *Confessions*.

32. Robinson does, however, maintain a diary and an account of daily "expenditures."

ble for adults to teach children "ce que sont les choses en elles-mêmes." The islands of *Robinson Crusoe* and *Rêveries* are fertile, but they are also infantile and asocial. "Nulle societé," argues Rousseau, "ne peut exister sans échange" (*Oeuvres*, 4: 461). The island is a pedagogic hypothesis with which to teach things to children. Defoe's narrative power derives from his attempt to establish the true value of things. The famous scene in which the uselessness of representative signs or money is described is, for the tutor, the happy theoretical foundation upon which his understanding of the novel is based. In *Robinson Crusoe*, however, the intersection of the verbal and economic systems of exchange and representation remains insular.[33]

Rousseau's integration of economic and linguistic theory is a comprehensive contribution to the social study of literature. Like Turgot and Rousseau, Karl Marx offers a theory of economic and linguistic exchange and representation (in which, however, the description of money is not identical to that of discourse). Marx did not devote as much time as he would have liked to the description of discourse, which he sometimes interpreted as a mere reflex of economic conditions. His thought therefore does not appear to be as wide in scope as that of Rousseau. For example, Marx does not integrate his theory of representation (whether of money or of language) and his interpretations of works of literature (such as the analysis of *Robinson Crusoe* in *Capital*). Despite its apparent incompleteness, however, Marx's analysis is more rigorous than that of Rousseau. Rousseau's pedagogically useful disassociation of word and thing, or coin and commodity, is misleading. He himself admits that gold can be both coin and commodity, so that sign and thing can be one. Such admissions are integrated into Rousseau's theory of representation in the form of questions that the tutor hardly detects—questions about the ontological status not only of signs but also of things.[34] The illusion of the presence of things is supported by the foxy diachrony of language representing supposedly synchronic images of those things. Rousseau never offers the sustained analysis of representation that Marx

33. In the "Cinquiéme Promenade," Rousseau admits that his ecstasy depends on separation from the rest of the world (*Oeuvres*, 1: 1048). The state of inner *repos* (pp. 1046, 1048) that he desires opposes the terrestrial social flux from which he would escape. "De rien d'extérieur à soi, de rien sinon de soi-même et de sa propre existence, tant que cet état dure on se suffit à soi-même comme Dieu" (p. 1047).

34. Outfoxing the fox, de Man interprets Rousseau's dictum "Commençons donc par écarter tous les faits" as though *faits* referred to all the things represented by signs. "Rousseau's theory of representation," writes de Man, "is not directed towards meaning as presence and plenitude but towards meaning as a void" (de Man, *Blindness*, p. 127).

offers in the first part of *Capital*. He does, however, exemplify how political and ideological criticism must study money and discourse together, whether or not they are structurally similar components of society.

Rousseau (and Marx after him) laid the groundwork for an inclusive social study of literature. Lesser Marxists than Marx, and lesser enemies of literature than Rousseau, argue for a very general correspondence between the history of the novel form and the history of economic life. They neglect, however, the study of language as monetary sign and also its relation to the narrative as a whole.[35] They avoid discussing precisely what Rousseau and Marx found most revealing in the study of language and ideology.

Rousseau's attack on literature is also an attack on social exchange value. The exchange value of literature is often misunderstood. Roland Barthes, for example, asks an incomplete question about narrative: "Contre quoi échanger un récit? Que vaut le récit?"[36] He means to discover the exchange value of *récits* within novels in which the narrator receives his own life in exchange for the story he tells. The *récit* of the fox in "Le Corbeau et le renard" is a clever exchange of words for cheese that sustains the fox's life and crafty nature. Rousseau suggests that bad tutors and even La Fontaine himself are exploiters like the fox. The fox's claim that his *leçon* is worth a cheese is, on a level deeper, perhaps, than La Fontaine's irony, a claim that the fable itself contains a worthy *leçon*. The fox bargains on behalf of the poet and ultimately on behalf of the tutor who teaches the poem or encourages his tutee to memorize its words.

La Fontaine's fable (like the fox's *récit*) turns out to be a kind of merchandise. It is a commodity to be exchanged for something else. At the same time it is a process of apparently counterfeit linguistic metaphors, or purchases and sales of meanings. Novels, too, are about counterfeiting, which one theorist has called the general subject of the genre.[37] If that which is imitated has no ontological status, however, then literature cannot even be counterfeit, for there is no original for it to copy.

That literature has exchange value does not mean that it has politically good value. The fable, in fact, is harmful to the student, and the system of exchange and representation by which it operates is poten-

35. See, for example, L. Goldmann, "Introduction à la sociologie du roman," in *Pour une sociologie du roman* (Paris, 1964).

36. Roland Barthes, *S/Z* (Paris, 1970), p. 95.

37. W. W. Holdheim, *Theory and Practice of the Novel* (Geneva, 1968), p. 259. (See André Gide, *Les Faux-Monnayeurs* [Paris, 1926].) Other theorists argue that the novel is informed by the heroic search for authentic value in a worthless or counterfeit world.

tially harmful even to the fox (himself a victim of society). Some would argue that literature precipitates a catharsis. For the child there is no catharsis; there is only the new disease that he catches from the fox. Lessing's translation of Richardson's version of "Le Corbeau et le renard" is, in this negative way, a safer pedagogical device. The food, which the fox takes from the crow, turns out to be poisoned; the fox is punished for flattering the crow. The terrified fox-admiring student will be less subject to perversion by Lessing's than by La Fontaine's fox. Despite this apparently moral twist, Lessing's fable would probably not have appealed to Rousseau, because it omits a crucial part of the articulation of words for things. The crow does not carry its booty in its mouth and is not flattered for the supposed beauty of its voice.[38] Lessing's fable cannot exemplify—as Rousseau shows that La Fontaine's version can exemplify—the subversion of human society by the falseness of language.

In his interpretation of "Le Corbeau et le renard," Rousseau suggests both an economics of literature and a theory of narrative. He attacks the language of modern society, in which representation is necessarily—and despite the intentions of the speaker—politically dangerous. He reveals a *mensonge* at the center of society.

Rousseau himself, of course, writes in the medium that he deplores. He flatters us with language; willy-nilly, he lies to us. However, Rousseau recognizes two kinds of untruths: lies proper, which harm or steal from the listener; and fictions, or Platonic noble lies, which benefit the listener as a tutor is supposed to benefit the tutee.[39]

---

38. Lessing's "Der Rabe und der Fuchs" (in *Lessings Werke*, ed. K. Wölfel [Frankfurt-am-Main, 1967], pp. 37–38) begins with a decisive change from La Fontaine's "Le Corbeau et le renard." "Ein Rabe trug ein Stück vergiftetes Fleisch ... in seinen Klauen fort." The *Rabe* does not put its poisonous prey into its mouth. It is able to do what the *corbeau* cannot do: speak to the fox without dropping its prey. In order to make the *Rabe* give him the piece of meat, the *Fuchs* must flatter something other than his voice. He calls the *Rabe* a messenger of the gods: "Sehe ich denn nicht in der siegreichen Klaue die erflehte Gabe, die mir dein Gott durch dich zu schicken noch fortfährt?" The flattery works. The *Rabe* does that for which he is flattered (giving) just as the *corbeau* does that for which he is flattered (opening his mouth to sing). The *Gabe* (gift) turns out to be a *Gift* (poison).

39. The fox insists that he does not lie. "*Sans mentir!*" writes Rousseau, "on ment donc quelquefois? Où en sera l'enfant, si vous lui apprenez que le Renard ne dit, *sans mentir*, que parce qu'il ment?" (*Emile*, in *Oeuvres*, 4: 354). Children cannot understand signs of things-that-are-not, such as "*phénix*" (of which the fox speaks) and "speaking animals" (of which the poet writes). (On the latter see *Emile*, in *Oeuvres*, 4: 353; and *La Nouvelle Héloïse*, in *Oeuvres*, 2: 581). The tutor is hard-pressed to explain these *mensonges* and to distinguish them from moral *apologues* (*Emile*, in *Oeuvres*, 4: 540; and *La Nouvelle Héloïse*, in *Oeuvres*, 2: 581).

In the *Rêveries* Rousseau distinguishes among kinds of *mensonges* by referring to

In his relentless attack on human society, Rousseau hopes to show how literary fictions—perhaps even his own—can help men to understand and change their world.

---

economic categories such as theft and counterfeiting. "Je me souviens d'avoir lu dans un Livre de Philosophie que mentir c'est cacher une vérité que l'on doit manifester. Il suit bien de cette définition que taire une vérité qu'on n'est pas obligé de dire n'est pas mentir; mais celui qui non content en pareil cas de ne pas dire la vérité dit le contraire, ment-il alors, ou ne ment-il pas? Selon la définition l'on ne sauroit dire qu'il ment; car s'il donne de la fausse monnoye à un homme auquel il ne doit rien, il trompe cet homme, sans doute, mais il ne le vole pas" (*Oeuvres,* 1: 1026). "Mentir sans profit ni préjudice de soi ni d'autrui n'est pas mentir," writes Rousseau. "Ce n'est pas mensonge, c'est fiction" (p. 1029). Good tutors and Rousseau himself (in the fabular "Cinquiéme Promenade") sometimes tell necessary untruths, which he defines not as "vérité nue" but as beneficial "vérité due" (p. 1033).

JOHN RUSKIN
AND THE POLITICAL ECONOMY
OF LITERATURE

[handwritten annotations: by relating political economy & art / literature, aesthetics & politics inseparable; we politicize art, make; politics]

John Ruskin attempted to hold in a single vision the theoretical and practical problems of esthetics and economics. In works such as *The Political Economy of Art* (1857), *Munera Pulveris* (1862–63), and *Sesame and Lilies* (1865), he sought to explain the economic value of art and the relation of esthetic taste to economic organization. For Ruskin, esthetics and politics are finally inseparable. The special considerations by which he binds them together are the most original aspects of his critical theory.

Many students have not understood the need for and significance of a political economy of art and literature. They have misunderstood Ruskin's economic and political theory and criticism of art and have almost entirely ignored the special "economy of literature." Even Marcel Proust, one of the most careful and sympathetic of his readers, refused to follow Ruskin's attempt to understand the relation between the arts and economy. Ruskin, wrote Proust, "chercha la vérité, il trouva la beauté jusque dans les tableaux chronologiques et dans les lois sociales. Mais les logiciens ayant donné des 'Beaux Arts' une définition qui l'exclut aussi bien la minéralogie que l'économie politique, c'est seulement de la partie de l'oeuvre de Ruskin qui concerne les 'Beaux Arts' tels qu'on les entend généralement, de Ruskin esthéticien et critique d'art que j'aurai à parler."[1] Ruskin did not use the term *Beaux Arts* "tels qu'on les entend généralement." Unlike the

An earlier form of this chapter appeared in *Journal of the History of Ideas*, January 1977.

1. Marcel Proust, *Contre Sainte-Beuve, précédé de Pastiches et mélanges et suivi de Essais et articles*, ed. Pierre Clarac and Yves Sandre (Paris, 1971), p. 106. All references to Proust are to this edition.

logicians (to whom Proust seems to defer), Ruskin explicitly rejected the definition of *Beaux Arts* that excludes *économie politique*. Proust, in fact, does consider the economic implications of Ruskin's esthetics. The easy separation of art from political economy, however, has helped many critics to avoid serious consideration of *The Political Economy of Art* and other political and economic works by Ruskin. Although they recognize Ruskin's attempt to join economic and literary studies, they make no real effort to follow him closely in this exciting experiment.

Even the chronologies of Ruskin's interest in art and political economy have been inaccurate because his biographers (like his critics) have not understood exactly what he meant by the "political economy of art." Ruskin's consideration of this economy predates both *The Seven Lamps of Architecture* (1849) and the chapter entitled "The Nature of the Gothic" in *The Stones of Venice* (1853). According to Ruskin, this most important interest began in 1828, when he was only nine years old. In *The Queen of the Air* he cites a curious poem written in his youth.

> Those trees that stand waving upon the rock's side,
> And men, that, like spectres, among them glide.
> And waterfalls that are heard from far,
> And come in sight when very near.
> And the water-wheel that turns slowly round,
> Grinding the corn that—requires to be ground,—
> **(Political Economy of the Future!)** . . .[2]

As Ruskin comments, this poem foretells *The Stones of Venice* and *The Queen of the Air*. The poet hears the sound of a water wheel, built by human specters and turned slowly by natural waterfalls, grinding the corn that men require. By the sudden interjection, "Political Economy of the Future," Ruskin, however ironically, interprets his early poetic art as a literary attempt to illustrate the "political economy" of man. Such an attempt is different from, but related to, the attempt to locate art itself within the whole economy.

In his first major publication, *The Poetry of Architecture* (1837–38), Ruskin analyzes architectural decoration (which he elsewhere calls "the costliness or richness of a building") as an example of art within the whole economy. "We can always do without decoration; but if we have it, it must be well done. It is not of the slightest use to economise; every farthing improperly saved does a shilling's worth of

2. *The Queen of the Air*, in *The Works of John Ruskin*, ed. E. T. Cook and A. Wedderburn, 39 vols. (London, 1903–12), vol. 19, pp. 396–97. All references to Ruskin are to this edition.

damage: and that is getting a bargain the wrong way" (*Works*, 1: 184–85). Ruskin argued that the economy of decoration in architecture should be like that in nature. (*The Poetry of Architecture* is pseudonymously signed *kata physin*, or "according to nature.") "We have several times alluded to the extreme *richness* and variety of hill foreground [in nature], as an internal energy to which there must be no contrast. Rawness of colour is to be especially avoided, but so also is *poverty* of affect. It will therefore add much to the beauty of building, if in any conspicuous and harsh angle, or shadowy moulding, we introduce a wreath of carved leaf-work,—in stone, of course. This sounds startlingly expensive; but we are not thinking of expense: *what ought to be*, and not *what can be afforded*, is the question" (*Works*, 1:182–83. Italics mine). The architect should carefully imitate nature's economy and mode of decorating. In *The Elements of Drawing* (1857), Ruskin similarly advises the painter to imitate nature's husbandry of colors. "Nature is just as economical of her fine colours as I have told you to be with yours" (*Works*, 15: 153). The addendum to this advice, entitled "Nature's Economy of Colours" (*Works*, 15: 217), is a foreshadowing of the "Economy of Literature," in which Ruskin advises writers about the proper economy of the verbal art.[3] Although he sometimes pretends to ignore the related economic problem of "what can be afforded," he knows that he must justify the expense of his recommendations to artists and statesmen. In the *Poetry of Architecture*, Ruskin raises the problem that is to dominate his thinking for the rest of his life: What value of art justifies its cost and locates it in the economy of a nation? In its fullest form this problem is at the center of the practical decisions about art in a free or planned market economy.

The expense of art and the unpleasantness of discussing the matter are factors that led Ruskin to begin to study art systematically in terms of its economy. This study of the economy of art is closely related to Ruskin's great argument that the quality of work produced by manual laborers is directly related to their conditions of labor. Indeed, in *The Stones of Venice* he tries to show that the society in which the worker lives is the most serious factor to consider when studying the reasons why the work of one period is great and that of another mediocre. This way of relating art and economic conditions was not original with Ruskin, but he does make strange and exciting applications of the principle to both painter- and poet-laborers. In *Modern Painters*

---

3. In the addendum to *The Political Economy of Art* entitled "Economy of Literature" (*Works*, 16, app. 6), Ruskin considers very briefly the writer's management of (verbal) materials and argues (as does Herbert Spencer in *The Philosophy of Style* [New York, 1882]) that "it is excellent discipline for an author to feel that he must say all that he has to say in the fewest possible words. . . ."

(1843–60), for example, he seems to protest that poetic production differs from that of other craftsmen: "A poet, or creator, is therefore a person who puts things together, not as a watchmaker steel or a shoemaker leather, but who puts life into them" (*Works*, 7: 215). However, in other works he is less certain about the differences between poetic and other labor. In *The Political Economy of Art*, as we shall see, he relies heavily on the metaphor that the labor of the poet is like that of a particular craftsman: the goldsmith. Ruskin's study of the political economy of art, however wide in focus, is never so diffuse that there disappears the significant and frequently ignored concept of the poet as a laborer who is or who produces some kind of economic value.

A work of literature may attempt to establish its own value for society by establishing the supposedly parallel value of a smaller literary unit within itself. For example, one critic has suggested that Balzac's *Sarrasine* seems to establish its own value by establishing the "exchange value" of the *récit* within itself; and as we shall see, Ruskin himself argues that Shakespeare's *A Midsummer Night's Dream* seems to establish its own special value by establishing the lack of "use value" in the tradesmen's play-within-the-play.[4] The economic relations of the *récit* to *Sarrasine* or of the tradesmen's play to *A Midsummer Night's Dream* are, however, not necessarily identical or even mimetically faithful to the economic relations of *Sarrasine* or *A Midsummer Night's Dream* to society. It is possible, then, that literature cannot truly establish its own esthetic or economic value. Therefore a friend to art and literature may wish (if only for rhetorical reasons) to write an apparently nonliterary work about the economics and value of literature. In such a work, literature itself would play a role similar to that of the *récit* in *Sarrasine* or the tradesmen's play in *A Midsummer Night's Dream*. This is one of the explicit goals in most of Ruskin's later works: to locate the work of literature within the actual world of production and exchange and to establish the true value of literature in that world. A reviewer of *The Political Economy of Art* wrote that it was Ruskin's "chief purpose to treat the artist's power, and the Art work itself, as items of the world's wealth, and to show how these may be best evolved, produced, accumulated and distributed."[5]

The economy of art, as understood by Ruskin, has two bases: first, that art is a value in a national economy, and second, that taste in

---

4. Roland Barthes (*S/Z* [Paris, 1970]) discusses *Sarrasine* and the *récit*. For Ruskin's comments on *A Midsummer Night's Dream*, see *Eagle's Nest*, in *Works*, 22: 152.

5. "Athenaeum," December 26, 1857; cited in introduction to *The Political Economy of Art* (Ruskin, *Works*, 16).

esthetics and morality in society are identical. He argues that the products of the "Fine Arts" are a valuable part of national wealth and that economists who do not understand the value of these products must necessarily be mistaken in their analysis of the laws of political economy. In the preface to *Munera Pulveris*, Ruskin insists that his works were the first to present the problems of political economy from this (proper) perspective. An "accurate analysis of the laws of Political Economy," he begins, cannot be made by "any person unacquainted with the value of the products of the highest industries, commonly called the 'Fine Arts. . . .'" (*Works*, 17: 131). Ruskin believes that his main thesis is original because it centers on the importance of artistic value. In *Munera Pulveris* he notes five principal groups of economically valuable things: "land, with its associated air, water and organisms; houses, furniture, and instruments; stored or prepared food, medicine, and articles of bodily luxury, including clothing; books; works of Art" (*Works*, 17: 154). The correct economic organization of these five valuable items differs, but their values are qualitatively identical. From this difference and yet identity arises the need for the specialized economies of art and books.

In his list of valuable items Ruskin omits gold. This is strange for two reasons. First, Ruskin states, in the chapter entitled "Commerce" of *Munera Pulveris*, that uncoined gold is a commodity with value like any other. Second, he frequently compares the value of art and books to that of gold. Indeed, he believes that not only art but also the artist or his talent is a kind of golden natural resource. The talents of the artist, like Ruskin's own innate "art-gift" (*Works*, 19: 396), cannot be manufactured any more than can gold. In the chapter entitled "Discovery" of *The Political Economy of Art*, Ruskin writes that "you have always to find your artist, not to make him; you can't manufacture him any more than you can manufacture gold. You can find him, and refine him: you dig him out as he lies nugget-fashion in the mountain stream; you bring him home; and you fashion him into current coin or household plate, but not one grain of him you originally produce" (*Works*, 16: 29–30. Italics mine). Ruskin argues that art or the artist is like gold because both are rare natural resources, "limited in use" (*Works*, 16: 30). Throughout "Discovery," gold is the artist or art object on which the statesman works.

In *The Political Economy of Art* as a whole, however, the metaphor of gold seems to play multiple, even contradictory, roles. In the chapter entitled "Application" (about the necessity not to waste the gold that is art), gold becomes, by a significant transformation, the natural resource on which the artist works, and the artist himself is discussed as if he were a goldsmith (*Works*, 16: 45–47). As the particular material

with which the artisan works, gold is both a commodity and a
medium of exchange. Ruskin maintains that if gold has a higher exchange value than artistic talent, then art is impossible. The
goldsmith will never be truly artistic until such time as he can be
confident that his golden plates will not be melted down and recast to
suit the fashions of some future decade. The metaphorical identity of
art and gold, which Ruskin asserted in "Discovery," is thus undermined by the argument in "Application": art can be destroyed by
melting, but gold is not destroyed even when exchanging its old
(possibly artistically superior) shape for a new (possibly inferior)
one.[6] The implication is that gold, not art, is a heavenly treasure that
neither rust nor moths can destroy and that art depends upon. As we
shall see, this dependency of the art of the goldsmith on gold is, for
Ruskin, not unlike the dependency of the art of the writer on wisdom.

The Political Economy of Art is about architecture, painting, and
sculpture. The value of literature is identical to that of these other
arts, but its laws of production and distribution differ. In Munera
Pulveris Ruskin considers "the economical and educational value" of
books, which consists "first, in their power of preserving and communicating the knowledge of facts" (which corresponds to the negative power of "disguising and effacing the memory of facts"), and
"second, in their power of exciting vital or noble emotions and intellectual vision" (which corresponds to the negative power of "killing the noble emotions, or exciting base ones"). Under these two
headings Ruskin discusses briefly "the means of producing and
educating good authors, and the means and advisability of rendering
good books generally accessible, and directing the reader's choice to
them" (Works, 17: 157). Moreover, he promises the reader an entire
lecture devoted to the economy of literature. He did not keep his
promise. One lecture in Sesame and Lilies, however, is intended to
open the doors to the treasures of books.[7] In this lecture, entitled "Of
King's Treasure," Ruskin does not use literature to illustrate his eco-

6. As both commodity and medium of exchange, gold tests the human ability to
distinguish between presumably true value (for instance, the value of the plate as a
work of art) and presumably false value (its value as a medium to be melted and
worked again). Gold, therefore, becomes a kind of institutional touchstone. Such an
idea is clearly presented in a popular song of Chilon, which Diogenes Laertius reports
(1.70–72): "By the touchstone gold is tried, giving manifest proof; and by gold is the
mind of good and evil men brought to the test." In this song, gold is both that which
tests and that which is being tested.

7. Ruskin would open the bibliothecal gates to wisdom with the words "Open
Sesame!"

nomic ideas about society; rather, he considers the special economic role of literature itself within society.

Throughout *Sesame and Lilies* Ruskin compares and contrasts the treasures of books and those of wisdom. In "Of King's Treasures" it is not clear whether Ruskin intends books or wisdom to be the real treasure of kings, "gold to be mined in the very sun's red heart" (*Works*, 18: 102). Sometimes Ruskin implies fearfully that art, artist, book, and writer are not valuable in themselves. Only wisdom (which "positive" literature may or may not contain and which "negative" literature does not contain) is truly valuable. The implication is that books are merely storehouses of easily accessible capital, containers of wisdom that can be extracted only by a terrific effort on the part of the reader who—like the critic seeking Ruskin's own economy of literature—must dig for it as for an especially valuable vein of gold.[8] The difference between books and wisdom is not clear because Ruskin tries to dissolve the very distinction between container and contained (or imitator and imitated) that he himself established. This conflation of books (as golden capital) and wisdom (as the gold that books contain and that the reader must mine) is like the conflation in *The Political Economy of Art* of art or artist (as the golden material upon which the statesman works) and the material upon which the artist works (such as gold or wisdom). Both conflations derive from an almost purposeful confusion of the differences between the value of gold as a commodity and its value as a medium of exchange. Ruskin seems to distinguish clearly between these two values, but actually he obscures their differences. He fears that art is not really like wisdom or gold insofar as art is not a real commodity. He fears that art—and literature in particular—is like gold only insofar as it is a medium of exchange. As we have seen, one of the values that Ruskin ascribes to books is their "power of preserving and communicating the knowledge of facts." This power of exchange is identical to that of money, a medium of exchange that Ruskin defines as "documentary expression of legal claim" (*Works*, 17: 157). But gold, as both medium of exchange and commodity, deceives many into believing that medium of exchange and commodity are identical; it is a documentary expression of legal claim that lays claim to itself as commodity. Similarly, literature is a medium of exchange insofar as it may hide or contain wis-

8. Ruskin suggests that the reader dig for wisdom as if it were gold. Compare, however, the warning of Heraclitus: "Seekers after gold dig up much earth and find little" (frag. 22). Ruskin's advice to the reader turns out to be the incorporation of capitalist ideas about gold into his own ideas about wisdom.

dom. When it pretends to be wisdom, it too conflates medium and commodity.

Sometimes Ruskin seems to believe that not only literature but all written language is a representation or documentary expression of a claim to wisdom. Throughout his later works he suggests that literature, like money, is only "the written or coined sign of relative wealth" (*Works*, 19: 402). Money, however, is "the transferable acknowledgment of debt," of which there are two kinds: "The acknowledgment of debts which will be paid and of debts which will not" (*Works*, 17: 203). If literature is valuable, then it must have good credit. The reader expects wisdom from a book as the owner of a bank note expects it to be transferable for gold.[9] Ultimately Ruskin fears that all literature is necessarily misleading, false, or counterfeit; that it is only foolishness in artful disguise, pretending to a wisdom that only the best literature admits it does not contain; that the lie of literature is ignoble. If this fear were justified, as Ruskin knew, it would entirely destroy his theory of the value of literature, which depends largely on the "economic and educational value" of books to make men good.[10] It is, then, "in defense of art" as he sees it that Ruskin confuses commodity value and exchange value.

9. In the economic world, a materialized form of Grace might transcend the necessity for debts and credits. Even if a Portia were able to accomplish such transcendence in Victorian England (as Ruskin believed she had accomplished in Shakespeare's Venice), it is difficult for Ruskin to conceive of a similar overleaping of the debtor-creditor problems implicit in the writer-reader and art-truth relations of literature. It is in literature alone that Portia exists. On Portia and *The Merchant of Venice* see "Commerce" (*Works*, 18), in which Ruskin etymologizes the words "Portia" (in terms of economic portion), "merchant" (in terms of divine mercy), and "grace" (in terms of that which is *gratis*).

10. Ruskin is uncertain whether books can truly educate men to be wise and act nobly. Sometimes he ignores this uncertainty by arguing simply that education is an end in itself. In "Of King's Treasures," for example, Ruskin intends to show "the use and preciousness" of books. He insists that bibliothecal education is not a means to an end and speaks disparagingly of those persons who think only of "the education befitting such and such a station in life" (*Works*, 18: 54). "It never seems to occur to the parents [of students] that there may be an education which, in itself, is advance in life; that any other than that may be advancement in death." Ruskin rejects "the mere making of money" as the end of education. Although he claims that education is an end in itself, it is clear that Ruskin considered wisdom to be the end of education, just as he considered wisdom to be the thing hidden in books. His arguments about education are strangely like those of the parents whom he disparages, except that he transforms their goal of money-making into his goal of wisdom-getting. Such a transformation, like that of *philokerdeia* (love of profit) into *philosophia* (love of wisdom) in the Platonic dialogue *Hipparchus*, is one of the keys to understanding the confused meaning of "value" in Ruskin's writings.

Perhaps, as Proust suggested in the brilliant introduction to his translation of *Sesame and Lilies,* Ruskin does not pay enough attention to the act of reading. Although frequently he does stress the importance of educated readers, Ruskin does not analyze closely enough *la lecture,* or the mining of wisdom from books.[11] Nevertheless, he is able to question both the possibility of *la lecture* within the confines of his understanding of reading and the very concepts of literary value that inform that understanding. This questioning is most apparent within the context of Ruskin's more conventional literary criticism, such as the famous passage about avarice and prodigality in *Munera Pulveris.*

In a remarkable note to the second edition of *Munera Pulveris,* Ruskin explains that paragraphs eighty-seven to ninety-four are "of more value than any other part of this book" (*Works,* 17: 208). He integrates these paragraphs into the second edition as the second part of the chapter entitled "Coin-Keeping," to which they were a mere addendum in the first edition. Usually this section of Ruskin's treatise on economics is read out of context, without considering the whole of *Munera Pulveris,* to which it has a relation justifying Ruskin's high regard for it. It should be read in the light of the whole book, in which literature, supposed to be one of the five values in political economy, itself illustrates principles of political economy. In "Coin-Keeping," literature illustrates its own value.

Ruskin begins "Coin-Keeping" by considering various problems of monetary currency. Currency is used to exchange equivalents in wealth—in any place, in any time, of any kind (*Works,* 17: 196–97). It is the great metaphor. The special power of gold in Victorian society (where it was the medium of exchange) is even greater than this exchange value because gold is also a valuable commodity. According to Ruskin (himself a coin collector), this double existence of golden currency leads many citizens to imagine its value as even greater than it actually is. Such citizens avariciously hoard their idolized gold. Money has the power of quantitative comparison, which appeals to those whose minds cannot conceive of other media of comparison, such as the linguistic or moral. Ruskin argues that both hoarding and

11. Ruskin did make the distinction between those books that are useful to read and those that are not (*Works,* 18: 60–62). It is not, however, analysis of what Proust calls *la lecture.* In a brilliant counterpart to Ruskin's consideration of reading, Proust suggests that although Ruskin was essentially correct to insist on the difference between speaking and writing, he was wrong to insist implicitly on the identity of conversation and the act of reading (*la lecture*). See "De la lecture," Proust, *Pastiches et mélanges,* pp. 160 ff.

prodigality have the bad effect on the economy of stopping the free or natural current stream of wealth. In paragraph eighty-six (the last paragraph of the original version of "Coin-Keeping"), he tries to bolster this argument with an illustration from Dante's *Inferno* and its interpretation of the Homeric Charybdis: "The *mal tener* and *mal dare* are as correlative as complementary colours; and the circulation of wealth, which ought to be soft, steady, far-sweeping, and full of warmth, like the Gulf stream, being narrowed into an eddy, and concentrated on a point, changes into the alternate suction and surrender [associated with hoarding and prodigality] of Charybdis" (*Works*, 17: 207). The metaphors throughout "Coin-Keeping" center on such words as *currents, streams, flows,* and *fluctuations.* Ruskin takes these metaphors seriously, so that, without accepting the protection of poetic license, he makes an easy transition from *currency* as the topic of a supposedly systematic economic investigation to *currency* with all its aquatic and literary associations.[12]

In the second part of "Coin-Keeping" Ruskin illustrates his conclusions about monetary currency with passages from great works of literature. Moreover, he considers the currency of literature itself in terms of a substantial golden truth on which he implies it is based. "It is a strange habit of wise humanity to speak in enigmas only, so that the highest truths and usefullest laws must be hunted for through whole picture-galleries of dreams, which to the vulgar seem dreams only" (*Works*, 17: 208). The enigmatic habit of speaking enigmatically is useless to the multitude and therefore its products can have no true currency for them.[13] Plato argued that all works of literature, and the Homeric epics in particular, do not hide truths useful to anyone. But Ruskin asserts that literature may be useful to those who know how to seek out esoteric truths. He defends his position by attacking Plato's imaginative capability. "Plato's logical power quenched his imagination, and he became incapable of understanding the purely

12. Ruskin's accurate and inaccurate etymologies are among the means he employs to establish connections between the supposed meanings of words. In "Coin-Keeping" he sets up such a connection between the currency of money and that of water. He pretends to defend that etymological link by arguing that "the derivation of words is like that of rivers" (*Works*, 17: 292). Ruskin uses the concept of currency not only to join etymologically the social movement of money and the physical movement of water, but also to explain the movement of words, or etymology itself. Although elsewhere he writes that a man thinks "economically" when he is aware of all of the etymological nuances of the words he uses, Ruskin often employs etymologies to avoid more complete linguistic or economic considerations.

13. According to Ruskin, currency "consists of every document acknowledging debt, which is transferable in the country. This transferableness depends upon its intelligibility" (*Works*, 17, p. 194).

imaginative element either in poetry or painting: he therefore somewhat overrates the pure discipline of passionate art in song and
music, and misses that of meditative art" (Works, 17: 208). Ruskin
seems to be siding with Homer against Plato. He admits, however,
that there is a deeper reason for Plato's distrust, which cannot be so
easily dismissed, namely, "his love of justice, and reverently religious
nature [that] made him fear, as death, every form of fallacy." Finally,
Ruskin only appears to agree with Plato that literature is merely the
coining of idle imaginations. He admits that "Homer and Dante (and
in an inferior sphere, Milton). . . have permitted themselves, though
full of all nobleness and wisdom, to coin idle imaginations of the
mysteries of eternity, and guide the faiths of the families of the earth
by the courses of their own vague and visionary arts" (Works, 17: 209).
In this sentence, significantly, Ruskin is trying to soften Plato's au-
stere and utterly devastating argument against art and artists. Plato
was not convinced that the poets were "full of all nobleness and
wisdom" or that truth lies behind the "fallacies" of art. Ruskin, however, insists that "the indisputable truths of human life and duty,
respecting which [all works of art] have but one voice, lie hidden
behind these veils of phantasy ["idle imaginations"], unsought, and
often unsuspected." These truths Ruskin himself would hunt in
"picture-galleries of dreams." "I will gather carefully, out of Dante
and Homer," he promises us, "what in this kind [the "indisputable
truths"] bear on our subject [currency], in its due place." The goal of
interpretation, as he understands it, is to find the truth hidden in the
fallacies of art. If Ruskin can do this, he will have shown either that
Plato was mistaken in his harsh judgment of art or that the Platonic
judgment was itself an esoteric enigma needing Ruskin's interpretation. He would take gifts of dust, show that they are potentially
valuable, and transform them into the truth that is wealth.

The section of "Coin-Keeping" that follows this brief but significant
"theory of interpretation" examines the possibility of the worthy uses
of material riches and illustrates its examination with passages from
many writers.[14] At the same time, however, this section purports to
be an example of the worthy uses of bibliothecal riches. Ruskin digs
into the "gold mines" of many writers (Plato, Dante, Homer,

14. In Ruskin's work, there are other ways in which economics and art mutually
illustrate each other. In Elements of English Prosody, for example, Ruskin refers the
reader to economic theories of possession, discussed in Munera Pulveris, to illustrate
and explain part of Pope's "The Rape of the Lock," Canto 4. And as Proust (citing
Joseph-Antoine Milsand) suggests, Ruskin uses not only literature but also painting
(for example, a Holy Family of Tintoretto) to illustrate his economic ideas (Proust,
Pastiches et mélanges, p. 107).

Spenser, Goethe, Herbert, Macé, and the authors of the Bible) in order to seek out the indisputable truths that he, an educated bibliolater, believes are hidden in books. Because Ruskin is not fully certain of the justice of his "idolatry of books," however, he integrates with his interpretation of these books an enigmatic critique of bibliothecal riches that questions their value and ability to illustrate accurately the problems of avarice and prodigality in the currency of material riches.

The Divine Comedy is one of the books Ruskin uses to illustrate his ideas about currency. In *Inferno*, a place of bad economy, the *mal tener* and *mal dare* "meet in contrary . . . currents as the waves of Charybdis." In *Paradiso*, the opposite place of perfect economy, there is a correspondingly perfect currency. In *Purgatorio* there occurs the wonderful transformation of those who have been prodigal and avaricious, but (unlike the sinners in hell) for love of earth. *Purgatorio*, then, is a kind of translation from false to true economy. It is a place where the apparently total falseness of sinners is purged until they can participate in the truth of heaven. As we have seen, Ruskin considers interpretation itself to be such a purgation of the apparent falseness of literature. Apparent falseness can become truth only if truth and that falseness have something in common (for example, love in *Purgatorio*) through which the metaphor from one to the other can happen.

In this section of *Munera Pulveris* the connection between the falsehood of literature and the truth of philosophy is a series of verbal juxtapositions by which Ruskin hopes to prove that Dante (the exemplar of literature) and Plato (the exemplar of philosophy) both agree with George Herbert about the nature of truth and economic value. Ruskin begins with a purposefully mistaken translation of a line from the *Purgatorio*: "Dante's precept for the deliverance of the souls in purgatory is: 'Turn thine eyes to the lucre (lure) which the Eternal King rolls with mighty wheels'" (*Works*, 17: 211). The Italian *logore*, however, is properly translated only by the English "lure," which Ruskin places between parentheses. He pretends that the English "lucre" has an etymological connection with either the English "lure" or the Italian *logore*. On the basis of a supposedly common etymon, then, he uses "lucre" (meaning money) as the principal English word to translate *logore* in Dante's precept for purgatorial deliverance.

Ruskin cites George Herbert as one who agrees with Dante about the relation of money (lucre) to stars (true wealth).

        Lift up thy head;
    Take stars for money; stars, not to be told
    By any art, yet to be purchased.

Herbert opposes money to stars. Similarly, Dante (according to Ruskin) opposes lucre to the lure of the mighty wheels of the "Greater Fortune," whose constellation (of stars) is ascending in the *Purgatorio*. Herbert makes the further point, however, that stars cannot be told (meaning "related" or "counted out") by any art. Ruskin seems to take no note of Herbert's artful questioning of the ability of art to "purchase" stars. He simply uses the passage from Herbert to make a slippery connection between Dante (to whom he compared Herbert by "false" translation and etymology) and Plato, from whose *Republic* (416e) he cites: "Tell them they have divine gold and silver in their souls for ever; that they need no money stamped of men—neither may they otherwise than impiously mingle the gathering of the divine with the mortal treasure, for through that which the laws of the multitude have coined, endless crimes have been done and suffered; but in theirs is neither pollution nor sorrow." The implication in paragraph eighty-nine (in which this series of passages from Dante, Herbert, and Plato occurs) is that Dante (a producer of "veils of phantasy") and Plato (a sharp critic of all art) are somehow in agreement about the nature of real or "stellar" value. In fact, however, Plato includes art as a species of "money stamped of men."[15] Art is not to be trusted, as Ruskin would trust the art of Dante and Herbert and his own artful conflation of "lucre" and "lure." For Plato there is only the noble philosophical lie, not the potentially truthful artistic lie. All art is guileful and counterfeit.

In considering the economy of literature, Ruskin wonders whether literary currency is necessarily misleading, false, or counterfeit. He distrusts his own artful pose or noble lie, not in defense of philosophy but in defense of and for the sake of art. By the end of the chapter "Coin-Keeping," the reader's credulity about the value of art has been stretched—purposefully and frequently—almost to the breaking point.[16] Ruskin is in the painful position of defending literature while knowing that philosophers (such as Plato) and poets (such as Herbert) suggest that it is useless. At one and the same time, he tries to defend literature from the point of view of political economy and to attack it vehemently from the point of view of literature itself.

15. On the counterfeitness of poetry in Plato: *Republic*, 580d, 583d.

16. Another crafty but exasperating attempt by Ruskin ("Coin-Keeping," in *Works*, 17, pp. 211 ff.) to conjoin art and truth is his interpretation of Circe and the Sirens in Dante. The Siren, according to Ruskin, "is lovely to look upon, but her womb is loathsome." She is the goddess of the "deceitfulness of riches." He draws upon Apollonius to argue that the Siren is also the daughter of the muses. Ruskin seems to argue, then, for the deceitfulness (of the daughter) of the artful muses. He approves, however, another artful figure from the *Odyssey*—Circe—and implies that there is a good kind of art (Circean) and a bad kind of art (Sirenic).

Ruskin's elegant attack is also strange praise of literature. In one of the lectures in *Sesame and Lilies*, entitled "Mystery of Life and Its Arts," Ruskin argues that the most significant characteristic of great art is its distrust of itself. Great writers differ from lesser ones in that great ones know they write nothing truthful. Whatever claim to truth is made by Plato (or Ruskin) is a rhetorical pose. Beauty, therefore, has to do with the knowledge of wrongness. The first principle of esthetics is "that the more beautiful the art, the more it is essentially the work of people who felt themselves to be wrong.... The very sense of inevitable error from their purpose marks the perfectness of that purpose, and the continued sense of failure arises from the continued opening of the eyes more clearly to all the sacredest truths" (*Works*, 18: 174). Yet sensing "inevitable error" with the partly closed eyes of the artist is not the same as knowing it, as Ruskin wishes to know it, with eyes wide open to the inevitability and degree of error. That some writers see "more clearly" than others does not mean that any one of them sees perfectly clearly, and that some works of literature are "more beautiful" than others does not mean that any work is able to be at all valuable to society by exciting noble actions and teaching wisdom.

Ruskin finds it useful to compare the relative clarity, or closeness to value, of three groups of thinkers: Christian writers, naïve writers, and capitalists. He finds the Christian writers to be unclear and wrong. Milton's account of the loss of paradise he supposes to be unbelievable even to Milton himself. Dante's *Divine Comedy*, to which Ruskin seems to refer seriously in "Coin-Keeping," is judged "a vision, but a vision only." According to Ruskin, the great Christian writers "do but play sweetly upon modulated pipes; with pompous nomenclature adorn the councils of hell." In "Coin-Keeping" Ruskin expressed his wonder at the arrogance with which writers such as Dante and Milton "coin[ed] idle imaginations." In "Mystery of Life and its Arts" he pretends amazement that the Christian writers have "filled the openings of eternity, before which the prophets have veiled their faces, and which the angels desire to look into, with idle puppets of their scholastic imagination."

Ruskin prefers the naïve poets such as Homer and Shakespeare, who show a greater truthfulness than the Christian writers in their relative silence about the greatest mysteries. In *Eagle's Nest*, he praises the "faultless and complete epitome of the laws of mimetic art" that is "Shakespeare's judgment of his own art" in *A Midsummer Night's Dream*: "The best in this kind are but shadows: and the worst are no worse, if imagination amend them." Ruskin interprets this sentence of Theseus, "spoken of the poor tradesmen's kindly offered art," to be a warning about the deceitfulness or counterfeitness of *mimēsis*. Ruskin chooses to describe the dangers of preferring art and shadows to the simplicity of truth by using not a truthful argument but merely a skillful, pleasant illustration from Prodicus (*Works*, 22: 152). Writers who question or mock their own *mimēsis* are more to be trusted than those who claim direct access to and reproduction of the truth.[17]

Ruskin's distrust of literature sometimes takes the extreme form of questioning language itself. Proust, a most sophisticated critic, cites Ruskin's sentence on the necessary fallibility of human language: "Il n'y a pas de forme de langage humain où l'erreur n'ait pu se glisser." As Proust suggests, Ruskin's argument invites us to question the works of Ruskin himself. "Ruskin aurait d'ailleurs été le premier à nous approuver de ne pas accorder à ses écrits une autorité infaillible, puisqu'il la refusait même aux Ecritures Saintes."[18] All written works are *mensonges* slipping forth from the intellectual sincerity of the writer "sous . . . formes touchantes et tentatrices." It is impossible for a writer to be truthful or to clarify completely any mystery. As Proust maintains, however, Ruskin was pleased to affect in his writings "'une attitude de la révérence' qui croit 'insolent d'éclaircir un mystère.'" Ruskin adopts the *mensonge* that he can clarify a mystery, in order to defend the concept of the value of literature. That defense lacks the obvious humility of the writers whom Ruskin professes to admire and instead resembles that of the capitalist class Ruskin professes to dislike.

Capitalists constitute the third group of thinkers whose access to truth Ruskin considers in the "Mystery of Life and Its Arts." They are the avowed enemies of art and the Economy of Life. Ruskin sarcastically gives them the power to know all things: "These kings—these councillors—these statemen and builders of kingdoms—these capitalists and men of business who weigh the earth, and the dust in it, in a balance. They know the world surely" (*Works*, 18: 116). Ruskin is ironic in suggesting that the self-assured capitalists know the world more surely than the Christian and naïve writers, but he has been able to assign to these latter writers no sure knowledge. His own uncertainty about the value of beautiful art and his dislike of capitalist

17. Ruskin allies counterfeiting with Platonic *mimēsis*, but ignores the more complex problems of numerical representation and homogenization and seems to confuse the Platonic theory of *mimēsis* with the Aristotelian adaptation of it. (See Chapter 2, "Esthetics and Economics" and note 11, and Chapter 3.) On imitation and economy, cf. Jacques Derrida, "Economimesis," in *Mimesis: des articulations*, ed. Sylvanie Agacinski, et al. (Paris, 1975).

18. Both the translation of Ruskin's sentence and the ascription to Ruskin of necessary and conscious fallibility are from Proust, *Pastiches et mélanges*, p. 135.

esthetics and morality combine to form a powerful invective against the capitalist economy of art. What is most strange in this invective is that it is a defense of art not merely on the basis of the value of art (which we have already seen is a kind of noble lie) but also on the basis of a supposed identity between esthetic taste and economic morality.

The ambiguities of the value of literature constitute one large problem in Ruskin's economy of literature. A second and corresponding problem is that of the relationship of taste in esthetics to morality in society. Ruskin pretends that this relationship is one of identity and that esthetics is ultimately an economic matter. His sociology of art assumes not only the Marxist formula that social conditions give rise to certain forms of art but also the non-Marxist formula that a morally good society gives rise to and corresponds to esthetically good art. He sometimes even judges or prejudges the morality of an age by the good or bad taste manifested in its art. For example, on the basis of his high regard for ancient Greek and Christian Gothic art, Ruskin concludes that the societies that gave rise to such art must have operated according to the laws of his "Economy of Life." Other writers, including Marx, argue that Greek art was good but that Greek society (which gave rise to it) was slave-based and, from the perspective of history, immature. Some writers, such as Plato, suggest that the best society would not produce the best art, but rather no art. The positions of these latter thinkers, whereby a bad society (for instance, bourgeois France) can produce a good art (for instance, Balzac's novels), is not without difficulties. Ruskin's assertion that only a good society can produce great art is politically dubious and finally self-contradictory.

Proust argues that Ruskin's *mensonge* about the identity of esthetic taste and economic morality (like his *mensonge* about the value of literature) was motivated by the desire to defend art. "Les doctrines qu'il [Ruskin] professait étaient des doctrines morales et non des doctrines esthétiques, et pourtant il les choisissait pour leur beauté. Et comme il ne voulait pas les présenter comme belles mais comme vraies, il était obligé de *se mentir* à lui-même sur la nature des raisons qui les lui faisaient adopter."[19] Ruskin renders politics esthetic, but he pretends that he is politicizing art. As Proust knew, the greatest problem in interpreting Ruskin is that he exhibits "sans cesse [cette] attitude mensongère." One of the clearest indications that Ruskin "insincerely" confused the relationship between art and politics is the

19. Ibid., p. 80.

famous treatment of architecture and society in *The Stones of Venice.* "Or, si Ruskin avait été entièrement sincère avec lui-même, il n'aurait pas pensé que les crimes Vénitiens avaient été plus inexcusables et plus sévèrement punis que ceux des autres hommes parce qu'ils possédaient une eglise en marbre de toutes couleurs au lieu d'une cathédrale en calcaire."[20] Proust concludes properly that Ruskin virtually idolized art, to the point of blinding himself to historical politics and its real relation to esthetics.[21]

Both the theory of the economic value of art and the theory of the identity of morality and esthetics, however, fortified Ruskin in his battle to reform the arts and finally society.[22] He stresses the importance of reforming the arts, arguing (like Wagner on opera and Morris on architecture) that art can transform society. When Wagner lost

20. Ibid., p. 82.

21. Patrick Geddes (*Patrick Geddes: Spokesman for Man and the Environment*, ed. Marshall Stalley [New Brunswick, N.J., 1972], p. 273) suggests that Ruskin was a follower of Jean de Sismondi. Sismondi, however, was one of "the spokesmen of Political Economy" (Karl Marx, *Capital*, trans. Samuel Moore and Edward Aveling, 3 vols. [New York, 1967], 1: 582) and knew well enough that a bad society could produce good art, "that 'Brussels lace' [which was generally admired] presupposed wage lords and wage slaves" (Marx, *. .Capital*, 1: 235). Geddes is more convincing when he argues that Ruskin was a "continuator of the 'Physiocratic School'" (*John Ruskin: Economist* [Edinburgh, 1884], pp. 41–42) and when he allies Ruskin's theories of money and value with those of William Stanley Jevons (Geddes, *Ruskin*, pp. 13, 41–42). Although he did not actually do so, Geddes might have noted that Ruskin's theory of currency is like that of the physiocrat Mercier de la Rivière (*L'Ordre naturel et essentiel des sociétés politiques* [Paris, 1767]; cf. Marx, *Capital*, 1: 114 ff.), that his theory of value is like that implicit in Richard Cantillon's study of artists' and artisans' wages (*Essai sur la nature du commerce en général* [Amsterdam, 1756]. Cf. Adam Smith, *Wealth of Nations* [New York, 1937], pp. 99 ff.; and Marx, *Capital*, 1: 555 ff.), and that Ruskin's bifocal interest in economics and language is like that of Turgot (see Introduction), "the principal practical representative of the school" (*Encyclopaedia Brittanica*, 11th ed., s.v. "Physiocratic School.")

22. Ruskin's suggested reforms in the arts are so well documented that they do not need listing but rather interpretation. In the particular case of the economy of literature, Ruskin carefully considered educational institutions as touchstones for discovering young talent. He also dealt with the publisher's dilemma that there is a modern plague of cheap, profitable literature but that the best literature does not pay. In some ways, the famous *Fors Clavigera* experiment (in which Ruskin himself actually instituted somewhat original means of publication, pricing, and distribution) followed logically from *The Political Economy of Art.* Ruskin argued that the price (or exchange value) of books ought not to be so low as to diminish their (use) value in the eyes of the public. Such an argument, implicitly defending the high selling price of his own *Fors Clavigera,* is a strange and important admission that the exchange value of a book may well affect its use value. (See esp. *Fors Clavigera,* letter 38, February 1874, para. 13; and letter 6, June 1871, pars. 1 ff.) Cf. James C. Sherburne, *John Ruskin, or the Ambiguities of Abundance* (Cambridge, Mass., 1972).

faith in the social power of art, he turned ever more strongly to reactionary opera and simple idolization of medieval Christianity.[23] Ruskin, too, has his idols, but he looks to social reform to make the good society that could give rise to good art. He questions the possibility of reforming the political economy of art without first forming a planned, nonsocialist economy. Although his understanding of society and economics was (as Proust argues) distinctively esthetic, Ruskin finally argues that great art is impossible without economic reforms. His famous desire for reforms, then, arises not only from moral indignation at the horrid conditions of the working class, but also from the fear that a society producing such conditions could never produce great art. In *Sesame and Lilies*, Ruskin fears that in Victorian England even "reading well" is impossible. The desperate conclusion he draws from this state of affairs is that literature cannot have an educative value in Victorian England, where good, self-evaluating literature cannot be produced and the works of past masters cannot be read properly. Such a conclusion may have pleased Ruskin, who was notoriously dissatisfied with his own literary production, but the supposed impossibility of good and therefore valuable art in his own time drove him to ever more bitter invective against his society and its false self-assuredness.

The most famous example of Ruskin's invective is his lecture "Traffic," delivered in Bradford. He addressed leaders of England's capitalist class who had invited him to advise them on how to build a beautiful building to house their Exchange. They wanted architectural, not moral, advice. However, Ruskin argued that good taste in architecture is (like all esthetic taste) "not only a part and an index of morality; it is the ONLY morality" (*Works*, 18: 434). Beauty, therefore, must be moral truth. Good buildings cannot be had by asking the advice of an expert in architecture, but by following the advice of an expert in morality and truth. Here Ruskin, pretending for rhetorical reasons to be an expert in both architecture and economic morality, claims no interest in the construction of the Bradford Exchange, which must be as ugly as capitalism is immoral. He does "not care about this Exchange of [theirs]" (*Works*, 18: 433). Instead, he focuses his attention on the conceivable Exchanges of more moral societies.

One such society, argues Ruskin, was that of the Gothic Christians, in which there could have existed an esthetic theory for the construction of beautiful Exchanges. He suggests that the decorations for his

23. On Richard Wagner and William Morris, see Carl E. Schorske, "The Quest for the Grail," in *The Critical Spirit*, ed. Kurt Wolff and Barrington Moore, Jr. (Boston, 1967).

proposed medieval Exchange would represent the morally admirable economic exchanges that took place in the medieval era: "On his houses and temples alike, the Christian put carvings of angels conquering devils; or of hero-martyrs exchanging this world for another" (*Works*, 18: 449). Only by its admirable moral heroism does Ruskin judge the worthiness of an action—such as exchanging—to give rise to imitation in the form of architectural decoration.[24] The practice of supplying poor people with food (for example, Jesus' miracle of loaves and fishes) is such an exchange. Because the audience is not interested in this "good" kind of exchange, however, Ruskin concludes that he is unable to "carve [as decoration for the Bradford Exchange] something *worth* looking at" (*Works*, 18: 450-51). He states that Christian or beautiful subjects are "inappropriate to the manner of exchange" to be represented by the decorations for the un-Christian Bradford Exchange, whose actions are more insidious and "cunning than any of Tetzel's trading." He describes the worthless decorations he deems most appropriate to the Bradford Exchange, and he makes an ironic suggestion that "in the innermost chambers of [the Exchange] there might be a statue of Britannia of the Market," his detailed and bitter description of which is an indictment of modern economic exchange (*Works*, 18: 450).

The lecture "Traffic" is rhetorically powerful because Ruskin argues for the identity of architectural Exchange and monetary exchange and insists that the first cannot be good unless the second is also good. He conflates Exchange (as work of art) and exchange (as economic organization) and opposes one bad society to two good societies. To the morality and art of Bradford capitalism Ruskin contrasts first those of the Gothic Christians and then those of the ancient Greeks. To the thought of Victorian capitalism, he opposes the *Republic* and *Laws* of Plato, who was one of the greatest enemies of "this idol of yours" and who taught men "to bear lightly the burden of gold." Ruskin is de-

---

24. In "Traffic," the focus on decoration is a particularly effective (if somewhat dangerous) rhetorical device with which to satirize capitalism, because it translates so easily into the medium of literature. Unlike some twentieth-century theorists of architecture (Le Corbusier, for example), Ruskin considered decoration to be an important part of a building. In "The Relation of Art to Use," he argues that "the entire vitality of art depends upon its being either full of truth, or full of use," and consequently, that good art must have "one of these main objects—either to state a true thing, or to adorn a serviceable one" (*Works*, 20, pp. 95-96). If, as Ruskin feared, art cannot itself be true and there is nothing serviceable to decorate or adorn, then there can be no good art. It has been argued by some modern thinkers that Ruskin's concentration on architectural decoration (to the exclusion of any consideration of structure, which may also be truthful or useful) is symptomatic of his theory of the relation between worker and product and, consequently, of a whole political outlook.

ceived (or wishes to deceive others) in judging the whole of Greek society by the art and philosophical writings it produced. The philosopher-king, so necessary to the Platonic "economy," exists only at the extreme margins of possibility in Greek society. Plato was able to produce great writing within and even define his philosophy against the conventions of classical Athens, just as Ruskin (a disciple of Plato and the prophets) lectures to an assembly with which he believes he is in some disagreement. The writing of "Traffic," and even the possible construction of the temple to Britannia of the Market, are proof that "good" critical art is possible in "bad" society.

Not all thinkers in Victorian England came to Ruskin's conclusion about the ineffectiveness or impossibility of good art in the society in which they lived. In a lecture entitled "Ruskin's Politics," George Bernard Shaw compares Ruskin's extraordinary power of invective with that of Karl Marx. Shaw argues perversely that Ruskin's skill is greater because, unlike Marx, he was a "Tory-Socialist" in his attitude to society: "When you read [the] invectives of Marx and Cobbett, and read Ruskin's invectives afterwards, somehow or other you feel that Ruskin beats them hollow. Perhaps the reason was that they hated their enemy so thoroughly. Ruskin does it without hatred, and therefore he does it with a magnificent thoroughness. You may say that his strength in invective is as the strength of ten thousand because his heart is pure. And the only consequence of his denunciation of society was that people said, 'Well, he can't possibly be talking about us, the respectable people;' and so they did not take any notice."[25] We have already seen, however, that Ruskin's heart was anything but "pure." His falsification of the economic value of art and the identity of taste and morality are, as Proust knew, signs of a certain intellectual evasiveness that he employed in the "noble" lie that is his defense of art. The power of Ruskin's invective derives from these falsifications. A biographer might even argue that Ruskin was so bitter because he believed that his own "art-talent" had been wasted in a bad society in which it could not flourish.

Marx had a different understanding of the roles of art and intellectual discourse in society, and of the solution to the ills of society itself. Like Ruskin, he attacked capitalism on the level of abstract political economy, but his principal goal was to understand not artistic reproduction in particular, but economic production in general. In "Traffic," Ruskin is strangely satisfied with his too-much-protesting opposition of the Victorian "Goddess of Getting-On" to the Greek

---

25. *Bernard Shaw's Nondramatic Criticism*, ed. S. Weintraub (Lincoln, 1972), p. 193. Shaw discusses "Tory-Socialism" on pp. 201–2.

"Goddess of Wisdom," comparing the mythology of his own age with that of the heroic Greeks. In an essay written in London in 1857 (when Ruskin was delivering his lectures on *The Political Economy of Art* in Manchester), Marx made a similar comparison. For him the *Crédit mobilier* is the symbol of modern economic exchange, just as Printing House Square is the symbol of modern linguistic exchange:

> We know that Greek mythology is not only the arsenal of Greek art, but also its basis. Is the conception of nature and of social relations which underlies Greek imagination and therefore Greek [art] possible when there are self-acting mules, railways, locomotives and electric telegraphs? What is...Hermes compared with the *Crédit mobilier?* All mythology subdues, controls and fashions the forces of nature in the imagination and through imagination; it disappears therefore when real control over these forces is established. What becomes of Fama side by side with Printing House Square?[26]

This passage is both elegy for the mythology of Greece and eulogy of the capitalist technology of France and England. Hermes—whether thief or messenger of the gods—is impossible in the Promethean age of the *Crédit mobilier.*[27] Ancient art (the technological and material basis of which have been transcended) can nevertheless give "esthetic pleasure" and in certain respects can be regarded as "a standard and unattainable ideal."[28] Marx explains this power of Greek art not by arguing (as does the *menteur* Ruskin) that it contains some sort of golden eternal truths, but rather by arguing that "the charm [that Greek] art has for us ... is a consequence of [the immature stage of the society where it originated], and is inseparably linked with the fact that the immature social conditions which gave rise, and which alone could give rise, to this art cannot recur."[29] Artistic production, perhaps, is a superstructure, and material production a substructure. If so, however, they correspond to each other not mimetically but dialectically. Unlike Ruskin, Marx does not need to argue that ancient Greece was morally superior to modern England and France because Hermes and the Goddess of Wisdom seem esthetically superior to the

---

26. Karl Marx, *A Contribution to the Critique of Political Economy,* ed. and intro. Maurice Dobb, trans. S. W. Ryazanskaya (New York, 1970), pp. 216–17. The cited passage is a translation of the introduction to the *Grundrisse der Kritik der politischen Ökonomie.*

27. On Marx's understanding of Hermes and Prometheus, see his "Difference between Democritean and Epicurean Philosophy," in *Activity in Marx,* ed. N. D. Livergood (The Hague, 1967). Marx later rejected such mythological references as mere substitution for real historical argument (Marx, *Political Economy,* p. 189).

28. Ibid., p. 217.

29. Ibid.

Crédit mobilier and the Goddess of Getting-On. Indeed, Marx sometimes admits to a grudging admiration of the heroic accomplishments
of Promethean capitalism. The "Tory-Socialist" Ruskin, on the other
hand, feared that if capitalist exchange were heroic, then good decoration would be conceivable for the Bradford Exchange. "There might
indeed, on some theories, be a conceivably good architecture for
Exchanges—that is to say *if* there were any heroism in the fact or deed
of exchange, which might be typically carved on the outside of your
building" (*Works*, 18: 448. Italics mine). But Ruskin pretends that
there is nothing serviceable or heroic about capitalism, just as he
pretends that Greek society was somehow "good." Such pretence, of
course, differs from the curious recognition of capitalist serviceability
and heroism in the writings of Shaw and also from the Marxist recognition of the heroism of the working class and of capitalist technology.

This respect for capitalism enabled Marx to offer his scathing
critique of it. His theory of a dialectical relationship between esthetic
taste and economic morality enabled him to understand how a work
of art could be of a period yet also in opposition to that period. It was
unnecessary for Marx, as it was necessary for Ruskin, to estheticize
politics by arguing that the societies that give rise to great artists must
be good societies. Because of this understanding, perhaps, Marx did
not feel the debilitating desperation that haunted Ruskin.

The great danger to literature is not the argument that literature
subverts citizens by teaching them falsehoods; it is the argument,
implicit or explicit, that literature has no real value or potential to
affect either good or evil, that it has no real role in human affairs and
ought not to be taken seriously. Although the student and lover of
literature may find his most theoretically exciting enemy in the arguments of those attackers of literature who (like Plato) take it seriously,
he finds his most threatening and politically insidious enemy in the
ignorance of those who do not bother to consider the economic and
political significance of literature. Assuming the social value of literature, they are unable or unwilling to define precisely the exact nature
of that value and trust hopefully that such things do not matter.
These enemies of the serious consideration of literature would shield
it from the significant and interesting analysis to which John Ruskin
attempted to subject it in his theoretical and practical writings.

Ruskin's attempt to write an "economy of literature" corresponding to his economies of the other arts was not totally successful. His
theoretical writings are mirror reflections, albeit unwilling, of capitalist
ideology transferred from the realm of economics to the realm of art.

They do not completely transcend the capitalist ideology from which they arise and against which they constantly inveigh with rhetorical ammunition. Ruskin protests against the abstract theories of classical political economy and only pretends to substitute for its concept of economic value a new understanding of Life. He knew the errors and dangerous implications of some of the theories he proposed in the economic defense of literature. He knew how unsuccessful were his attempts to treat literature and wisdom as commodity and as medium of exchange, and to identify esthetic taste and economic morality. Ruskin himself felt the wrongness of these theories. Most interesting, he felt a certain necessity to continue in that wrongness in order to defend what he believed to be the proper place of art in a national economy. His pose of certainty (what Proust calls an "attitude men-songère") was like the very capitalist self-assuredness that he mocked sarcastically throughout his lectures. Both capitalist and his own ideological defenses are too-much-protesting assertions without rigorous argument. Fortified with such assertions, however, Ruskin suggested and supervised many excellent reforms in the arts, some of which surpass in vision many of his theoretical writings.

John Ruskin's economy of literature is much more than a self-contradicting attempt to apply a special variation of classical political economy to the economy of art. To the extent that Ruskin did analyze his own thinking, he found it inadequate. He recognized the hidden capitalist ideology of his theory of literary value and the politically dangerous implications of his theory of the identity of taste and morality. That he recognized and criticized implicitly his own theoret-ical *mensonges* is a great example and contribution to the sociology of literature. That he persevered in these *mensonges* is the sign not of his intellectual dishonesty, but of his tremendous desire to understand and interpret the relation between art and economics in his own time.

CONCLUSION

This book about the economy of literature seeks to understand dialectically the relationship between thought and matter by looking from the formal similarities between linguistic and economic symbolization and production to the political economy as a whole. We have seen that literary works are composed of tropic exchanges (for example, the simile and metaphors of Heraclitus's Fragment 90 and the plot of Sophocles' *Oedipus Tyrannus*), some of which can be analyzed in terms of economic content and all of which can be analyzed in terms of economic form. The economy of literature seeks to understand the relationship between literary exchanges and the exchanges that constitute a political economy.

The chapters in this book pose specific questions. For example, why did coinage, tyranny, and philosophy develop in the same time and place? What is the sociology of the distinction between the invisible, private realm and the visible, public one? What is the semiology of coins as material media of exchange and as symbols or works of literature? What is literary disposition and dispensation? What are the relationships among verbal, monetary, and political representation? Other problems and other times and places might have been considered.[1] Those discussed here, however, should be representative enough to suggest the general way of the economy of literature.

Aspects of the money of the mind toward the analysis of which the chapters in *The Economy of Literature* move include the internalization

1. For the medieval period and the *topos* of the cornucopia, for example, see Marc Shell, "The Economy of the Grail Legends," *Canadian Review of Comparative Literature* 5, no. 1 (Winter 1978); and on modern propaganda and the relationship between economic form and language, see Marc Shell, "The Forked Tongue: Bilingual Advertisement in Quebec," *Semiotica* 20, nos. 3–4 (1977).

the money of the mind

monetary Authority

of monetary form in the modern dialectic and the internalization of monetary inscription in the modern critique of the concept of truth.

"The Ring of Gyges" noted the symmetries in Plato's *Republic* between economic hypothecation and philosophical hypothesizing and between moneychanging and dialectical division of genuses into species. Similar symmetries in the dialectics of Kant and Hegel elucidate their ideologies and theories of production. For example, Kant defines *Aufhebung*, or sublation (the principal movement or trope in later German dialectic), as the mutual cancellation of real opposites. His necessary illustrations of such opposites are debt (*Aktivschuld*) and credit (*Passivschuld*), when both *Schulden* are predicates belonging to a single subject and are quantitatively equal to each other.[2] Hegel, on the other hand, defines *Aufhebung* as the cancellation and transcendence of opposites. Relying on the meaning of *Aufhebung* in eighteenth-century commercial discourse, he treats it as a "cancelled (*aufgehoben*) note or bond which still has positive value as a receipt or discharge from debt."[3] In the *Phenomenology* Hegel would demonstrate how this simultaneously negative and positive bond helps to articulate genuses and species, to explain metaphorization, and finally to reveal absolute truth.

"The Language of Character" proposed a numismatic "epigrammatology"[4] or logic of the relationship between inscription and in-

---

2. In *Versuch, den Begriff der negativen Grössen in die Weltweisheit einzuführen* (in *Werke in zehn Bänden* [Darmstadt, 1968], vol. 2) Kant applies Newtonian physical mathematics (in the terminology of which *Aufhebung* means "cancellation") to the metaphysical world. He considers two kinds of opposition: logical opposition, or affirming and denying something about a single subject; and real opposition, which arises when two predicates of a single subject are opposed, but without logical contradiction. Kant exemplifies real opposition by referring to the two directions in which a physical body (for example, the earth) may be pulled, and to debt and credit. "A person who owes a debt to another person of 100 florins must find the sum. But suppose that the same person is owed 100 florins by another. The latter is then held as reimbursing the former. The two debts united form a ground (*Grund*) of zero. There is no money to give and no money to receive" (my translation). In economics, as in physics, the zero produced is supposed to be a relative nothing, the final result of monetary *Aufhebung*.

3. Cf. W. T. Harris, "Note," in *Hegel: Selections*, ed. J. Loewenberg (New York, 1929), p. 102. The similarity between Hegelian *Aufhebung* and Aristotelian *anairesis* (an opposite of *diairesis*) is suggested by the latter's meaning "taking up a lease," "withdrawing money from the bank," or other acts of economic cancellation, and also "taking up bodies for burial." Antigone, for example, does this to the body of her brother (cf. Hegel's analysis of *Antigone*, in *Phänomenologie des Geistes* [Frankfurt-am-Main, 1970], ch. 6) and all people must do this with those things that they wish somehow to incorporate and transcend.

4. On the term "epigrammatology," see Geoffrey Hartman, "Monsieur Texte: On Jacques Derrida, His *Glas*," *Georgia Review* 29, no. 4 (Winter 1975): 761. Hartman plays

scribed thing. As we saw, a coin is a numismatic epigram that cannot be thought of apart from the material where it is inscribed. A coin comprises both an inscription and a thing on which the inscription is stamped, to which the inscription refers, and together with which it becomes legal tender. This epigrammatology is internalized in the definition of truth. Many works of literature and philosophy compare coins to truth.[5] Nietzsche, for example, would upset the West by metaphorizing that "truths are ... metaphors worn out and without sensuous power; coins which have lost their impressions and now matter only as metal, no longer as coins."[6] Heidegger adapts the Nietzschean argument and takes issue with the traditional concept of truth as adequation of intellect and thing (*adaequatio intellectus et rei*).[7] His principal essay on the essence of truth, however, relies uncritically on propositions about coins in order to exemplify the possibility or impossibility of such adequation. Heidegger fails to note that a coin is not only a thing (an ingot) but also a proposition (an inscription) about, and even part of or "adequate" to, this thing.[8] He does not see the relationship between epigrammatology and adequation. The essay systematically and symptomatically distorts things, metaphorization, and the concept of truth. The economy of literature sets out to reveal the philosophical and political tendencies of such distortions. It warns against adopting theories that ignore the economics of dialectic and truth to which *The Economy of Literature* is prospective.

Some thinkers may try to nullify this economics by noting that *The Economy of Literature* begins with a mere story whose historical content can be disproved or whose political tendency can be disapproved of. Rousseau himself exhibits a sophisticated distrust of stories and a classical distrust of classical wisdom. Yet his critique of La Fontaine's translation of a fable of Aesop, who was a foxy slave during the age of

---

on the title of Jacques Derrida's *De la grammatologie* (Paris, 1967). Cf. Eugenio Donato, " 'Here, Now'/'Always Already': Incidental Remarks on Some Recent Characterizations of the Text," *Diacritics* 6, no. 3 (Fall 1976): 25.

5. For example: G. E. Lessing, *Nathan der Weise*, act 3, scene 6, in *Werke* (Köln and Berlin, 1962), vol. 1, and *Briefe antiquarischen*, in *Gesammelte Werke* (Berlin and Weimar, 1968), vol. 5, pp. 604–5, letter no. 52; F.W.J. von Schelling, *Vorlesungen über das akademische Studium* (1802), in *Werke* (Munich, 1927–28), vol. 3, p. 290; and Hegel, *Phänomenologie*, p. 40.

6. F. Nietzsche, "Über Wahrheit und Lüge im aussermoralischen Sinn," in *Werke in drei Bänden* (Munich, 1966), 3: 314.

7. Martin Heidegger, *Sein und Zeit* (Halle, 1929), pp. 212 ff.

8. Martin Heidegger, *Vom Wesen der Wahrheit* (Frankfurt-am-Main, 1954). See Marc Shell, " 'What is Truth?': Lessing's Numismatics and Heidegger's Alchemy," *Modern Language Notes* 92 (1977): 549–70.

Moneying the mind

the Greek tyrants, displays the tyrant-sophist of the modern world.
Our tale of the ring of Gyges or of the origin of the moneying of the
mind is a similarly theoretical inquiry. It is a rhetorical trope which we
set up and put down. In the end, Gyges the tyrant is a fall guy. But
tyranny, which the tale of his ring sets forth, has made its pratfall
neither in literary nor in legal theory and practice.[9] We still look for
ways to reform the political economy, as does Ruskin, or to free men,
whom Rousseau says are born free,[10] from the visible chains by which
some men, and from the invisible chains by which all men, are
bound.[11]

   Thinkers may wish to avoid the economics of literature. Like the
speaker in Archilochus's poem, they may insist that to them things
Gygean are out of sight or invisible: "I care not for the wealth of
golden Gyges, nor ever have envied him; I am not jealous of the
works of gods, and I have no desire for lofty tyranny; for such things

9. The tale is a trope, but the economics of language that it tells is not merely topical.
In the work of some thinkers, perhaps, economics appears to be merely one *topos*
among many similar *topoi* (for example, the sexual). Geoffrey Hartman thus interprets
Derrida's turn toward relating esthetics and political economy (in *Glas*) and Lukács's
turn toward relating the experience of art and the lessons of political economy (in his
"große Ästhetik"): "Any grand Aesthetics, I suspect, will turn out to be an Xthetics:
where 'X' signifies something excluded, something ex-d from a previous system and
now redeemed: the 'ugly,' for instance, or 'low' or 'mad' or economic factors" ("Cros-
sing Over: Literary Commentary as Literature," *Comparative Literature* 28, no. 3 [Sum-
mer 1976]: 275–76). The economy of literature does not need to exclude from considera
tion the troping of specific *topoi* (Aristotle, *Rh.* 1.2.21) such as those to which Hartman
refers. As I have noted in the Introduction, however, there is a theoretical necessity for,
as well as the historical fact of, the internalization of economic form in language. Unlike
specific *topoi*, this internalization is general; it invades and pervades everything.
Whether or not we employ terms like "rhetoric" (the Platonic knack [*tribē*] or the
Aristotelian art [*technē*] of making persuasive tropes) and dialectic (of which rhetoric is
supposed to be the counterpart [*antistrophē*] [Plato, *Grg.* 465d; Aristotle, *Rh.* 1.1.1, cf.
1.3.9]) or "poetry" and "philosophy," and whether or not we pretend to synthesize
them, theory fulfills itself (if at all) only in its encounter with and account of its own
internalization of monetary form, which is the architectonic *poseur par excellence*.
   10. Jean-Jacques Rousseau, *Du Contrat social*, in *Oeuvres Complètes*, 4 vols. (Paris,
1959–), 3: 351.
   11. Jean de La Fontaine ("La Vie d'Esope, le phrygien," in *Oeuvres complètes de La
Fontaine*, ed. René Groos and Jacques Schiffrin [Paris, 1958], vol. 1) tells how Aesop
freed himself from slavery. Aesop, who was born mute, learned to use his tongue
(*langue*) so well that he could tell how tongues (*langues*)—the human kind by which
men speak and the animal kind that men eat—are, like human languages (*langages*), both the best and the worst of all things (p. 19; cf. p. 14). When the seal-ring of
his master's polis (Samos) was lost, Aesop had an opportunity to speak slyly enough to
"purchase" his freedom (pp. 22–23). La Fontaine notes that the freed Aesop sent fables
to Croesus of Lydia (p. 24), the fifth descendent of Gyges. (Cf. Jean de La Fontaine, "Le
Roi Candaule et le maître en droit," in *Oeuvres complètes*, 1: 576–84.

are far beyond my sight."[12] The speaker denies that he desires the wealth and tyranny of Gyges and asserts that he would not wish to be an "equal to the gods" (as Gyges is called in the Platonic inquiry). Like Ruskin, however, he knows enough to see what not to see on the horizon. He is already uneasy about Gyges or else he would not speak these words. The speaker's protests are, like the *mensonges* of Ruskin, symptoms of his Gygean entrapment.[13]

The critical thinkers I have studied in *The Economy of Literature* know and are uneasy that a special logic, the money of the mind, informs and cannot be expelled from their thinking. As a god or an "equal to the gods," Jesus tried to eject from inside the walls of the Temple the classical moneychanger (*kermatistēs*) and his changing coins (*kermata*).[14] He wanted to keep the monetary agents of homogenization and uniformity out of view of the ark where he supposed the divine One to dwell. Plato, however, knew that money could hardly be eliminated from the Academy where human lovers of wisdom conversed. He knew that hypothecation informs hypothesization and that change-making informs the dialectical division of the One (*kermatidzesthai*). Plato recognized and took into his account of metaphorization and truth the symmetries between money and the Idea or between rhetoric and its counterpart, dialectic.

The history of theory from Aristotle to Hegel and Heidegger is a series of swollen footnotes to Plato. These notes try—as does this book—to understand and define themselves against his thought. In the end, however, there is no easy way out of the field where theory encounters and tries to account for its own internalization of economic form. Wagner's operatic characters, perhaps, could return to the Rhine maidens the gold from which was fashioned the ring of the Nibelungen, and perhaps Rousseau could reject the hypothetical offer of a ring of Gyges. The literary and political theorist, however, cannot ignore the economy of literature. There is no retreat from, no safe lookout onto, no island in the midst of, this intellectual battlefield.

12. Archilochus, frag. 25.
13. Archilochus's metaphorization does, perhaps, resemble the exchanges of a barter economy and not those of the monetary economy of Gyges' Lydia, and Longinus does call his poems uneconomic and sublime, but the content—if not the form—of Archilochus's work is already affected by the powers of Gyges.
14. John 2: 14–15. Cf. Matthew, 21: 12.

economic thinking begins w/ Plato ...

PLATES

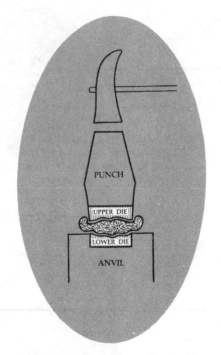

1. Instruments of the Greek coinmaker.

2. Tetradrachm of Syracuse (c. 412–400 B.C.), inscribed KIMON (the artist's signature) on both obverse and reverse.

3. Tetradrachm of Syracuse (c. 415 B.C.), showing EYAINETO (the artist's signature).

4. Denarius of Rome (124–103 B.C.), showing abbreviated signature of Publius Maenius Antiacus (the artist).

5. Tetradrachm of Syracuse (c. 412–400 B.C.), showing signature of Eucleidas (the artist).

6. Tetradrachm of Clazomenae (c. 375 B.C.), inscribed *Theodotus epoie* (Theodotus made it).

7. Stater of Ephesus (c. 600 B.C.), inscribed *Phanēos eimi sēma* (I am the *sēma* of Phanos).

8. Stater of Gortyna (c. 450 B.C.), inscribed *Gortynos to paima* (This is the coin of Gortyna).

9. Gem belonging to Thersis, inscribed *Therios eimi sama, mē me anoigē* (I am the *sēma* of Thersis, open me not).

10. Didrachm of Selinus (c. 520 B.C.), showing wild parsley leaf (canting badge).

11. Stater of Rhodes (c. 375 B.C.), showing rose (canting badge) and inscribed *Rodion*.

12. Stater of Melos (c. 420–416 B.C.), showing apple (canting badge).

13. Stater of Euboean League (411–410 B.C.), showing cow (canting badge).

14. Stater of Side (c. 460 B.C.), showing pomegranate (canting badge).

15. Stater of Phocaea (c. 550 B.C.), showing seal (canting badge) and inscribed ϕ.

16. Florin (fiorino d'oro) of Florence (1252), showing lily (canting badge).

17. Ducat of Venice (1284), inscribed SIT.T.XRE.DAT.Q.TV.REGIS.ISTE.DUCAT.

18. Noble of England, Edward III (1351–77), inscribed I H C AUTEM TRANSIENS PER
MEDIUM ILLORUM IBAT.

19. Dinar of Beni Nasr, Granada, Muhammad IV (1325–33).

20. Dinar of Ayyubids, Saladin (1175–76).

21. Onlik of Ottoman Empire, Ahmad III (1703).

22. Mohur of Mogul Empire, Jahangir (1606).

23. Denier of France, Carolingian, Charlemagne (781–814).

24. Three-pound piece, England, Charles I (1643). Minted by Nicholas Briot (?).

25. Tetradrachm of Camarina (c. 410 B.C.).

26. Tetradrachm of Athens (480–400 B.C.).

27. Stater of Croton (c. 550–530 B.C.), incuse.

28. Stater of Ami- (or Asi-) (c. 550–530 B.C.), incuse.

29. Stater of Metapontum (c. 550–530 B.C.), incuse.

30. Coin of Byzantium, Romanus IV Diogenes (c. 1067–70), inscribed OS ELPIKE PANTA KATORTHOI / PARTHENE SOI POLUAYNE.

31. Decadrachm of Acragas (c. 412–411 B.C.).

32. Coin of Britain, Marcus Aurelius Carausius, inscribed *Expectate veni*.

Index of Names
and Principal Works

Index of Subjects

Adequation, 154
Alchemy, 13n, 42
"Algebra" in language, 84, 108, 110, 117
Alienation, 4–5, 58, 122
Allegory, 106; of cave, 44–46
Alphabet, 11n, 68, 74, 123
Anthropology, 6
Architecture, 130–31, 144–50
Art, 8–10; economic and chrematistic, 24, 92–95, 101; reform of, 145n, 151; supposed neutrality of, 22–23; as technē, 97–100, 155n; truth hidden in, 139–41. See also Architecture; Chrematistics; Economics; Goldsmithy; History; Minting; Photography and cinematography; Rhetoric; Sculpture; Shepherding; Writing
Athens: coin of, 76–77; Ruskin on, 148–50

Barter, 32–33, 49, 55–57, 121
Beauty, 8, 104; as eidos, 14–17, 21, 43
Bradford Exchange, 146–47
Britain: coins of, 70–71, 75, 81; Rousseau on, 123; Ruskin on, 146–50
Bureaucracy, 17–19

Calligraphy, 73–77
Canting badges, 68–69
Catharsis, 126–27
Cave, 27, 44–46
Charaktēr (stamp), 62n, 64, 67n, 85
Chrematistics (chrematistikē), 24, 37, 45–48, 92, 94, 100–101; and philosophy, 26, 136
"Coin-Keeping," 137–41
Coins, 51–60, 63–88 passim; Byzantine, 79; calligraphy on, 73–77; as canting badges, 68–70; in China, 12n; illustrating literary works, 80–81; incuse, 77–79; and letters, 74; Muslim and Persian, 72–75; and nomos (law), 64–66, 68; and number, 66n; origin of, 11–14; ring-coins as, 35; as sculpture, 63n, 77–79; as

symbola, 33; and tyranny, 12–13; and words, 3, 38. See also Inscription; Minting; Symbol and thing
Contract, 32–35; social, 122–23. See also Deposit
Convention (nomos). See Law
Counterfeit, 7, 101, 126, 141, 143; Oedipus as, 96; monetary inscriptions prohibiting, 73–74n
Credit, 5, 7, 8, 11n, 33, 59–60, 104; and debt, 49, 136, 153

Democracy, 8, 12n, 86, 121–23
Deposit: as down-payment, 34; of the Good, 46, 104; as hypothec and hypothesis, 45–48, 60; monetary, 22, 25, 29, 33–34, 45–48, 49, 60; as principal, 46–47, 95; as "put-down," 43, 62, 155; of truth, 46n, 95; of weapons, 22, 25, 45
Diachrony and synchrony, 6, 118–19, 125
Dialectic, 2, 9–10, 39–40, 45, 50–62, 145, 155n, 156; confutation (anairesis) and sublation (Aufhebung) in, 45n, 153; and the divided line, 42–46; division (diairesis) in, 45–48, 153n, 156; as exchange (antamoibē), 50; hypothesizing in, 9–10, 13, 26, 45–48, 125, 153, 156. See also Deposit; Moneychanging; Polar opposition; Truth
Dikē (justice): as end of economics, 91, 94; vs. kerdos (profit), 91, 94
Drama: about Gyges, 16; economy of, 90–91, 102, 109; fear and pity in, 91, 101; and fable, 124; of Oedipus Tyrannus, 95–101; peripeteia in, 96n

Economics (oikonomikē), 24, 27, 89–112 passim. See also Chrematistics
Education, 106, 113–28 passim, 134, 136, 142. See also Truth, economy of
Ephesus, 60–61, 66–67
Esotericism, 107, 139
Esthetics, 8, 63, 85–88, 90, 129–31, 144–51

Library of Congress Cataloging in Publication Data

Shell, Marc.
  The economy of literature.

  1. Economics in literature.   I.   Title.
PN51.S364   001.5   77-21640
ISBN 0-8018-2030-8